# How Concepts Solve Management Problems

# How Concepts Solve Management Problems

Mike Metcalfe

*University of South Australia*

**Edward Elgar**

Cheltenham, UK • Northampton, MA, USA

Published by
Edward Elgar Publishing Limited
The Lypiatts
15 Lansdown Road
Cheltenham
Glos GL50 2JA
UK

Edward Elgar Publishing, Inc.
William Pratt House
9 Dewey Court
Northampton
Massachusetts 01060
USA


A catalogue record for this book
is available from the British Library


Library of Congress Control Number: 2013949874

This book is available electronically in the ElgarOnline.com Business Subject Collection, E-ISBN 978 1 78347 108 9

ISBN 978 1 78347 107 2 (cased)

Typeset by Servis Filmsetting Ltd, Stockport, Cheshire
Printed and bound in Great Britain by T.J. International Ltd, Padstow

# Contents

# Preface

How would concepts solve the problem of my car breaking down? If it did, I might, explicitly or implicitly, generate a list of what I might do next. This list might include:

- fix it myself;
- breakdown service;
- friendly local mechanic;
- get new car;
- burn and run.

If I decided to use the first of these, 'fix it myself', I might move on to using one of the concepts below:

- fuel;
- engine mechanics;
- electrical;
- transmission;
- computer chip

Then I might use the concepts of 'fix', 'replace' or 'work around'.

Pragmatic concepts are experienced patterns of activity. This includes numbers, colours, sounds, feelings and objects. Things are what they do.

This book offers a process for conceiving of and enacting solutions to complex, 'wicked' (see p. 11, this volume), messy, swampy or socio-technical problematic situations. It explains how and why pragmatic philosophy provides a preferable means of solving this sort of problem. Pragmatism argues that humans use linguistic concepts, words, to perform complex thinking. Thinking, including scientific, practical and complex problem-solving, is an act of using concepts. These concepts are often named, sourced from past social interaction experiences. Humans only have language, memories, past experiences, social interaction and a pattern-recognition capacity to think with. What pragmatic concepts are, and how they provide a means of making sense of large and complex problems, involving numerous conflicting stakeholders, is explained and applied in this book.

Another, more relevant, example may help. Think about the global issues of immigration, the environment, poverty and the impact of new information technologies. You cannot think about these unless you have some past experience of these four conceptual ideas (linguistic concepts). You know what immigration, the environment, poverty and new technologies do, and you have emotions or feelings associated with each of them. To be able to think about any one of them you need some other concepts to use. For immigration this might be justice, security, culture or the environment. For new technologies it might be immigration, the environment or poverty. Each new concept will make you remember different things. Thinking is a process of using linguistic concepts, implicitly or explicitly. Conceptualizing problems is therefore a process of selecting the set of useful concepts which will be used to think about the problem situation. Actions that follow from these reasons will seem rational.

To explain why and how to formulate reflective, pragmatic or concept driven problem-solving, this book uses the conceptual ideas or concepts of:

- pragmatic inquiry;
- stakeholders' concerns;
- idea networking;
- solution concepts;
- paradoxical outcomes; and
- intent (with related actions).

The first chapter explains the role of reflection in thinking. The next chapter explains the pragmatists' understanding of thinking as a social process of inquiry. It is assumed that complex problem-solving is a participatory process of human inquiry that cannot use strictly scientific research methods. The book then moves on to the practical task of how to collate stakeholders' concerns using idea networking into a handful of useful concepts or organizing principles. These are used to make sense of, or structure, future actions related to solving the problem. Once a set of concepts and related actions have been agreed these need to be communicated as decision-making criteria.

At the end of each chapter is a short section called 'Application'. It is hoped that this book will be read with a particular problem situation in mind. This end section will make suggestions as to how you might apply the contents of each chapter to your problem. This provides a chapter-by-chapter (step-by-step) process of using concepts to solve problems. The last step suggests you draft a report justifying how and why you recommend a problem be solved.

# Acknowledgements

I would like to acknowledge the assistance of my Masters and PhD students in helping me to articulate the practicalities of how pragmatic concepts can help in their careers. I have drawn on the empirical research of numerous people and hope to have referenced their work correctly when in appears in this work. However, I have worked closely with most of them and wanted explicitly to acknowledge that their presence and work did act to motivate mine. I hope they got as much help from me as I did from them. They are, in random order, Kate Harris, Eva Balan Vnuk, Peter Balan, Tony Hookins, Mathew Hillier, Nahmeh Hassanli, Colin East, Maureen Lynch, Carmen Joham, Saras Sastrowardoyo, Jing Gao, Libby Hobson, Luke Houghton, Allen McKenna, Dennis List, Marisa Maio Makay, David Matthews and Scott Armstrong.

# 1. Reflective thinking

## OVERVIEW

All thinking is reflection. This chapter explains the pragmatic argument of how humans think, how they inquire and problem-solve. Heidegger, in *What Is Called Thinking* (1968 [1817]) explains thinking as bringing 'things' into our presence, to our attention. Pragmatism, as you would expect, provides a means of doing that. It argues that all useful, rigorous, creative or purposeful thinking is foremost a process of reflection on concepts.[1]

## PROBLEM-SOLVING

The mainstream advice about how humans think about complex problems is thought to be wrong. Many writers including Mason and Mitroff (1981) and Mintzberg and Westley (2001) have reported a mismatch between what concerned people actually do and the traditional 'steps' of objective problem-solving. The modern foundations of the 'steps' root metaphor appear to be from Dewey's (1982 [1910]) *How We Think* but they seem to have been misinterpreted by overlaying them with objectivism. The misinterpretation is identified and typified by Mintzberg and Westley (2001) as defining the problem, diagnosing the causes, designing solutions, choosing and implementing the solution. At the core of these steps is the idea that the solution comes after the impartial collection and thinking about all the relevant information.

This chapter will re-present Dewey's argument that the stepping stones to thinking start with tentative solutions or conjectures (to use his word) prior to a process of reflection and rational justification. These tentative conjectures come from seeing analogies with prior experiences. The evidence that will be used to support this argument starts with Dewey's own words and examples. It goes on to look at Polya's (1945) problem-solving advice, Popper's (1972) writings on conjecture, Rittel and Webber's (1973) 'wicked' problems definition, Crosswhite's (1996) argumentation theory, as well as Guindon's (1990) and Klein's (1989) empirical findings. It is believed that there is a thread through this work which the mainstream problem-solving literature has ignored.

Checkland (2000), Rittel and Webber (1973) and Mason and Mitroff (1981) argue that alternative problem conception or appreciation is problem-solving or, as Ackoff (2007) would say, moving towards problem dissolving. They argue that the process of problem conception is thought to define what will be seen as a rational solution. Put another way, until you can (dis)solve a problem you have not fully appreciated it. This needs more explanation later, but those readers who pride themselves on their scientific, methodical, impartial thinking may be uncomfortable with the idea that solutions arrive in our minds prior to any deliberate or controlled thinking process, including the methodical, explicit collection of information over time. This uncomfortable feeling would seem to come from deeply held early science assumptions reinforced in Sherlock Holmes's advice to Watson not to guess 'who done it' until all the evidence has been collected. However, it is being suggested that these traditional scientific stages to rational thinking are a non-evolutionary interpretation of experiential self-conscious humans. Dewey presents the evolutionary approach.

## JOHN DEWEY (1859–1952)

Dewey, described by some as the most influential philosopher on thinking and education in the twentieth century, spent the second half of his life in the Department of Philosophy at Columbia University, US. Like Schon, he is thought of as a writer on educational philosophy, yet both of their works have been seminal to the management literature. Newell and Simon cite Dewey in their own oft-cited book *Human Problem-Solving* (1972), as does Churchman in his oft-cited book *The Design of Inquiring Systems* (1971). Simon won a Nobel Prize and Churchman was short-listed. In more modern times Mintzberg and Westley (2001), seminal figures in the management research literature, directly attribute the rational steps of decision-making to Dewey. Dewey spells out the steps (or as he says, constituents) of reflective thinking, in his small book *How We Think* (Dewey 1982 [1910]).

Dewey's book starts by defining thinking, which he wants to distinguish from 'daydreaming'. He specifically means focused, purposeful, rational and intelligent thinking. He uses the label 'reflective thinking' in the way that we might talk of 'critical', 'careful', 'considered', or 'deep' thinking today, but importantly he inserts the word 'reflective' apparently in order to emphasize critically reflecting on a prior belief, 'first thought', conjecture or some other 'supposed form of knowledge':

> Active, persistent, and careful consideration of any belief or supposed form of knowledge in the light of the grounds that support it, and further conclusions to which it tends, constitutes reflective thought . . . it is a conscious and voluntary effort to establish belief upon a firm basis of reasons. (Dewey 1982 [1910], 3)

Later in this book Dewey's work is used to explain how this 'established belief upon a firm basis of reasons' might be analysed (where analysed is distinguished from synthesized). The analysis or 'picking apart' (zooming in) provides the 'steps' (constituents, parts) and is spelt out under his chapter heading, 'The analysis of a complete act of thought'. He starts by presenting three everyday examples of thinking. The first of these is:

> 1. The other day when I was downtown on 16th Street a clock caught my eye. I saw that the hands pointed to 12.20. This suggested that I had an engagement at 124th Street, at one o'clock. I reasoned that as it had taken me an hour to come down on a surface car, I should probably be 20 minutes late if I returned the same way. I might save 20 minutes by a subway express. But was there a station near? If not, I might lose more than 20 minutes looking for one. Then, I thought of the elevated train, and I saw there was such a line within two blocks. But where was the station? If it were several blocks above or below the street I was on, I should lose time instead of gaining it. My mind went back to the subway express as quicker than the elevated; furthermore, I remembered that it went nearer than the elevated to the part of 124th Street I wished to reach, so that time would be saved at the end of the journey. I concluded in favour of the subway, and reached my destination by one o'clock. (Dewey 1982 [1910], 69)

After presenting two other examples Dewey sees some emergent properties in thinking:

> Upon examination, each instance reveals, more or less clearly, five logically distinct steps: (i) a felt difficulty; (ii) its location and definition; (iii) suggestion of possible solution; (iv) development by reasoning of the bearings of the solution; (v) further observation and experiment leading to its acceptance or rejection; that is the conclusion of belief or disbelief. (72).

This appears to be the origins of the idea of what has become the five stages of decision-making. Dewey quickly explains that steps (i) and (ii) frequently fuse. So mapping the steps on the example that he provides, my interpretation is as follows:

*Problem Conception*:
The other day when I was downtown on 16th Street a clock caught my eye. I saw that the hands pointed to 12.20. This suggested that I had an engagement at 124th Street, at one o'clock. (Thus he could be late for the appointment)

*Possible Solution 1*:
(He could take a surface car)
*His reflection*:
I reasoned that as it had taken me an hour to come down on a surface car, I should probably be 20 minutes late if I returned the same way.
*Possible Solution 2*:
I might save 20 minutes by a subway express.
*His reflection*:
But was there a station near? If not, I might lose more than 20 minutes looking for one.
*Possible Solution 3*:
Then, I thought of the elevated train.
*His reflection*:
And I saw there was such a line within two blocks. But where was the station? If it were several blocks above or below the street I was on, I should lose time instead of gaining it.
*Possible Solution 4*:
My mind went back to the subway express as quicker than the elevated;
*His reflection*:
I remembered that it went nearer than the elevated to the part of 124th Street I wished to reach, so that time would be saved at the end of the journey.
*Conclusion/Decision*:
I concluded in favour of the subway, and reached my destination by one o'clock.

As a flowchart, his steps of thinking might look like Figure 1.1. The feature being highlighted is that a quickly guessed or 'first' solution seems to come before the collection of supporting evidence (as reasoning or as empirics). This is why Dewey calls it 'reflective thinking', that is, thinking back on a possible solution. Dewey provides synonyms for 'possible solution', 'first thought' or 'quick idea'. He suggests, 'conclusion', 'supposition', 'conjecture', 'guess' and 'hypothesis'.

This idea of placing the solution prior to the thinking will be a novel suggestion only to those unfamiliar with the ideas behind argumentative inquiry, or of the pattern recognition literature from psychology. Of course, the example provided is very simple, as are the other two examples that Dewey discusses, both of which have the same form. Seeing them as simple examples of thinking might, however, mistakenly open up the possibility of distinguishing reflective thinking as alright for quick everyday decisions, but not for important scientific thinking or project management. This would allow a return to the line of argument that 'jumping to

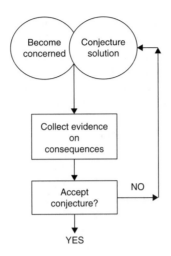

*Figure 1.1   Dewey's steps to thinking*

conclusions' needs to be avoided until after some careful consideration of the facts. It is being suggested that any split between everyday thinking and 'big project' thinking is an error, as the big project thinking only includes what is happening in the heads of the individuals involved in a project.

## EMPIRICAL SUPPORT

Guindon (1990) accidently provides empirical support for Dewey's examples. He compiles a two-hour protocol analysis of three professional designers who are designing lift (elevator) control software. He struggles to apply Herbert Simon's (1975) ideas of ill-structured problems to describe the type of trial-and-error heuristic processes the designers went through to complete an effective design. These designers were well qualified, and very experienced. He concludes: 'This study shows that the early stages of the design process are best characterised as opportunistic' (Guindon 1990, 336).

He found that designers frequently guessed at solutions, and then thought about whether these would work when compared to the requirements. The 'guesses' were accepted, modified or rejected after further thought or testing. There was no linear process of appreciating the requirements, collecting facts and selecting alternative solutions, and then selecting a solution. Although Guindon does not mention Dewey, his description of how his designers solve their problem has similarities to the three examples provided by Dewey. Guindon, however, is concerned that his designers are not following Simon's interpretation of the traditional steps, suggesting that this may be because humans have only bounded rationality and are imperfect at reasoning. This assumes Simon's problem-solving algorithms are an idealized form of human problem-solving that somewhat inadequate humans should aspire to. Dewey's interest is in how humans think.

Klein (1989) observed the actions of experienced firefighters, nurses, data programmers, soldiers, paramedics and design engineers. He describes their problem identification and conception as 'recognition primed': they appeared to observe the problem domain until they recognized a pattern such as the firefighter recognizing a particular colour of flames in certain locations. They then knew how to respond: the solution. The task was one of situation assessment not option selection; their efforts went into sizing up the situation. He found that once an option was apparent, 96 per cent of the time the experts did not attempt to generate more options in order to make comparisons. Rather, they moved on to thinking through whether their conjecture solution would work, or how it would have to be modified to work. Problem identification and conception was not a comparison of alternatives but rather a process of editing their first thought conjectures. This is much what Dewey described above.

Mintzberg and Westley (2001) have also noted that some problem-solving seems to jump to the solution before any reasoning or evidence has been collected. He calls this the 'seeing first' approach (having insights) and contrasts it with the traditional step approach which he calls the 'thinking first' approach. Part of Mintzberg and Wesley's (2001) critique of the 'thinking first' approach includes the experience that people often seem to have solutions in search of problems: hammers looking for nails. This seems to be a bit like Chalmer's (1982) theory-laden observation. Mintzberg cites March as characterizing problem-solving as: 'collections of choices looking for problems, issues and feelings looking for decision situations in which they may be aired, solutions looking for issues to which they might be an answer and decision makers looking for work' (Mintzberg and Westley 2001, 90).

Mintzberg's 'seeing first' approach uses the example of a family out shopping seeing a black stool and declaring that this was the solution to the problem of the colour scheme for a new apartment. The apartment is then totally redesigned, successfully, around this stool. The thinking approach would have been to set the colour scheme (plan) and then find furniture and coverings to suit (actions) the plan.

Mintzberg's third option of 'doing first' thinking aligns with the action learning or practitioner ideas of Argyris and Schon (1978) which suggest that when a problem is identified, just guess some action, do it and then think about what happened. Again, the thinking comes after the guessed solution. The doing is expected to provide some experiences to think about. This might be seen as similar to the 'seeing approach' where the action is to 'see' rather than to act.

**Therefore**

Philosophers, researchers and experienced decision-making theorists seem to have noticed that humans, when faced with a concern, jump to a tentative solution and then can choose to act to rationalize that conjecture using more critical thinking such as observation, reasoning and experimentation. If the solution is found wanting then it is rejected and another guess evaluated. This is different from the traditional view of rational thinking for coping with concerns, which required evidence to be collected first, some process of selecting from alternatives, and then a solution selected. The essential difference is that the reflective, opportunistic, seeing-first approach starts with a conjecture.

Is there any sort of theory to suggest that the conjecture-first approach is rational? Suggested below is a three-stranded, but not mutually exclusive, set of justifications. One is an evolutionary perspective (stigmergy), one from a theory of knowledge and another from a child psychology perspective.

## CONJECTURE FIRST

Rapid and instinctive response to recognized threatening phenomena does appear to be justifiable in evolutionary terms. Being able to recognize instantly a cliff edge or tiger's face in long grass would seem to give survival advantage. Other examples include rapid hand closure on touching something painful and rapid eyelid closure on exposure to excessive heat. These can be seen as a very instinctive form of problem-solving. The rapid instinctive action would seem to involve the brain recognizing and responding to what it sees as a danger. However, some readers may want to distinguish this sort of instinctive reaction from 'rational thinking'. Yet these instant pattern recognition mental responses at least open the door to an approach to thinking that aligns with the idea that the brain very quickly jumps to conjectures; the brain seems to be a rapid recognition organ. In the psychology literature this is often referred to as 'automatic thinking' (Allport 1954). As Dewey seemed to be suggesting above, reflecting carefully, rationally, scientifically, methodically and systematically upon an intuitive response may be a preferable way of understanding human thinking.

The 'automatic thinking' line of argument from psychology is that the human brain develops schema or mental models to enable us to interpret what we see. This is similar to Kant's *a priori*, Churchman's perspectival thinking, boundary shifting in systems thinking (Ackoff 2000), Chalmers's (1982) theory-laden observation and the ethics literature on framing (Werhane 2002). At the cognitive level 'vision' can be explained as the brain very rapidly recognizing a stream of input through the senses. This is perhaps appreciated by recounting the experiences of adults who undergo eye surgery to successfully correct birth defects causing blindness. In some cases the blindness is caused by a physical fault in the eye that can be corrected by surgery. After the operation, while technically their eye 'works', they are unable to decipher the confusing pattern of colours and lights entering their eye. This is apparently not due to some further fault with the optical nerves but rather because their brain has no memories, no schemas, to use to call upon to interpret the shapes and patterns of light entering their eye.

This may be analogous to how we think. We mix experience as recognized phenomena with new sensory inputs. This reinforces the suggestion that when we think we automatically perceive the problem from historic schemas or perspective (frames, theories, values, system boundaries) which are likely to be the result of genetic, childhood and broader social influences. This schema of perspective provides an explanation of what is thought about; it gives recognition. Creative thinking can then be defined as suggesting a new recognition, a new perspective on an old problem, one that the others involved in the problem had not considered.

Stigmergy is a term used in the self-organization biology literature (Camazine et al. 2001) for what is observed in some swarm insects; they seem to react automatically to different physical cues. The experiments usually referred to are those of ants in laboratory Petri dishes. Individual ants have been observed to move sand about in a meaningless random manner until they spot a recognizable shape such as a pupa cavity, after which their actions switch to constructively building an extension to this cavity. The shape seems to trigger a responsive action. We can see a similar response in humans who see a person, word, structure, noise or some other phenomenon and respond intuitively from prior experience. An experienced problem-solver can therefore be expected to respond rapidly to recognizable situations, jumping to very tentative conjectures.

The conjecture-first approach can also be aligned with writings in the theory of knowledge philosophy. Many philosophers comment that questions are at the beginning of human thought. Crosswhite (1996), in his support for argumentative reasoning, argues that we should really start with the tentative conjectures, not the later verbalized question. Children, as well as dumb and deaf people and species without language, all of whom do not have the linguistic device of questioning, or without knowing what a question is, can solve problems. They can be expected to become confused as they try to impose a pattern on sensory input. They can also be expected somehow to make sense of these images or noises if only to classify them as 'problematic' by thinking up conjectures (solutions, ideas) that do or do not 'fit'. However, unless these people without questions have rational reasoning skills they might not justify their conjecture in an explicit manner which could aid community learning. Crosswhite, as philosopher, seems to agree that the brain jumps to conjectures based on genetics or experience almost instantly upon our receipt of new sensory input; it gives pattern and meaning to these inputs. If the patterns work then there is no problem; conversely if the guessed-at patterns do not seem to fit the sensory input, then a problem is declared. Inductive science suggests we should somehow suspend this instant pattern recognition, and rather collect evidence in a state of suspended judgement. Crosswhite feels this is not really possible and repressing this first impression will distort what is seen as relevant evidence. Rather, he suggests we acknowledge explicitly what our brains have conjectured and set about justifying that conjecture to ourselves and others.

The theory of knowledge literature also suggests this conjecture-first approach in two further and related ways. One way is Popper's (1972) ideas of presenting conjectures for falsification. The other is inherent in argumentative inquiry. Popper's conjectures are meant to be more thought-out than instinctive responses, but the basic layout of having an upfront explicit conjecture that needs to be proved to a sceptical audience is the analogous notion. It was intended to be contrasted with the discovery approach of seeking evidence prior to finding some solution. The difference seems to come down mainly to whether you believe that the first thought conjectures can be completely set aside prior to evidence collection and whether non-theory-driven observation can be undertaken.

The use of competitive argument (reasoned debate, not quarrelling) as a means of argumentative inquiry, rather than primarily persuasion, now has a number of advocates (Eemeren and Grootendorst 2003; List and Metcalfe 2004; Perelman and Olbrechts-Tyteca 1969; Walton 1998). As with Popper, the idea is that an advocate declares a knowledge claim to start a competitive inquiry process with a sceptical knowledgeable audience. From this process it is intended that an improved and fully justified knowledge claim emerges. Churchman extends this to seeking participants' perspectives of complex social problems. These perspectives need to be justified to the sceptical audience.


## POLYA

Another strand of thinking that appears to support the conjecture-first approach to thinking may be drawn from the words of that classic problem-solving text by Polya (1945), *How To Solve It*. This booklet is aimed at mathematicians. It provides a suggested methodology to tackle the creative process of solving mathematical and geometric problems. His steps are:

> First. You have to understand the problem.
> Second. Find the connection between the data and the unknown. You may be obliged to consider auxiliary problems if an immediate connection cannot be found. You should obtain eventually a plan of the solution.
> Third. Carry out your plan.
> Fourth. Examine the solution obtained. (Polya 1945, xvi)

When saying 'understand the problem', Polya seems to simply mean read or observe the problem: a first cut. The argument of this chapter is that while this is being undertaken possible solutions will jump into the reader's head. It is only identified as a problem if none of these tentative conjectures is thought to be viable. Polya provides advice on what to do next with his second step, which advises the need to seek analogous problems that have been solved. He suggests using existing solutions to old problems. This could be described as an act of further appreciating the problem. This is still further elaborated on in the third step which Polya states as testing to see whether the old analogous solution, or at least similar concepts, work for the new problem. Polya, who is a well-respected author on problem-solving, is therefore not suggesting that solutions come after reasoning about alternatives. Rather, he suggests that you search for a tentative conjecture solution (from an analogous problem) and then think about its usefulness for the current problem. This perhaps does not directly address the issues of prior experiences providing automatic analogies, but it does align with Dewey's ideas and the advice of argumentative inquiry to not seek alternatives and compare them, but rather to conjecture something that might work, and then think about editing this to fit the problem at hand.

# WICKED PROBLEMS

Polya's advice was aimed at mathematical problems while Dewey's was aimed at everyday problems and social research. This raises the issue of whether there is a need to distinguish simple from complex problems in terms of how solutions are sought. Rittel and Webber (1973) seem to have influenced Churchman and his students, Mason and Mitroff (1981), into thinking that wicked problems need a significantly different approach than simple problems. Simple problems are typically identified as mathematical or physical sciences problems and wicked problems are complex social problems, such as poverty and organizational strategy. Rittel and Webber (1973) define a wicked problem as one where:

1. There is no definitive formulation of a wicked problem.
2. Wicked problems have no stopping rule.
3. Solutions to wicked problems are not true-or-false, but good-or-bad.
4. There is no immediate and no ultimate test of a solution to a wicked problem.
5. Every solution to a wicked problem is a 'one-shot operation'; since there is no opportunity to learn by trial and error, every attempt counts significantly.
6. Wicked problems do not have an enumerable (or an exhaustively describable) set of potential solutions, nor is there a well-described set of permissible operations that may be incorporated into the plan. Every wicked problem is essentially unique.
7. Every wicked problem can be considered a symptom of another problem.
8. The existence of discrepancy representing a wicked problem can be explained in numerous ways. The choice of explanation determines the nature of the problem's resolution.
9. The planner has no right to be wrong. (1973, 161–66)

Dewey's problem of how to get to his next appointment matches the first nine[2] criteria. It does not match the traditional problem-solving advice to first identify all the possible solutions and then to fully evaluate each. Leaving aside the definition issue for a moment, items 2 and 6 (numerous problem definitions and solutions) do, however, seem to match the conjecture-first approach as they suggest that the problem-solver is free to think up as many conjectures as the situation permits. Given the likely influence of Dewey on Rittel this may not be surprising. Items 3 and 4 (no best solutions) were covered because there was no definitive proof that the evidence of the goodness of any conjecture solution was not absolutely 'true '. Rittel writes of problem 'resolving' in place of problem-solving in order to suggest that the solution is both socially constructed and likely to be open to re-solving later.

Items 5 and 7 (solutions are not generalizable) are covered in Dewey's appointment example because he has to get to this particular appointment, at this particular time. All the conjectures and supporting evidence are only relevant to this one-off situation. Repetitive experiments for generalized results are not possible.

Item 8 reminds me of Ackoff's (2000) call for problems to be dissolved not solved. Typically, this involves zooming in or out on the problem system to some sub- or supra-system and looking at the problem with that new conception. For example, his dissolving of an industrial dispute between bus conductors and drivers involved zooming out the problem conception to that of the 'wider' systems view of the bus company's operations. He wanted to consider the relative number of buses to bus stops. Dewey's appointment example problem could also be shifted to a wider city transport system problem, a multi-campus lecturer's problem as well as an appointments scheduling problem. Dewey did not discuss these conception-shifting opportunities, but it does seem an obvious next step – one that Ackoff takes. Conjectures-seeking can make use of this shifting of conceptions, only one way of which is to zoom in or out on the problem.

This issue of selecting an appropriate conception of a problem provides an understanding of how complicated a problem is, or is wanted to be. Dewey's appointment problem is not seen as complicated because it appears to be solvable at the level within his immediate and sole control. Zooming out and suggesting redesigning the city transport would then be understood to be a much more complicated problem involving numerous different groups of people.

Put the other way around, a problem can be made simpler by zooming down to one of its sub-components; a very science solution. If Dewey had decided to do this and reduced the problem to how to get there by, say, the subway, then the issues would have become: where is the station? which platform do I need? and so on.

So in summary, in situations of socially constructed problems, perhaps best called concerns, given imperfect knowledge and time constraints, the approach of finding solutions by exploring conjectures seems to be appropriate. These conjectures are generated from experience in an opportunistic (brainstorming) manner. There is no possibility of exploring all the possible solutions and fully evaluating them. It may appear to be a suboptimal approach, but the situation is too complex and too socially constructed for a complete set of solutions to be useful. The concern-solving task becomes one of finding a solution that works well enough to stop those involved being concerned.

## APPRECIATING AND SOLVING

As discussed earlier, those assuming the 'traditional' steps of decision-making tend to assume that appreciating a problem comes before, but is relatively independent of, the correct solution to a problem. With a wicked problem there is much more of a 'producer and product' relationship: how the problem is explained influences the solution. This is item 8 in Rittel's list, 'The choice of explanation determines the nature of the problem's resolution'. How a problem is set, defined, explained or appreciated is believed to determine what is seen as a satisfactory path to solution. For example, Dewey presented his appointment example from the conception of a choice between three transport alternatives. He did not present it from the conception of a city transport design problem. His presentation influenced the range of conjecture solutions (patterns) that his brain supplied. The way a problem is conceived is an important part of determining what appears to be the rational solution.

Gilbert (1991) argues that 'as perception construes objects, so cognition construes ideas'. He draws on the experimental psychology finding to compare Descartes's ideas on how we move from an idea to a belief with those of Spinoza, opting for Spinoza. Descartes suggests we appreciate ideas in a neutral form and then later decide if they are to be believed or not. Spinosa suggests that the act of appreciating an idea is synonymous with believing it. We have to actively then set about a process of critiquing this belief if we are to disbelieve it later. The evidence Gilbert provides to support his argument is quite extensive, including noting that children have to be taught to be disbelieving, and that our language defaults to belief: it takes more words to state something in the negative. Gilbert reviews the psychology literature on people making decisions when stressed. Their default position is to act as if anything they have been told was correct. Moreover, subjects told the information they were being given was false, when stressed, used it as if they believed it. This all aligns with the human information processing research which shows a general failure of people to seek disconfirming evidence as part of their inquiry strategies. This line of reasoning explains, at the cognitive level, how conceiving a problem is believing it, and that how it is appreciated will influence what and how it is believed. How we believe something is likely to affect our initial conjectural solution.

Better problem-conceiving methods are therefore thought to be the key to purposeful thinking. The multiple conception approach, called a system approach by Churchman (1971), suggests the need to ensure problem-solving is set in the context of seeking differing conceptions or interpretations. There are some multiple conception generation methods for problem conception beyond Ackoff's zooming in and out on the problem situation. Some are: multiple rich picturing (Checkland 2000), Morgan's (1986) metaphors, a word generation software such as 'Randomword' (http://www.infinn.com/randomword.html), Linstone's (1999) technical, organizational and personal perspectives, and Mitroff and Kilmann's (1975) storytelling. These are designed to encourage a range of intuitive solutions derived from first generating multiple interpretations of how the problem might be viewed. These exercises, done in groups, are believed to generate first thought conjectures from novel conception of the problem using differing conceptions in at least some of the minds of the participants. New conjectures will follow new interpretations of the problem, but these alternative interpretations may need to be generated and made explicit, perhaps in a confidential manner.

List and Metcalfe (2004) suggest debate can also be used to generate alternative conceptions of the problem by asking participants to edit a conjecture written out in the form, 'That X is Y and not Z'. This publically argued editing is intended to assist the group to think through the perspectives suggesting the conjectured solution in more detail. Having articulated a conjecture, falsifying (disconfirming) evidence could then be sought. Falsification can also be seen as generating new conceptions – further appreciation. It is possible to say that a problem is not really appreciated until it has been explained from a multitude of conceptions.

## CONCLUSION

This chapter has argued that the brain rather insists on jumping to conjectured solutions to a concern as soon as it thinks it has understood the situation. This makes the process of needing to generate multiple understandings or conceptions of a concern critical for creative, purposeful, rigorous thinking. Dewey's illustrative example of selecting transport to get across town was mentioned. Using the conception of timeliness immediately suggested a different solution to that of saving the environment. A reflective understanding of how we do and should think suggests that our brains will be going through an endless process of 'jumping to conclusions' as the problem is appreciated and made sense of. This is believed not to be human frailty but rather a strength, provided tentative conjectures once generated are methodically and rationally justified. It does, however, mean that careful thinking involves more than justifying conjectures. It means care needs to be taken over what conceptions of the concerns are generated.

The way concerns are presented becomes important; multiple conceptions of the problem situation are essential. Being pragmatic means accepting that these conjectured guesses are going on, but being sceptical about their reliability and inquisitive about the conception used to set the problem in the first place. This is how we humans should and actually do think carefully. It is different from how computers think. Accepting that the brain jumps to conclusions can become the basis of reflection. We arrive at a problem situation with conjectures based on prior experience; not to do so would be unprofessional or inexperienced. Practices that make us sceptical about our prior experiences being relevant for a new problem need to be made explicit and formalized into processes for careful rational reflective thought.

Creative, purposeful problem-solving formulation is therefore seen as a deliberate process of reflection which involves the setting up of alternative conceptions of the problem situation in the minds of those involved. It is thought that how this problem conception is done will automatically stimulate a number of conjectured solutions for what needs to be done. What makes the thinking purposeful is what mental concept(ion)s are used to conceive a problem and, therefore, likely conjectured solutions. The pragmatic or concept-driven approach to problem-solving is based on the assumption that thinking is about purposeful reflection against explicit concepts.

## APPLICATION

Pragmatism is about reflecting on experiences, learning from doing, actions. This book develops, chapter by chapter, a pragmatic way of conceptualizing problems so as to decide upon appropriate responses. It would therefore be internally consistent to read this book with a problematic situation in mind, some thing or event you are concerned about. At the end of each chapter there will be a short application section suggesting, in line with the contents of the chapter, what you might do next to more carefully conceptualize your problem.

This chapter has argued that thinking, and therefore problem-solving, starts with a conjecture of what might be done. This is how our brains have evolved. Clear thinking later requires the careful explicit selection of alternative concepts with which to reflect on the initial conjecture. Therefore, you might want to briefly articulate a problem as a conjecture of what might be done. As assistance with how to do this, seven examples are provided:

1. That Australia needs to be careful about getting caught up in any *conflicts between the US and China*. This is because the US is a traditional and cultural ally, but China is a growing massive market for Australia's cheap coal and iron ore.

2. That *oil and gas hydraulic fracturing* (fracking) is appropriately used in managing reducing carbon levels in the atmosphere. This is because there are concerns over carbon dioxide levels in the atmosphere. Gas, supplied without large-scale digging operations, may provide a temporary *midterm reduction* in carbon emissions.

3. That if you want to anticipate the *behaviour of organizations*, then you need to understand the *mindset of stakeholders*. This is because an analysis of assets, markets, products, norms, regulations, histories and capabilities may not provide sufficient information to predict (or manipulate) the behaviour of organizations.

4. That universities *need to restructure* in response to the threats and opportunities generated by the available free online courses offered by prestigious universities (massive open online courses – MOOCs). This is because in 2012 over 3 million students, and growing, have enrolled in free online courses offered by 62 of the world's most prestigious universities. It is unclear how this will *impact* upon the less prestigious universities.

5. That the *emergent informal industry* (strategic group) of house-owners offering cultural tourist accommodation in Iran needs to form a community of practice if it is to avoid inappropriate government intervention. This is because this fledgling group wants to define itself independently of the strong centralized government bureaucracy in that nation.

6. That a bathroom equipment manufacturer needs to *align the future thinking* of market analysts, senior managers, staff and what is portrayed in its image and policy documents. This is because the markets have changed due to the ongoing global financial crisis, causing some *fracturing of response plans*.

7. That the actual and potential *business models of social enterprises* in Australia need to be made explicit. This is because there is a growing interest in the possible alternative business models for this emerging industry that offers a *free market social welfare system* compared to that of assuming the welfare state.

Note the italicized concepts used in these conjectures. These are the default concepts being used.

# NOTES

1. This chapter is based on: Metcalfe (2007b, Chapter 1).
2. Rittel and Webber's point number 10 appears to introduce a moral imperative into solving wicked problems so as to avoid unethical experimental actions which affect people's lives.

# 2. Problem-solving as pragmatic inquiry

## OVERVIEW

Know where your rationality comes from. This chapter provides an explanation of the philosophical basis of a pragmatic approach to problem conceptualization. Pragmatism is practical but it is also a philosophy of how humans inquire to identify and solve problems. Pragmatists' 100-year-old approach involves assisting a concerned community to surface and reflect on a handful of linguistic concepts they want used to interpret the future. Problem conceptualization is assumed to be a process of participatory inquiry: how the concerned might act in the future.[1]

## PRAGMATISM

Menand (2002) provides a useful historical discussion on the early pragmatists: Peirce, Dewey, James and others. This chapter focuses on slightly different details in its aim to design a system of steps or principles for thinking. More emphasis is placed on the pluralist thread of pragmatism (Rescher 2005). Mao Tse-tung's (1967) academic work might be added because of his belief that knowledge lies within the 'doer', those with the action experience, rather than those who theorize from their imagination. It is agreed that pragmatism can be seen to effectively start with Peirce in the nineteenth century, although Nietzsche's (1979 [1873]) influence has to be acknowledged. In modern times, Rorty (1982) and Putnam (2001) are seen as the modern advocates. Given the disputes in public administration journals (Shields 2005) a distinction might be made between pragmatism and neo-pragmatism. Most ideas develop offspring with slightly different characteristics. Neo–pragmatism seems to play down certain characteristics of pragmatism, such as the role of experience in thinking, and play up other characteristics such as pluralism. The personal construction of pragmatism explained here might be guilty of being closer to the linguistic pragmatism, a theory of knowledge that includes peoples' experiences as interpretations through default concepts. This contrasts with some of the modern pragmatists such as Rorty who are concerned that experience relies on our sensory inputs, which can be problematic.

Menand's book *The Metaphysical Club* (2002) describes the meetings of the early pragmatists as being a search for a better way of reasoning, following the carnage of the American Civil War. It had been a bloody war over ideas such as federation, human liberties and the removal of servitude, with both sides claiming to be right. The mood of the pragmatists was progressive, humanistic and critical of the very structured and privileged 'European' society. They must have been aware of the work of early critical social theorists, but rather than looking at politics and economics as Karl Marx did, Peirce (1878) looked to emancipation from a study of how we reason, and thus of knowledge, and of epistemology: how we inquire. Starting from a very solid understanding of logic he argues that what is logical is dependent on what concept(ion)s are being used to see the world. What is logical is dependent on prior actions that, through our senses, become experiences. This puts his work a long time ahead of Kuhn, earned him the admiration of a few well-respected analytic philosophers, and seems to echo Nietzsche's 'there are no facts, only interpretations', 'what then is truth' and 'the doer alone learneth'. One form of short-sightedness in thinking is to insist that our own logic is the only correct one.

This then can be seen to be one of the distinguishing drivers of pragmatism: it looks at knowledge from the viewpoint of inequality or interpretation and vice versa. Habermas's book *Knowledge and Human Interests* (1972) argues for the sociology of knowledge. It has a largely commendatory chapter on Peirce's writings, which were from nearly a century earlier. Habermas argues that knowledge is not built up from a foundation of logic and/or empirics but rather by communities of doubters debating. Both pragmatism and Habermas are anti-foundationalist. The Metaphysical Club, like those who were reacting against the inequity of European culture in the eighteenth and nineteenth centuries, argued the new world needed a new epistemology; a new social order needed a new epistemology but one that still had science at its core. Knowledge was not only a process of impartially building one fact on another, as advocated by the rationalists and empiricists, but rather logic and empirics needed to be interpreted through alternative perspectives or conceptions. Quine (1961) and Quinton's (1966) conception or concept of the web of knowledge makes analogous the structure of our brain, the World Wide Web with its linked websites, and our knowledge. Events can have numerous interlinked 'websites' each representing a different concept(ion) used to generate a different interpretation. A problem seen through the concept of 'power' provides a different interpretation from the same problem seen through the concept of 'effectiveness'.

*Principle 1: Assume each community uses different prior experiences to interpret physical events.*

Boland and Tenkasi (1995) talk of communities of practice (Wenger and Snyder 2000); these communities each have their own default concepts for thinking about particular problems. When we think, reflect, we start by using the conceptions learnt from our childhood, our community. Clear thinking requires that we try to be aware of these conceptions. Deconstruction is one way: a historical construction of these conceptions. An alternative suggested by James is comparison and contrast. So, the first principle of thinking about complex social situations is to remember that different people conceive of situations differently.

This principle reflects the post-Civil War history of pragmatism and its desire to allow in multiple rational conceptions as part of any thinking by or for communities. It wants to accept that different communities may have different but rational conceptions of past events. Pragmatism tends to use the term 'inquiry' rather than thinking or research. Inquiry, communal thinking, is thought to be more of a social act within or across communities than is usually recognized in much of the thinking literature (e.g. Simon 1975). Thinking to produce knowledge claims in pragmatism is explicitly seen as being a process of social interaction or of involving justification specific to each community of doubters. This comes close to Popper's ideas of conjecture and refutation when talking about justification to a sceptical universal audience (Popper 1972, 1971 [1945]). Communities of practice do, however, contrast with Popper's ideas that conjectures need to be convincing to a 'universal' audience. Habermas talks of justification to civil societies. The term 'doubter' is used in place of the word 'sceptical', the latter suggesting a need for only empirical evidence. Doubters need to be convinced using whatever works in their particular community. This suggests that pragmatic thinking is a process of interacting with different communities (inquiry) to construct understanding and design actions. This seems particularly relevant to those trying to solve problems in a conflictual environment.

Pragmatism is therefore more explicit about alternative 'communities of practice' (Wenger and Snyder 2000), each having its own background experience and default concepts for reflecting on that experience. Justifying a knowledge claim, even in terms of it being useful knowledge, is expected to be significantly different for each different community. Science, of course, has its equivalent in Kuhn's paradigms or schools of scientific thought.

What is a reasonable explanation in one community is nonsense in another. Therefore, problem solutions will need to be justified in ways relevant to the alternative stakeholder communities.

It can be seen that this pragmatic view of thinking not only decides how to think about a concern; it will also determine what concerns need to be studied. A Muslim community might feel there is some urgency in better understanding alternative interpretations of the Koran. For a medical community it may be AIDS, and for an environmental community it may be global warming. The research problem is socially constructed, and only deemed solved, by a community. Rittel and Webber (1973) explain this using the concept of 'wickedness'. Useful thinking is, like a community's morals, also socially constructed. They go on to say that the system is self-referencing, in that situations can only be understood by using concepts with which a community is comfortable. These concepts in turn determine what a concern is, and what it is not. We see concerns depending on the concept used to explain them. For example, a review of a concern by using a concept such as 'face' would then see a 'face-saving' problem. Pragmatic thinking should therefore recognize the concepts influencing us and those being used by communities involved in the problem situation, but also those required to stimulate new thinking in a community.

An egalitarian consequence of the pragmatists' use of community-generated concepts is that those being thought about are reflective and having a significant impact on the thinking of the thinker. Their concepts will be washing into any new thinker interacting with that community. This is sometimes called being mentally captured by the opposition in negotiations: becoming sympathetic. Social interpretation of how we think differs from objective interpretations. It recognizes that our thoughts come from others not ourselves. This counters the Descartian lone scholar assumption of the thinker as a separate unaffected mind able to think differently and separately from those being inquired about, who are not some form of unreflective automaton.

So, the focus on group experiences, and the concepts used to reflect, places a different emphasis on how to inquire in pragmatic thinking. Scientific inquiry places a lot of emphasis on method, on exactly how the evidence in support of a knowledge claim was collected. At the extreme it is assumed that, if a rigorous method is used, then the evidence collected to support a proposed solution will be thought to be 'true' regardless of who collected it or to whom it is presented; the communities involved are thought of as being merely part of some universal audience. Pragmatism distinguishes thinking from scientific research by saying that thinking is community-based rather than sole or universal, aligning it with Hegel, Heidegger and Habermas. The emphasis is on having a community of doubters who force those who think something to justify their claims reasonably. To be a community of doubters, it has to be motivated and competent. This provides an alternative way of seeing the rise of science. Rather than being a community of Methodists, it can be seen to be an ever-increasing number of paid professionals who want to advance their careers and can do so by doubting the knowledge claims of others (Latour and Woolgar 1986). Thinking is advanced not so much by method, as by doubters.

*Principle 2: Identify a dialectic of useful concepts.*

Pragmatism, as constructed here, does not attempt to discover a single best interpretation of physical events, rather it attempts to understand by constructing multiple well-justified interpretations or conceptions. Events happen – why they happen needs multiple conceptions. Pragmatic thinking is not a matter of discovering the one correct interpretation perhaps built up from a foundation of correct smaller interpretations, like bricks in a house, aiming slowly to discover the entire picture. Rather, pragmatism sees thinking as reflecting on physical events through a variety of concepts (lenses, theories, perspectives, stances, viewpoints, concerns, frames, priorities or ideologies). To use a classic scientific example, the experience of the event of the movement of planets was once interpreted using the concept of clockwork. This reveals a certain pattern of interrelated movement. Interpreting the same experiences of planetary motion using Newton's concept of 'attraction' reveals different insights, ones related to mysterious forces acting between bodies not in contact with each other; forces apparently much like electricity or magnetism. Experiencing those planetary movements using Einstein's 'time space distortions' results in yet another set of insights about how objects at some distance from each other can still affect each other, now with the absence of invisible forces.

The consequence of this understanding of pragmatic thinking is that it becomes being as interested in what concepts are used to 'see' events or experiences, as the events themselves. As will be discussed in more detail later, concepts to the pragmatists are patterns of activity. Calls for theories as explanations (why things are as they are), for pragmatists, become a call to understand the concept or perspective used to generate particular explanations or interpretations. Calls for theories as idealized models of how things should be, such as power relationships, are interpreted in pragmatism as ways of seeing, sense-making (Weick 1995) the construction of a multifaceted concept. So for example, in Markus's oft-cited article (Markus and Bjorn-Andersen 1987) on technical power determining the solution to technical problems, pragmatic thinking would use the language that they looked at the event of information technology (IT) managers' actions by using the concept of 'technical power'. They would not be thought of as being involved in any process of generating a theory of technical power.

This pragmatic intent to see the world through differing concepts, to provide a non-foundational view of knowledge, means that calls to stand on the shoulders of those who went before, for foundational courses and for the development of theories, are inappropriate. This is not to say that it is impossible to develop the facets of any concept being used to interpret physical events. For example, the facets of the concepts of power (Markus and Bjorn-Andersen 1987), systems (Ackoff 1971) and behaviour (Forgas and George 2001) have been extensively developed in the literature. The newer concept of 'becoming' is still being developed (Bearman and Stovel 2000), while the concept of self-organization has had some development (Fuchs 2003; Joham 2006). Pragmatism is not comfortable with the suggestion of there being one best universal concept for interpreting certain experiences. However, there may be certain concepts that are more useful than others, depending on the particular situation.

The soundbite most associated with pragmatism is 'what works best' or 'what fits best'. This is a shortening of, 'what works best in a particular situation' (James 1910 [1907]). Extending it further, the pragmatic construction of the most useful concept for interpreting particular experiences of physical events is what 'fits best'. This seems at first glance too relativistic. Surely one person might be deceived. For example, some soldiers' experience is that the concept of 'flatness' (i.e. two-dimensional) is what works best at explaining the earth's surface. There is a risk this 'works best' definition of knowledge may mean that a soldier's knowledge would not move beyond thinking that the earth is flat. The concept of flatness works best to explain their experiences, but excess zeal insisting it is the one truth raises the danger of conflict with sailors, global navigators. The use of the concept of 'roundness' works best for them, it best explains their experiences. However, the tension is resolved to the satisfaction of most soldiers that a round earth concept can also explain their flat earth experiences. The round earth explains some experiences of farmers that the flat earth concept cannot explain, such as the horizon. The round earth concept explains to sailors how far the horizon is. On balance, the concept of roundness is more 'useful' than that of flatness; it provides more explanations than the concept of flatness applied to our experiences of the earth. Thus, the 'what works best' requirement of pragmatism does not mean knowledge will not enlarge; rather it grows by comparing concepts.

The popular use of the term 'pragmatic', when not meant as 'practical', is usually to provide a contrast to 'idealistic'. So an organization can say it is being pragmatic when it offers bribes to access some information. The alternative would be to say that the organization is guided by some absolute, universal or idealistic ethical standards, suggesting it is not willing to compromise them. Pragmatism objects to universal interpretations of anything. This idealist stand is resisted because it is saying there is only one correct concept with which to see the situation. The pragmatic organization is saying it is willing to tolerate practices such as bribery by understanding this as simply a different construction of persuasion.

The use of multiple concepts is being suggested because the obvious critique of pragmatism's anti-foundational stance – its unprescribed methods, its calls for communities of doubters, and its multi-perspectivalism – is relativism. Of course, this is rejected by the modern pragmatists such as Rorty (1982) and Putnam (2001). In their definitions of knowledge, they focus on reasoned justification. The concepts used need to be justified to communities of doubters who trade in reasoned justifications. Earlier, Churchman (1971) had recognized the problem and provided a system for reasoned justification of any knowledge claim resulting from an inquiry. Metcalfe (2006) explains Churchman's system as having five elements: logic, experiences (empirics), explanations why, counters to alternative explanations, and voice to all. The last element means that any thinking, to be ethical, should ensure it gives a voice to all those involved. Churchman argues that these sorts of elements need to be present if thinking is to have at least some chance of being convincing to a community of doubters. Most thinkers would automatically use most of Churchman's elements and see little wrong with using the rest methodically.

The term 'concept' has been used here as it is thought to be the modern equivalent of Peirce and Dewey's use of the term 'conceptions'. Also, it is the term used by modern exponents of pragmatism such as Baggini (2005). It may be opportune to compare it to similar terms. The generation of systems-thinking pragmatists – Mason, Mitroff and Ackoff – often use the word 'perspective'. Alternatives appear to be viewpoint, lens, framework, frame, stance, ideas, world-view (*weltanschauung*), and even ideology (although these last two words now have some very political overtones). Some may be considered more deep-rooted than others and some intuitive, while others may be considered to be derived from the command of language.

It has been suggested that pragmatic thinking should identify the differing concepts participants use to understand a problem, and to use multiple concepts to see a problem in more detail. Extending this, using contradictory concepts is advised as this is thought to generate more insight. For example, seeing the problem of funding university places using the contradictory concepts of elitism and egalitarianism is expected to be productive. Dialectic, contradictory, ironic or paradoxical concepts can be particularly decentring and therefore creative: useful for encouraging creative thinking (Hatch 1997).

*Principle 3: Make concepts operational as conjectured ideas or solutions.*

This principle suggests that whatever concepts are used to think about problems, they need to be made operational into a conjecture (hypothesis, argument or proposition). This is because the concept needs to be turned into practical means of thinking about what action is to be taken. The conjecture is better in the form of a statement that suggests what action might be taken rather than as a 'research' question. For example, if the concept is 'technological determinism', what conjectured solutions or ideas does this concept suggest? Markus (1994) used the literature to derive the conjectured idea 'that social effects are determined by the characteristics of technology, regardless of users' intentions'. This suggests what actions can be taken to 'test' whether the conjectured idea works or not. Different technologies can be tested for their impact on users' behaviour.

The conjecture ideas do need to be justified. This often means identifying the questions that the conjecture will raise in the mind of a sceptic. These might then be used to design what evidence is collected to suggest that the conjecture is useful. This evidence collection might use observation, document analysis, a survey or an interview. Ultimately, it will need to use an action: an intervention. Continuing the Markus example, action may mean asking participants to use one technology over another. Their actions or comments in response to this action are then interpreted using the conjectured idea. For example, you might ask participants if they felt one technology forced them to be conservative, or to act differently to their intentions. Further evidence might be collected from noting the reactions of those affected by the users of alternative technologies.

*Principle 4: Trial conjectured ideas, use these to act on the conundrum, then carefully note what happens.*

Continuing from the previous principle, this principle is saying: enact the conjectured idea – that is, act or at least imagine acting on the conundrum (problem situation) – and then note the responses. Peirce argues for setting up this dialectic between our prior conceptions and what actually happens when we act (Rescher 2005). This acting in the physical world provides us with experiences. Experience is a series of inputs we have sensed with our five bodily senses, through our eyes, ears, skin and so on. For there to be a sensory input there has to be an action, a physical event. For us to see, light has to strike our eye, and we have to process it. For us to hear, some action has to generate a noise. More generally, when we trial an action, we provide input to our senses and acquire knowledge. So, for example, the old project may have had to be modified to accommodate some stakeholders. The senses of those involved would have detected dissatisfaction from stakeholders, be it verbal or gestural. Then they might have experienced the project being changed. Next there would have been a revised set of stakeholder community reactions which, if the change was successful, would be interpreted as less hostile than previously. This set of sensory inputs needs to be reflected upon for learning to occur.

However, this chapter is arguing that the interpretation of these events will be influenced by what concept is being used, either explicitly or by default. Reflecting on the effects of the action needs to reflect also on the usefulness of the concepts used and whether alternative concepts would have been useful. The action being reflected upon may be an intervention, or a formal controlled experiment. With a formal experiment, there is methodical control over perceived elements of the conundrum using a series of 'if – then' hypotheses. This indifference between real-life actions and formal experimentation makes pragmatic thinking less vulnerable to the 'rigour versus relevance' debate. Rather than treat practitioners' experiences of prior actions as unreliable or biased, pragmatic thinking asks what would be the most useful concept to reflect on what happened. For example, the medieval sailor may have sailed around the world implicitly using the concept of the flat earth to interpret their day-to-day existence. Later in life, this sailor may hear about the concept of the world being round and use that to reflect on past experiences. This comparison could generate valuable new knowledge about the concepts of flatness and roundness. While logic and laboratory experiments are often presented as 'concept-free', Peirce's work on identifying logic as concept-dependent rather undermines the uniqueness of experiments except as providing experiences that might not be possible in everyday events. Past experiments can also be reflected upon later using different concepts.

The importance of experience of past actions in pragmatic thinking aligns with its concern with the egalitarian consequences of how knowledge is defined. The pragmatic definition of knowledge needs both those that do (have experiences) and those that think (develop innovative concepts). The classic example here must be the extent to which Darwin consulted breeders to develop his evolution theory. The breeders provided the breeding intervention experience, and Darwin the concept of 'natural selection' by the environment. Mao's famous paper (1967) makes the case that it is the workers who have the knowledge of the means of production; capital cannot produce anything without the experience of the workers. Pragmatism would say the workers are only half the story: someone also needs to provide useful concepts to reflect on those workers' experiences. These useful concepts may well be provided by the workers but they often come from alternative innovative experiences such as Darwin's overseas travels. This led to useful knowledge derived from both breeding experience and a novel concept. The 'intellectual' may think of different concepts but these will not resonate with, be thought useful by, the practitioner unless they fit into his or her experiences. This recognition of the need for both functions to create and define knowledge is to some extent egalitarian.

Turning the pragmatic use of experience on its head, the purpose of pragmatic thinking is also to affect the future. Some scientific thinking places the emphasis on validity or truth rather than on the immediate usefulness of the findings. Pragmatism has a further egalitarian strand in being about seeking 'useful' knowledge, being full of uses. Useful knowledge provides those with a conundrum more choices on how to act differently and so overcome their problems. The idea that thinking could be done 'for its own sake', to merely increase the universal body of knowledge or to conquer nature, is not pragmatic. Pragmatic thinking needs to conclude in recommendations for how to act.

*Principle 5: Reflect on the consequences of the acting on the conundrum.*

Having acted on the conundrum (problem situation), there will be consequences. Reflecting on these consequences using explicit concepts, a post-mortem, is thought to be very educational. Care needs to be taken to separate the concepts used to design the action and the physical events that were experienced as a result of that action. Dewey (1982 [1910]) defines thinking as carefully noting the consequences of an action chosen based on a prior conception. That is, inquiring carefully into the logical sequence of events that follows from an action. Dewey uses the example of catching transport across town to get to a meeting. What are the consequences of taking a bus rather than a taxi, intended or unintended? When using the concept of 'timing', different consequences are highlighted compared to using the concept of 'environment'. This 'consequencialism' of pragmatism has been criticised for requiring prediction skills when actions are not possible. However, this criticism seems to be applicable to all thinking aimed at improving people's choices in the future.

James (1996 [1911]) argues that concepts are best defined by their consequences if acted upon. He provides various examples including 'freedom' to mean that if you have the concept of 'freedom', then you would have no more feeling of sensible constraint. Having the concept of 'necessity' means your way is blocked in all directions save one, and having the concept of 'God' means that you can dismiss certain kinds of fear. This seems to be a straightforward suggestion, one likely to impact on how a concept is made operational. Moreover, requesting that the entire design of any thinking include consideration of the consequences is likely to change its scope and focus significantly.

One means of thinking about the consequences of an action might be to extend the scope of the thinking to include a study of an attempt to implement any recommendations. For example, the study of the impact on social behaviour caused by particular technology might recommend particular communications protocols and then see what impact they have. An alternative response to the call to study consequences would be to design the whole thinking process to focus specifically on consequences of actions. This already happens, but perhaps not as the result of an epistemological driver. An example of a study that focused on consequences is that of Ash and Coiera (2004). They studied the error rates as a consequence of the implementation of a new computer system that had been justified on the basis that it would reduce errors. Incidentally, they found that the error rate increased.

Locke used the term 'experience' in his classic book *An Essay Concerning Human Understanding* (1690). Its connection to the term 'experiment' attests to the fundamental role of sensory inputs to empirical science. However, pragmatism puts more emphasis on experiences following an action rather than independent observation. Observation is an action, even a weak form of intervention, but perhaps in danger of not engaging enough senses. This point can be made using the old story (Scudder 1874) of a young scientist being mentored in the ways of science. The young scientist is asked to observe a dead fish as part of his training to be a scientist. He stares at it for some considerable time, only to discover he is not able to answer detailed questions about the fish's appearance. He is then mentored to try to draw the fish as a way to improve his quality of observation. The student is very impressed by how much more of its details he then appreciates. This is a point Latour (1986) makes. Merely observing the fish is considered insufficient to know the fish, but not only because of the number of senses used. Drawing it means using the concept of 'representation' as well as the action experience. However, that drawing the fish moves the student's thinking to using the concept of 'representation' from the concept of 'observation' is silent in the original story.

The obvious way to collect empirics or experiences for pragmatic thinking is therefore to be involved in an action, as this stimulates the senses providing experience, especially actions that involve dynamic change. Gaining access to situations where actions can be trialled may simply be a matter of good timing, being there when change is occurring. Or it may require an 'intervention' (Midgley 2003). By 'intervention' is meant orchestrating a change, disturbing something, the action. The resultant change is then reflected upon, using an explicit concept. For example, the intervention may involve installing a system in an organizational department. The experience of this intervention could be reflected upon by using the explicit concept of 'capability' or of 'flexibility'. What is learnt is expected to inform how the new system is implemented elsewhere as well as the usefulness of these two concepts. Such system interventions align with the complex systems ideas which suggest that conundrums, like frogs and caterpillars, cannot be understood by picking them apart; rather they need to be studied in the context, in their environment, as a whole. Picking apart to study something is often called identifying 'variables'. Rather, pragmatic learning is thought to occur from disturbing the whole system, and then reflecting on the overall reactions, this being closer to the world of the practitioner. An example of simple intervention is provided by Braa and Vidgen (1999). They intervened in an action that involved a large aerospace company's wiring loop installation. They simply arranged for the software programmers to meet the users of their 'wire looming' programme, something that had never happened before. The thinking reflected on the impact of that intervention using the concept of 'quality'.

Placing the focus on the consequences of an action, that were identified because of a reflection on a particular concept, provides thinking output different from that which would be obtained from generalizations. For example, carefully using a random sample may provide a valid generalization of the behaviour of the wider population. However, it does not provide consideration of the consequences of the population acting in this way.

## A SYSTEM OF THINKING

The intent of this chapter was to argue for a useful system of group social thinking or inquiry that was derived from pragmatism. 'Useful' in pragmatism means it has many uses and/or provides new choices of how to act. The evidence in support of this argument started with reconstructing pragmatism. This is always a personal interpretation. In this case a lot of emphasis was placed on pluralism and experience and on some of the issues concerning planners. These issues include relevance, concern with how to act as much as understanding the physical world, design, having to deal with powerful stakeholder communities each having used different concepts, having to undertake ethical problem-solving and with having to balance outcomes against social needs. All these issues are well accommodated within pragmatic thinking.

To end simply with a list of unconnected elements or principles would be very unpragmatic; they need to be connected, preferably into a purposeful

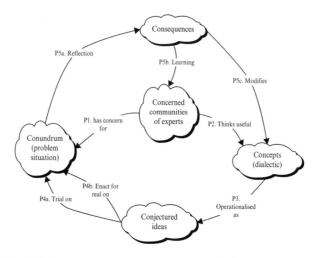

*Figure 2.1    Thinking system (pragmatic inquiry) diagram*

system (Churchman 1971). Their interconnection might have been appreciated from the discussion principles above. The suggested system of interconnections is shown diagrammatically in Figure 2.1. The idea for the overall design of this diagram comes from Checkland's LUMAS model (Checkland 2000), which uses different terms but which otherwise is an exemplar of what has been presented here as a pragmatic system of thinking. The diagram does not really have a starting point but the selection of concepts defines everything. The nodes represent the principles and the arrows represent actions. The five principles are indicated as P1 to P5.

The principles, shown as stages in this diagram, may best be explained by providing an example of them being applied, so a small case study follows.

## SMALL CASE STUDY

An organization perceived it had the problem (conundrum, situation) of its capital expenditure decisions not reflecting its strategic plan. The reasons given were operational pressures outweighing long-term ones, disagreements about the core purpose for the existence of the organization, and the strategic plan being constantly changed. This was a significant problem because this organization operated in the heavy engineering industry where capital expenditure items took years to implement fully, then needed to be in place for decades to recover costs.

The preparation of the strategic plan included the use of scenario planning which attempted to identify several realistic 'tipping points' likely to occur in the next 25 years. These were defined as being significant changes to the market, the technology or the organization's mode of operating. The organization also prepared a management concepts document, which was intended to guide managers when making day-to-day decisions. There were six concepts, or statements of how to operate, in a hierarchy. These replaced the one vision, mission, intent and objectives approach to organizational planning. The concepts were intended to assist managers to decide how to deal with what had been identified in the scenarios. For example, if a scenario identified a significant competitor arising in India within a decade, then the 'quality not price' management concept would suggest an appropriate response. However, despite having these scenarios and concepts, unfortunately they were not resulting in capital buying decisions that logically followed. Rather, items were purchased which reflected neither the scenarios nor the concepts.

The organization was looking for an appropriate epistemology to justify how the scenarios, concepts and purchasing decisions could be developed more holistically. It could only insist on scientific inquiry methods to a point. Simulations and experiments on a possible new plant were used to test their effectiveness. There was still need for creativity and participatory planning to identify what needed to be tested and how best to use whatever was being tested. Pragmatic thinking appeared to be the logical choice, therefore aligning their planning and decision-making with the stages in Figure 2.1. Principle 1 suggests the planning process started by preparing the scenarios by first itemising all the relevant stakeholder communities, including competitors and governments and identify what they say was the problem and their intuitive solutions. This might reveal their prior experiences and what they were using as their default concepts for thinking about the problem. It was necessary to try to understand how these communities saw the world and how they saw the organization. Principle 2 suggests the organization then needed to determine a new, widely accepted set of management concepts, and some contradictory ones, with which to think about the future. The group decision-making method of 'consensus groups' was used for this, using representatives from the alternative communities debating (mildly) against each other. These concepts, remembering the scenarios from principle 1, were then used to generate conjectured ideas of how to act next: what buying decision to make (principle 3). The idea generation process again involved small groups brainstorming but this time only made up of staff from the organization. The resulting conjectured ideas were then enacted for real a few months later, after a further series of 'red-teaming' trials, simulations or group mind experiments. These were intended to help the organization understand more clearly how competitors might react (principles 4a and 4b) to their planned actions. Next, the physical consequences of enacting the decisions were recorded. These records were then used by a 'post-mortem' group to provide for reflection on the effects of the decisions (principle 5a). This reflection drew on both the new state of the communities' concerns and on the usefulness of the concepts used. Lessons from this thinking process were then documented to be available to inform later rounds of planning (principles 5b and 5c).

Having briefly outlined how the pragmatic thinking system principles might be applied when strategic planning, it may be worth remembering that any 'scientific' research might apply the principles in the same manner. The 'researcher' first needs to identify what communities they are doing the research for, for example psychologists, physical scientists, designers or historians, and their default concepts. What are they concerned about and what will they accept as well-justified knowledge (principle 1)? The derivation of the dialectic set of concepts can be used in the next round of research (principle 2). The use of the term 'concept' is thought to be analogous to using multiple rival conceptual frames, or theories. The concepts have to be made operational in experimental designs, models, research hypothesis, arguments or propositions, intervention designs or research questions (principle 3). These are then enacted either in an experiment (principle 4a), or into the population (principle 4b), and the consequences of these actions carefully recorded (observed). This is where the scientific concerns over precision, analysis and validity can be used to record the physical effects of the actions taken. Last, the consequences of the actions need to be reflected upon (principle 5a); this often appears as the 'discussion' section in research reports which often includes advice to future researchers (princibles 5b and 5c).

It is thought that perhaps the principles of pragmatic thinking can be applied to most problem-solving situations. In Australian Royal Commissions, the terms of reference determine the concerned communities and the concepts to be used. In criminal courts, the concepts used are personal accountability and public safety. In a police investigation the starting concepts for a 'who did it' investigation are suspects, physical activities at the time of the crime, self-reported versus witness reports, and motivations. In Native Title (indigenous land rights) negotiations in Australia, the concepts often used are equity, development and reconciliation. In engineering design, the concepts used are often materials' strength, weight and cost.

## CONCLUSION

While understanding that each context is different, this chapter has introduced some general principles for problem-solving (Feyerabend 1975).

It provides some concepts for sense-making the formulation task (Weick 1995). These principles were informed by pragmatism. This provides a group interactive view of community problem-solving that uses but goes beyond the principles of scientific inquiry. Pragmatism is an extension of science but it focuses more on the interpretation of physical events and on providing choices of how people might act in the future, preferably to improve lives. There is dialectic between pragmatism and science because they are similar in many ways, yet different enough to be challenging.

The key difference may be that pragmatism starts not from assuming a universal audience but rather from assuming a constructive conflict of multiple communities. Popper expressed concern in *The Open Society and Its Enemies* (Popper 1971 [1945]) that, without requiring science to be open to critique from anyone, the 'nationalistic' science of the twentieth century might return. The conflicting communities' principle from pragmatism does not compound this problem, but rather turns it into an advantage. Anyway, Kuhn has suggested that science only needs conflicting paradigms or schools of thought when these communities do not acknowledge each other. It thought, or at least hoped, that creativity can occur from the constructive interaction of paradigms.

The pragmatic principle of seeking useful dialectic concepts comes close to the scientific idea of good research involving the testing of rival theories. The difference between concepts and theories may come down to which is more general. It is thought that theories come from some conception. For example, string theory uses the dialectic of the concepts of waves and particles (a violin string is both). Darwin used the dialectic concepts of survival and competition to develop his evolution theories. Theories are explanations why, or how, derived from a particular concept. They may fall somewhere between the concepts principle and the conjectured ideas principle in pragmatism. The similarities are underlined by Popper's calls for conjectures as the way to advance science (Popper 1972). Science tends to focus more on conjectures that state cause-and-effect relationships. Pragmatism tends to assume a complex system, so its stance on causal relationships is characterized by the remark, 'the acorn does not cause the oak tree'.

An important consequence of distinguishing traditional scientific theory from concepts may well be that using concepts means admitting that undertaking an inquiry requires 'bias'. The inquirer admits he or she is looking from a predetermined conception, and is not pretending to have an empty, inexperienced, objective and unbiased mind (Dennett 1995; Gilbert 1991). However, if being biased, or if not being objective, means misreporting what was experienced through the senses, then both pragmatism and science are aligned against this behaviour (MacCoun 1998).

In terms of acting on the world and observing what happens, pragmatism and science are also complimentary. Pragmatism tends to be interested in interventions rather than controlled experiments. This may be because pragmatism assumes complex social systems where independent variables cannot be separated out and individually manipulated.

Note, however, that this chapter has argued against starting the problem-solving process by setting visions, missions or objectives. It also argued against the notion that unbiased information can be collected, and that all the options of how to act in the future can be known and evaluated. Any information collected must be interpreted through whatever concepts are being used to interpret the world, implicitly or explicitly. Problem-solving involves making these concepts explicit.

## APPLICATION

This chapter has argued for problem-solving to use the elements of pragmatic inquiry (see Figure 2.1). In the previous chapter the conundrum was introduced. Next, the concerned community need to be identified. Stakeholder groups can be derived using numerous different sets of concepts. For your problem you want to identify your stakeholders using the following classification methods:

- Systems: owners of the problem (decision-makers), actors (doers), clients (being solved for whom).
- Ecology: food, sexual partners, competition, predators, other species.
- Government: citizens, enemies, United Nations, global businesses, ex-pats.
- Commercial: suppliers, competitors, industry, regulators.
- Public sector: public, government, adjacent agencies, similar agencies.
- Power: the powerful, the affected, the interested.

Try not to exclude anyone.

An alternative is to use classification systems that include non-humans and anthropomorphize them; what would the thing or profession say if they were able to express a viewpoint about the problem?

- Things, organizations, people.
- Technology, sociology, psychology, religion.
- Technology, skills, knowledge, ideas, beliefs.
- Groups, skills, ideas, things.

*Table 2.1  MOOC Stakeholders*

| Category | MOOC provider | Students | Universities | Lecturer/ researcher | Government/ funders |
|---|---|---|---|---|---|
| Things | Internet<br>IT software<br>Proctoring equipment<br>Mobile technologies | Certificates<br>IT<br>Costs | Lecture facilities<br>Campus activities<br>Laboratories | Office<br>Books<br>Lecture notes<br>Equipment | Universities<br>Regulations |
| Groups | Directors<br>Academics<br>Marketing<br>Finance | Undergraduate<br>Postgraduate<br>Part time<br>Alumni | Lecturers<br>Admin<br>Unions<br>Researchers<br>Friends<br>Funders | Teachers<br>Researchers<br>Tutors<br>Professors<br>Science vs arts | Politicians<br>Bureaucrats<br>Voters<br>Suppliers<br>Regulators |
| Skills | Software<br>Finance<br>Teaching theory<br>Hardware | Study<br>Timetabling<br>Social<br>Motivation<br>Referencing | Proctor<br>Records<br>Performance management<br>Appeals | Classroom<br>Marking<br>Researching | Regulation<br>Performance management<br>Finance<br>Marketing organization |
| Ideologies | IT solutions | Learn from teachers<br>Get qualified<br>Social interaction | Public good<br>Commercialisation<br>Financial responsibility<br>Economic development<br>Personal development | Truth-seeking<br>Honesty<br>Impartial<br>Fair<br>Helping<br>Examination<br>Publish or perish | Voters<br>Rights<br>Taxes<br>Global markets<br>Justice<br>Economic development |

Perhaps see this set of four short flash files on stakeholder analysis using systems thinking, TOP (things, organizations and people) and rich pictures: http://www.youtube.com/user/ideasresearch.

So, using example number four about massive open online courses (MOOCs), the 'groups, skills, ideas and things' classification of stakeholders, and identifying the groups of provider, students, universities, lecturer and government, Table 2.1 is constructed. Later the items listed inside the table will anthropomorphize to be given a voice (thought bubble, sound bite).

## NOTE

1. This chapter is based on Metcalfe (2007a).

# 3. Concerns as default concepts

## OVERVIEW

Participatory problem-solving requires consideration of stakeholders' concerns. The previous chapter recommended that this include identifying useful concepts to reflect on the problem situation. It is thought that a failure to do this forces us back on to our default concepts. These are our concerns. Unless explicit alternatives are provided, stakeholders can be expected to use their default concepts, their concerns, to solve whatever problems they encounter in the future. This chapter explains how and why stakeholders' concerns provide a starting point for problem-solving through identifying explicit appropriate concepts.[1]

## CONCERNS VERSUS PROBLEMS

'[O]rganisms must have begun with a concern for their internal problems and prospects, eventually graduating to a concern for proximal problems and prospects at their boundaries, before advancing to the concern for, cognitive appreciation of, ever more distal problems or prospects' (Dennett 1996).

Without thinking, there are no problems; without people thinking, there are no problems. The physical cosmos has no problems; thinking beings interpret problems onto situations. For lower-order organisms this thinking is about evolved concerns such as eating, being eaten and reproducing. These concerns interpret their world; they use them to reflect on what is brought to their attention. Humans do the same, but the range of concerns is far greater.

Problem identification is often presented as a situation that anyone would have seen as a problem. The very language of calling a situation a 'problem' objectifies it, making it appear not to have any particular owners. This 'objectivist' language encourages the assumption that problems are universal objective facts that exist independently of the human mind. But there is a subjectivist interpretation of why problems appear universal or at least commonly conceived. Take the claim that everyone would see world poverty as a problem. Everyone has the same hunger concerns; we seem to be born with a concern for hunger. We use this concern, and other concerns, as a default concept to interpret events that come to our attention. Empathy can be seen as reflection using shared concerns. Anyone concerned about hunger would interpret the situation facing those in poverty as problematic.

Seeing that our concerns act as default concepts becomes clearer when there is a difference of opinion about what the problem actually is. Efficiency is an example. The 'problem' of process efficiency is commonly used to undertake organizational change. However, who has this problem with efficiency? It is more often than not only a problem perceived by the managers of capital rather than the workforce. Certainly those concerned with the environment often resist more efficient extraction of the earth's resources. The workers are concerned with working conditions so do not see an efficiency problem, the capitalists are concerned with world competition so do see a problem with relative efficiency, and 'greenies' are concerned about use of natural resources so see a different problem with efficiency. Perhaps none of these three communities would have acknowledged that their thinking involved reflecting off concepts, but it is possible to see that they are.

Objectifying problems, by calling them 'problems' rather than some particular person's concerns, disconnects them from the concern creating them and discourages consideration of who has what concern. This bypasses the important step of explicitly discussing what concepts ought to be used to reflect on the problem situation. This can become a form of oppression. Minority 'others' have the concepts of the dominant thrust upon them without consultation. Acknowledging what makes something a problem is the concept used to reflect on a situation, clarifies thinking, opens an approach to negotiation and encourages pluralist solutions. In the absence of agreed explicit concepts, the concerns of the dominant will be used as default concepts.

There will be a number of situations where we are asked to think about a problem situation when it is not possible to discuss what concepts will be used. In these cases, consideration of the concerns of those involved is thought to be a means of providing the concepts participants are using by default. It is therefore necessary for those interested in thinking about problems to have some understanding of people's concerns.

## CONCERN-SOLVING

Wilson (1983) defines concern as a readiness to exert influence: a readiness to act. A failure to be able to act often heightens concern. Use of the word 'concerns' does come up in the problem-solving, research and inquiry literature. Baskerville and Wood-Harper (1998) use it frequently in their explanation of research as studying an 'area of concern'. This, they argue, needs to be determined upfront in any investigative process. Keen (2000) also talks about exploring communities' concerns rather than 'topics' when looking for research agenda. Dewey (as cited in Argyris and Schon 1996) uses the term 'doubts' as the driver for human inquiry. This must be a similar concept to concerns, as must be Habermas's cognitive interests (Ulrich 1983).

Concerns would seem to derive from nature (instinctive) or nurture (communicated). For primal survival concerns, language is not thought paramount. Small children instinctively know to stay away from rows of sharp teeth, whereas concerns over being burned may be learned either from touching a fire or from observing the panic-like actions of parents. More complex concerns, such as promotion at work, are socially constructed through dialogue later in life. Barnes and Bloor (1982) argue that humans not only have, like all species, instinctive concerns, but also uniquely appear to have a concern-anticipation and concern-solving disposition. Humans do seem to have an environmental competitive advantage in our desire, supported by our language skills, to create and solve concerns of our own perception. For example, National Aeronautics and Space Administration (NASA) scientists are exploring for water (oxygen and hydrogen) on planets to allow the building of life-support systems and for resupplying rocket fuel. Is there a problem here that 'needs' to be solved, or is the real driver merely curiosity or threat anticipation? Extreme sports are another example: in this case, solving the problem of how to get a safe thrill. If dealing with threats is seen as concern-solving, the evolutionary advantage becomes clearer. Those humans who have avoided death by anticipating threats may have produced more offspring. Technological advancement itself can be seen as overcoming basic human concerns about controlling nature and food resources.

Wilson (1983) uses the term 'cognitive authority' to describe those people who influence our concerns. Influencing people's concerns may act to alter their information wants. Persuasion is really about altering people's concerns – a practice well versed in advertising. Resolving a problem can be perceived as being an act of manipulating people's concerns, anywhere from the identification to the solution of the problem. This will include appreciating those concerns, trying to clarify them, trying to satisfy them and trying to alter them. Put another way, thinking about a problem requires consideration of the conceptions of those involved, which, in turn, affects the thinker's concerns.

Landry (1995) tracks the history of organizational problem-solving in the twentieth century, criticizing an overemphasis on the objective side of problems, which he describes as leading to a view of a problem as 'like an island' that anyone can circumnavigate and therefore understand. He calls for more appreciation of the fact that problems are conceptions in people's minds. Therefore, solutions require changing those conceptions, sometimes by altering the performance of the object of the conception and sometimes by redirecting the perception. We see these conceptions as being determined by concerns.

Metcalfe and Powell (1995) argue that it is people's concerns (real interests) that they use to interpret the millions of messages they constantly receive from the environment. This author believes that these 'concerns' are the primary concept for processing information. The idea being that, if you are concerned about something, this 'determines' your priorities to these messages. Put another way, your personal ethics or values act to interpret how you evaluate the world, so concerns and values (and ethics) appear to be linked and provide conceptions of life and its problems.

Haynes (2000) revisits Polanyi's work on tacit knowledge. He argues that one way of interpreting Polanyi's definition of tacit knowledge is that experience will change a person's conception of a problem. Using concern as that which gives the conception, this can be translated as saying that an experienced person will conceive a problem differently from an inexperienced one. Learning from the experienced therefore involves the inexperienced trying to understand the difference in their concerns compared to those of the experienced.

## AN ILLUSTRATION

It is being argued, in line with Dennett's quote at the opening of this chapter, that we are born with survival concerns. We learn others from our families, friends and tutors. Upon receiving an external message (stimuli) through the senses, such as the presence of someone or food, these concerns motivate our brains to make assertions (claims, decisions) from which we decide to try some action. In babies, this action might cause a missed grab. In a community setting, it may be a member successfully clicking on a computer menu or having the idea to develop a new product. This action may be just to move, to say something or to build something. If the action is long enough, as in building something, then information will be sought to sustain that action. The action creates new knowledge (or a new conception) and will be followed by a period of reflection, regardless of whether it is successful or not.

A 'problem' occurs when this reflection on a responsive action identifies a gap between what was thought desirable and what is now perceived to exist. It is so all-pervasive that it is hard to envisage, with a person going around this 'concern resolution loop' hundreds of times a day, sometimes dealing with trivia and sometimes working on an innovative complex task. Consider a simplified example: while designing a new policy, an employee may be talking through options at a meeting while scratching her nose. In this situation there are at least three iterations:

- First, the nose scratching started with a sensory input of an itch. Concerned over the presence of a bug on her skin, the manager uses her memory to come up quickly with a possible action; she rubs her nose. Information from her fingertips suggests there is no bug. The rubbing worked, there was learning through action. No external information was required and a moment's reflection saves the experience in her memory.
- Second, assume at the meeting someone boldly states, 'Let's take that section out of the policy altogether.' The woman's concerns make the thought (claim) jump into her mind that, if this is done, her job may be affected. She thinks about it for a while (information from her memory), asks for a point of clarification (confirming information from outside), then agrees, maybe asking for it to be put in writing (creating explicit knowledge). The whole meeting agrees and the woman reflects, maybe even making a note, on who said what, and why. She thinks that more information should really have been called upon before the idea was verbalized, but it was a good solution, one she might use herself sometime, in some form or another in the future.
- Third, the meeting mentioned above was part of a three-monthly review of progress on a project the woman had initiated. It involved designing a policy. The project was the result of complaints about the old way of doing things. She had felt the need for something different. She started thinking about how best to do the changes, calling on some colleagues and reading the manual for a few suggestions. While not yet finished, she had learned a lot and was reflecting on what she had learned and could be useful in the future.

In all three cases, the woman is going through the 'thinking system' outlined in the previous chapter but using default concerns rather than explicit concepts. In one case, there was a need for external information, beyond her memory, for the more complex tasks. The more complex the task, the more iterations were taken as the task was broken down into smaller concerns and 'claims'. Further, the more complex the task, the more formal the reflective process needed to reinforce the storage of memories. This is also happening in the minds of those involved with the woman.

## REAL CASES

To better understand how appreciating concerns can be used to interpret problems might work in practice, a series of actual events are described below.

Being a government minister (senator) is very much about being in tune with people's concerns. As a manager of a totally social process, success is defined by those involved. This contrasts with purely engineering tasks where some outcomes can be demonstrated objectively enough. With 'political solutions', a minister has to define success depending on whether those with influence over him felt it was a satisfactory outcome. Saying that politicians are concerned with other people's concerns is not being a bit utopian. What is being suggested is that their advancement depends on the feelings of a select group of people, typically the collective electorate, party members, or in the case of a minister, the premier (chief or prime minister). These 'colleagues' decide whether the member of parliament (MP) has been successful. This may well be true for most, if not all, careers.

The minister in this study had a very acute sense that his role was to do things that other people appreciated. For example, the sale of public assets was not decided upon by following some pseudo-mathematical analysis. Rather, it was undertaken because the 'right' people would be appreciative of the sale, but it was not to be done without a clear appreciation of how the 'wrong' people would react. The job was about communication, in and out, not about calculations. Information came from experts' written or verbal reports. All discussions were aimed at minimizing controversy and in addressing someone's concerns. If the premier was concerned about something, that took priority. The minister had concerns, as did the public, public servants and industry representatives.

Company representatives would arrange to meet with the minister so they could outline their concerns or lack of them. Concerns had to be communicated and balanced. Stories carrying concerns were told by people claiming to represent large numbers of people. The more credible the story, which was rarely formally confirmed, and the greater number of people it claimed to involve, the more priority was given to the story. People's apparent accuracy, sincerity, past reputation and general level-headedness was also important in making the stories have influence.

What follows are samples of the typical problems handled by a Minister in Australia. Each is intended to illustrate the usefulness of interpreting problems in terms of the participants' concerns rather than as being about the thing these concerns are revealing.

## The Emergency Services Communications Problem

The police, ambulance service and fire brigade were looking to upgrade and integrate their communication systems to digital, for more reliable coverage and to carry a lot more traffic, such as graphics files. (That was the professed object under consideration.) The state had a mishmash of different systems managed by a range of public service departments including fisheries and the utilities. It was an innovative information technology (IT) project, which had the risk of blowing its budget. Moreover, attempts in London and Melbourne had been disasters, with the new systems simply not being clever enough to replace human operators. The state had a recent history of an IT project cost blowout and of emergency services communications failures leading to a fatal error.

The concerns involved were about value for money, whether integration would rob the smaller departments of their autonomy, about a failure during an emergency and about the Minister losing financial control because of the technical nature of the project. In previous cases, it is suspected, public servants had received Cabinet permission for projects, knowing the budget estimates were too low, but relying on the government becoming so publicly committed to a project that further requests for funds were reluctantly approved. As so many government agencies and commercial consulting companies were involved, the task of keeping all the parties involved was massive. This included first creating concerns about the complexity of this project in participants' minds and then working through solving them. The project did go to large cost blowouts.

It would be hard to suggest that thinking about this problem was primarily about detailed analysis or identifying alternative decisions paths. It was about the identification of the concerns of participants. The police were concerned with being in control of the project as well as there not being any 'incidents' that put the police at the scene in any unnecessary danger. As 'owner' of the project, the Minister was also concerned about financial liability. The other emergency services wanted coordination of services but did not want to come under the direction of the police. A lot of knowledge was sought to argue for alternative designs using the experience of those who operated similar systems elsewhere. Each side had their own numbers to support their arguments, none of which seemed to impress the other side. A lot was learned about how all the agencies involved operated. Had the Minister used an analysis approach then no real progress would have been made.

### The Problem of Norwood's Trees

The state-owned electricity utility was pushing the Minister to pass legislation to empower it to cut roadside trees in danger of touching overhead electricity wires. The utility wanted to cut back the trees to an extent that meant it would not have to revisit the tree for three or four years. As this considerably reduced the tree size, local residents in the established leafy suburbs wanted a modest annual trim, but preferably to have the wires put underground. They were making it an election issue in a marginal seat.

The utility was concerned with repair costs and the residents with aesthetics. As 'owner' of the utility, the Minister tended to be more concerned about financial liability than aesthetics but wanted an agreed outcome so as not to overly affect votes. A lot of knowledge was sought about tree growth rates, about treatments to slow down tree growth, about horizontal boring to insert underground wires, and about the effect of tree branches growing between wires. Each side had their own numbers to support their arguments, none of which seemed to impress the other side.[2] Again a lot was learned about how all the agencies involved operated, about tree growth and the law on an owner's liabilities. At the end of the day, all sides compromised because of the threat of an election changing the balance of power in Parliament. An independent arbitration process was established. It took many hours of meetings which ended up focused on participant concerns, not on cost analysis.

The clever thinking in this situation was not in the provision of information to test claims. Concerns were managed using news releases, articles, posters, letters, email listservs and talkback radio. Domination of these allowed concerns to be manipulated and aggravated by both the residents and the utility. During discussions, access to detailed information on costs, such as undergrounding, did not speed up the negotiations. Often, more information led to the opposite effect as contrary information was sought. Participants seemed to keep themselves informed by telephoning[3] experts for estimates. For example, several horizontal boring companies, local and overseas, were contacted for approximate estimates. The drafting of the legislation that settled the negotiation provided controls that reflected the concerns of those involved.

### The Gun Buy-Back Problem

Following the massacre of tourists in Tasmania by a disturbed lone gunman, the Australian national government funded compensation for the states to insist on the forced surrender of certain types of weapons. Typically, these were semi-automatic weapons. The gun lobby objected, arguing for the right to carry arms. In South Australia, the legislation was passed quite quickly, while there was a need for the careful enactment of the content of the legislation, including ensuring the budget was not exceeded. The Minister was concerned that those administrating the buy-back process were doing their job effectively. Numerous requests for special consideration were received, plus numerous threats.

The concerns are obvious. From the state Minister's conception, this issue was created by the passing of federal laws. His role was to arrange the buy-back to minimise voter dissent at the local level. Information was sought from police records about numbers of registered guns, and estimates provided of the number of unregistered guns. Much of the debate was about personal liberty rather than being based on care analysis of factual data. The media was used to heighten and then alleviate participants' concerns.

To repeat, the point about all these cases is that the optimum problem-solving approach was to focus on the various participants' concerns, not primarily on the objective analysis of objective evidence. Evidence was collected and used but it was worked around, as lawyers tend to do in court. The primary task was to get from, or communicate to, participants a clear understanding of the other participant's concerns – this defined the problem. In some cases, this was to make participants concerned and in others to alleviate those concerns. There were endless meetings but the thinker's task was to ensure these led to an improved understanding of concerns. From these, the Minister could make decisions after weighing the pros and cons of participants' reactions. Thoughts of impartial evidence-based analytical solutions were considered to be naive.

## IDENTIFYING CONCERNS

It is thought that the importance of the 'thinking system' depicted in the previous chapter is that it makes the connection between concerns, participants and perceived solutions. Problems are interpreted by different concepts or, by default, people's concerns. Identifying these gives clarity of thinking and participants a voice. Satisfactory solutions may require these multiple concerns (default concepts) to be addressed.

While a more formal method for revealing the concepts or concerns participants are using to interpret the problem situation will be discussed later, a very useful first step is simply to ask, using a simple set of semi-structured questions. The intent is to separate the concerns from the object, event or thing perceived to be the problem situation. This uses the assumption that the object concerned about exists and differs from the concerns.

Typically, the questioning might start from saying that there is a problem

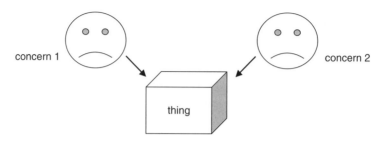

*Figure 3.1    The object–concern separation*

that others need to fix. The first step is to separate the thing under consideration from the person's concerns. First ask, 'What exactly is the "object" or thing under consideration?'. Let us say the answer is 'production efficiency'. This can be drawn up as the box in Figure 3.1, with the object as 'efficiency'. As there are many different issues over efficiency that could concern someone, the next question that is asked is, 'What is it that "concerns" you about efficiency?' Let us say the response is, 'How best to redesign the organization.' 'Redesign' can then be written up next to the cartoon face (concern 1). Typically, the discussion is not as straightforward as this. If the client has several concerns then these may need to be identified as different problems. Usually there will be some very important debate about these two parts; they may switch, or change noticeably. The dialogue is very important not only so that the person with the problem takes some ownership of the two parts, but also to help clarify the two parts as separate entities.

However, all this will only make explicit the concerns of one person. The strength of reflecting on concerns is to make explicit the range of concerns that exist for one problem. With the example above, another concern may be 'redundancies' (concern 2 in Figure 3.1). It is important to seek out purposefully as many different concerns on the problem as can be found, as this will develop a collective concern for the problem – one very relevant to a collective solution. Seeking these concerns can be justified on both moral and rational grounds given the extensive small-group performance literature demonstrating the innovation of group solutions when concerned people are involved. Moreover, this collective concern is suggesting consensus decision-making or imposing some excessively bureaucratic process.

## CONCLUSION

This chapter argued that concerns are the default concepts people use to interpret situations as problematic, and therefore what they see as viable solutions. This may appear to be a small linguistic turn but it explains how we construct and solve problems without being aware of the concepts we are using. Purposeful thinking is about appreciating how those concerns are acting on stakeholder participants. Giving primacy to participants' concerns over the collection of evidence-based data when problem-solving is not only thought to be more realistic but it also opens the possibility to a more collective and therefore possibly emancipatory approach to thinking about problems. Focusing on concerns aligns with Argyris's (1994) call to identify 'theory in action' as opposed to espoused theory, meaning what participants are really worried about, rather than the so-called rational evidence produced to support those concerns. Focusing on concerns gets to the root of the problem. Moreover, it discourages the 'superman' view of thinking whereby privileged gurus, who have not lived the situation, feel they can outthink all others and solve complex social problems with little consultation.

The justification for the concern appreciation language has drawn on the pragmatism literature that has long held that social situations are far too complex to model, and anticipate-in-change due to the massive complication of dynamic interconnectivity. The pragmatic thinking solution is to give primacy to understanding the concepts used by participants. Unless explicitly constructed, these concepts are simply going to be the stakeholders' concerns. Managing these concerns and the introduction of other explicitly agreed-upon concepts is thought to provide a basis for developing a coordinated solution able to bind the differing stakeholders into one common means of sense-making their shared if dynamic situation. The next chapter explains how community discussions might be structured to identify concerns.

## APPLICATION

To draft a collaborative strategy we need a large number of statements that express concerns about the future of your organization. One of the skills of the analysts is in soliciting a good set of statements. As a starting position, imagine what you think the stakeholders would say about your problem.

These concern statements are central to how you conceptualize the area of concern so they do need to be creative. They should be forward-looking; suggestions of how to act rather than repeating that there is a problem. Zoom in and out and see the area of concern as a life form trying to survive in a swamp. Try to spot trends, threats and opportunities locally and overseas.

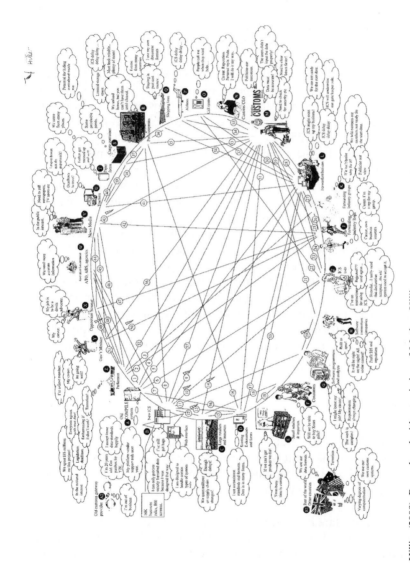

*Source:* Hillier (2009). Reproduced with permission of Mathew Hillier.

*Figure 3.2 The problem with Australian Customs' new computer system*

Draft at least 80 (many more is better) conditional concern statements of about 10–20 words. Number them from 1 to 80+. Avoid repetition, as well as calls for more information to be gathered, for more meetings and/ or for policy to be set; try and be specific about what outcomes are sought.

Using the running examples, below are examples of concern statements:

1. US and China: The US Ambassador might say that Australia has strong historical, military and cultural ties to the US; it should not be too quick to abandon these just to sell coal to China.
2. Fracturing: An environmentalist might say gas is still a finite commodity; we should preserve it for future generations.
3. Organizational mindset: An experienced manager might say that it does not matter what is going on in someone's head; rather, all that matters is what they do.

The next chapter will elaborate on the drafting of these concern statements.

Figure 3.2 provides a representation of the concerns (as thought bubbles) of those involved in installing a new computer system at Australian Customs a few years ago. The lines across the middle represent tensions between people (Hillier 2009).

## NOTES

1. This chapter is based on Metcalfe and Hobson (2001).
2. The more experienced ministers avoided using quantitative or statistical evidence – which then had to be fully validated – in arguments as it usually turned out to be open to alternative interpretation.
3. Reinforcing the suggestion that the best piece of technology for problem-solving (addressing concerns) is a mobile phone.

# 4.  Collaborative planning

## OVERVIEW

This chapter is about how to facilitate a problem-solving or planning meeting to source stakeholders' and analysts' concern statements. These can later be concept mapped to identify meta concerns or organizing principles. Prior to the meeting, industry analysts, scenario planners and forecasters will be asked to reflect on their expertise and experiences. This may include their undertaking analysis methods such as SWOT (strengths, weaknesses, opportunities, threats), PEST (political, economic, social and technological), Porter's Five Forces, war gaming, value chain analysis, force field analysis, scenario networking, focus groups systems dynamics modelling and so on (see Wikipedia). Those involved should bring their subsequent concerns and/or optimism to the planning meeting.

The proven method used for idea generation and evaluation by science over thousands of years is argumentation, reasoned evidence-based debate (not quarrelling) as used in the adversarial justice system. Argumentation, done well, is creative, using controlled competition to reveal underlying assumptions and different perspectives in a way that encourages critical appraisal of those perspectives. This approach can be very useful when dealing with social issues and a diverse community. Therefore, this chapter will explore the proposition that well-managed argument is a useful design for planning meetings. However, the traditional debate format is thought to be too confrontational, not resulting in a set of agreed concern statements. The consensus group format uses argument, but overcomes many of the confrontation problems.[1]

## COLLABORATIVE THINKING

When planning for complex situations with long time horizons, collaboration is required. This involves seeking qualitative inputs from experts and potential end-users. In such contexts participatory thinking, involving a wide range of stakeholders, is more effective than relying on an elite group of experts to come up with their plan. Real problems arise when trying to get it implemented by people not genuinely involved in the reasoning behind the plans.

The task of problem conceptualization includes attempting to appreciate and manage the present influences that are likely to act on some future event. This involves first identifying those influences and then appreciating their dynamic nature. Influences may be from people, nature and/or tradition. Looking at historic trends of past outcomes may help, as might trying to understand a wide range of different perspectives. Having made these influences explicit, argumentation can then turn to appreciating and discussing alternative futures in a manner appropriate for those present. The method for seeking input to a problem solution suggested here includes an attempt to communicate, to appreciate and to gain some commitment to agree on alternatives.

Beyond focus groups, the socio-technical systems movement in the 1960s originated a variety of group intervention processes for facilitating meetings of communities of stakeholders and analysts (for more details see List and Metcalfe 2004). They now seem to overlap in how they are conducted, but include:

1. The search conference, originated by Emery and Trist (1965): a method by which organizations and communities can examine their likely and preferred future actions.
2. The future search method of Weisbord and Janoff aims to assist diverse communities seek common ground by helping them create ideal future scenarios by combining diverse ranges of stakeholder types.
3. Participatory rural appraisal, developed by Chambers, encourages the use of local residents to collect information and utilizes methods such as semi-structured interviewing, focus group discussions, preference ranking, mapping and modelling, seasonal and historical diagramming.
4. The scenario workshops of Andersen and Jaeger use a panel of citizens to question experts under their procedural control to build up a future scenario.
5. Appreciative inquiry, with its 4Ds of 'discover, dream, design and develop', encourages members of an organization, typically through structured interviews, to discover what they regard as successes, and to build on that. In the 'dream' stage, often run as a large group conference, members work on envisioning a desired future for the organization.
6. The KJ method of Kawakita Jiro: an approach adopted by the school of total quality management in Japan, involves the use of small

workgroups to generate and evaluate ideas for improving production processes.

7. The interaction meetings method developed by Doyle and Straus attempts to ensure that all participants in a meeting have an opportunity to be heard, and that the meeting process considers all relevant views.

8. Warfield's interpretive structural modelling (ISM) is a software-aided form of collaborative model building. With ISM, a group models relationships between goals and subgoals by making a series of binary comparisons using focused argument. (See List and Metcalfe 2004 for references.)

Some of these techniques were primarily designed as research methods, while others are methods for planning or problem-solving. However, some have fallen into disuse (to judge from the lack of recent citations) for a range of reasons, among which was that they had no explicit guarantor that justified, reasonably consensual knowledge would be produced.

## ARGUMENT

The dialectic, reasoned, rhetorical or argumentation process is about the only non-violent mechanism that humans have to construct, refine, apply or challenge diverse perspectives. People who claim to have a new idea or perspective are asked to justify their claims by providing supporting evidence, while others are allocated the competitive task of thinking of ways to counter this evidence. Structures for organizational argument have developed over the centuries, typified by the English justice system. This process of organizational argument goes to the heart of democratization of community groups between and with government services. This research attempts to turn this ideal into a routine facilitation process.

Complex problem-solving thinking is a social activity and, as such, alternative perspectives will typically exist. Ignoring these, treating them as unfortunate noise or simply not appreciating that they exist means forgoing an opportunity to use these forces as motivation to better understand a situation; see Churchman (1979), Mason and Mitroff (1981) and Linstone (1999). Put the other way around, the solutions and groups' needs and wants can be viewed as the end result of an argument between vested interests, which is dependent of what ideas are raised, who got a voice and how well the ideas are communicated. Problem-solving thinking, as argument, aligns with what Crosswhite (1996) and Walton (1998) call persuasive dialogue reasoning: that is, it assumes you are trying to convince cynical, yet competent, opponents of your claim or vision, prior experience or preferences. The philosophical basis comes from Socrates', Plato's and Aristotle's dialectic reasoning, revisited through Walton (1998), Eemeren et al. (2003), Perelman and Olbrechts-Tyteca (1969) and Habermas (1984). The 'guarantor' of a justified knowledge is the establishment of effective rules of verbal competition (or questioning) between the participants. For some meetings between stakeholders and analysts this competition has to be encouraged, but very mildly, in others it needs to be restrained and depersonalized. An argument is not a quarrel. But it is a competitive process of creating knowledge through reasoned debate. In this way it is an inquiry method.

Both in the sense of providing good information for making decisions and for assisting with the act of actually making the decisions, setting up a well-managed process of argumentation research appears to have an explicit philosophical basis and is well integrated with the inquiry epistemologies. Tracey and Glidden-Tracey (1999) propose three elements that are related to conducting inquiry as a reasoned argument: '(a) focus on underlying assumptions, (b) avoidance of compartmentalizations of inquiry components, and (c) iterative comparisons of assumptions across components'. This emphasis on revealing underlying assumptions is an integral part of argumentation and something that makes this approach particularly relevant to forecasting. Ulrich (2002) refers to this as making 'boundary judgements'.

Tracey and Glidden-Tracey (1999) go on to say that to argue before a critical audience for a specific approach from among identifiable options requires careful thought and more careful articulation of assumptions. This aligns with the extensive management literature on the use of argument in both problem formulation and decision-making. For example, Niederman and DeSanctis (1995) report that the argument approach leads to a greater combination of both coverage of critical issues and higher satisfaction with group problem-solving, leading to a greater commitment to implementation. Meyers and Seibold (1989) also summarize the extensive empirical research on analysing argumentative processes in everyday commerce, while Fischer and Forrester (1993) report on research being undertaken on the role of argument in government policy formulation. They again report that it was helpful in drawing out issues and in improving understanding between parties.

As problem-solving includes communication and motivation, the argument approach doubles up in this role. Users are more likely to be committed to a new design if they have been involved in a reasonable argumentative process or if their questions are anticipated by reporting the arguments or evidence. If nothing else, the perceptions of the purpose and context of the solution will be better communicated. The management literature supporting the role of argument to assist communication is even more extensive than the decision-making literature. Meyers and Seibold (1989) summarize it by saying that, from the discipline's beginnings in late nineteenth century as forensics pedagogy, the study of argument has been a rich intellectual tradition in the field of communication.

A further attraction of the argument approach is that it makes bias explicit. Pretending to be impartial where repeat experiments were not possible has stressed scientific inquiry and is unconvincing in the political competition of modern organizational life. Much time and emotion is saved if each actor openly states their preference, or claim, upfront, rather than pretending to present impartial questions, and is then asked to justify this claim in a public arena.

## PLANNING MEETINGS

Given the long history of the use of public debate both in the justice system and in politics, and its importance in democracy, it was thought that this was a pragmatic approach for designing participatory or collaborative problem-solving thinking. However, this needed to be tempered by or fully integrated with what has been learned about participatory processes. This suggests that planning meetings to help with problem-solving need to be designed around a process that, after some initial discussion, articulates a set of claims (or one-line concern statements, propositions) around which some form of debate needs to be managed. Rather than adopt the classic 'Western' approach of eventually voting for or against the statement, our experiences suggest that the debate be used to edit the statement until a clear majority are willing to vote either for it or against it. This suggestion comes from List (2001), who developed a method entitled the 'consensus groups', so named because of similarities to the nominal group technique.

From one viewpoint, this consensus group technique is the opposite of a survey. With a survey, the questions are fixed: all interviewers must ask each question using exactly the same wording, even if this does not seem relevant to the respondent. The only possible variation, given the way a survey is designed, is in the result; for example, how many people gave each possible answer to each question. Naturally, these results are expressed numerically, for example '37 per cent strongly agreed that they supported government policies on education'. A consensus group works in the opposite way: a percentage threshold is fixed (typically around 75 per cent) which indicates consensus. Without this agreement a question, or rather a statement, still needs to be edited. The main use of consensus groups is in assessing public opinion when the underlying concepts are ambiguous, as is the case with many human activity questions.

Unlike a focus group, in which the moderator or analyst usually decides on respondents' behalf the nature of their opinions, the consensus group is essentially participative. The participants themselves decide, not the outside expert. The moderator of a consensus group is there only to aid the process, not to decide on the findings. For this reason, consensus groups are well suited for inclusion in approaches such as participatory rural appraisal (PRA), as developed by Chambers (1994) and later broadened into concepts such as participatory learning and action (PLA) and partici-patory rural communications appraisal (PRCA).

Collaborative problem-solving thinking using argument, in consensus groups, has been gradually developed and evaluated since the late 1980s. It began within the Australian Broadcasting Corporation (ABC), which then had 54 regional radio stations across Australia that all wanted some audience research done. The ABC, unable to handle the demand, set out to develop a method that the regional managers could use. Their training was mainly in journalism; they had very strong verbal skills, but no education in statistics. Therefore, it was necessary to avoid survey methods and focus on developing a group discussion method that could be effectively run by regional staff.

The method settled on was to run a discussion in three distinct phases. In the first phase, each member of the gathered group is asked to describe their radio listening habits and to evaluate existing programmes. Having thus established a starting point based on current behaviour and prefer-ences, the participants move on to a second phase.

In this phase, participants discuss likely and desired futures within the topic area, and then what might be the indicators of success. While listen-ing to this discussion, the secretary records a series of tentative (deperson-alized) concern statements (or claims, or propositions), such as, 'in future talkback radio will be most effective when it improves listeners' daily lives in some ways'.

In the third phase, the concern statements are presented to the group to argue over, modify and sharpen. The secretary, facilitator or participants may suggest edits to the wording of the original statement to clarify it. If it is discovered to embody more than one issue, it is split into several other statements, which are then discussed separately; the same criteria apply as with the wording of questions in a survey. With some community groups, the debate needed stimulating by appointing one member as a 'devil's advocate'. In South-East Asia, many participants were unwilling to express disagreement, and the nominal group method of providing anonymous statements written on index cards (before the forecasting phase) proved more effective. When all participants in a group agree that the statement is clearly worded, and the majority agree with it, then it is voted upon. The outcome from the session is a set of statements, with varying levels of recorded agreement.

Consensus groups are usually done in sets of three, each involving 10–12 participants, a moderator and a secretary. The principle is that if three completely different groups of people arrive at similar results (and they often do) then these results should be typical of the whole population. Though it is easy to run a consensus group, it is not a simplistic research method, and the skills of moderator and secretary steadily grow with practice.

The consensus group technique can also be adapted and extended into a more rigorous format. A linked series of consensus groups, typically done during a full-day session involving both the management and the clients of an organization, in which each group forms a tacit understanding of the other, can work together in the later stages to produce plans and normative forecasts. List and Metcalfe have named this process the 'co-discovery conference', in recognition of its roots in the search conference of Emery and Trist (1965). We plan to report on the theory and practice of the co-discovery conference later.

## AN EXAMPLE

In order to provide a better understanding of the method, an example is presented, based on work done in Indonesia. Indonesia is undergoing a reawakening of democracy. The political system is now less biased in favour of the interests of the rich and powerful, there is a relatively high level of press freedom, a new public awareness of the power of democracy, and a growing mutual dependence of the government and the media on each other. Indonesia is no longer classified as one of the very poorest countries: the 2002 United Nations Educational, Scientific and Cultural Organization (UNESCO) Human Development Index ranked it 110th of 173 countries for which data are available. With an adult literacy rate of 86.9 per cent, it now has a relatively well-educated population. Around 80 per cent of households have access to radio, and around 50 per cent have television. The average city dweller has access to about six daily newspapers, five TV channels and 20 radio stations.

Because of the small scale and relatively low cost of radio, it is believed that if a reasonable proportion of Indonesia's 212 million population can develop a two-way relationship with radio (by providing a channel for direct feedback), then it may be the next most direct route for mediated democracy. Radio Republik Indonesia (RRI) is the government broad-caster, which has one national network and around 50 local radio stations. For years, RRI was the mouthpiece of the government; most of its news was supplied directly by the government-controlled Antara news agency. Thus, RRI has low credibility in some quarters and now faces competition from a wide range of new commercial radio stations.

A major current issue for RRI is how it can adapt to serve the purposes of democracy. Sida (the Swedish government aid agency) has been funding a new project to enhance Indonesian democracy through RRI, by inculcat-ing the principles of public service radio. The programme is administered by the Media Development Office of Swedish Radio. RRI, it seems, had never had much direct contact with members of the Indonesian public and, accordingly, needed to develop a set of new directions for responding to the post-Sukarno political and social environment in Indonesia. Therefore, the Swedish project placed a strong emphasis on audience feedback. It was in this context that List (see List and Metcalfe 2004) was asked to use his extensive experience in audience research in developing countries to apply the consensus group technique for this project. The consensus process involves four stages: preparation, discussion, consensus and summarizing.

**Preparation**

1.  Decide on how to subdivide the audience into three contrasting groups. In this Indonesian example, the three groups used were (a) people living in villages; (b) younger and more educated town dwellers; (c) older/less educated town dwellers.
2.  Recruit a sample of people in the study area. Generally, a purposive sample rather than a random sample is used, in order to ensure the representation of various stakeholder types within each group. List (2001) found in Indonesia that women needed strong encouragement before they would attend.
3.  Train RRI staff – generally middle managers and journalists – as moderators and secretaries for the group discussions.
4.  Develop an initial agenda, similar to the type of outline used in semi-structured interviewing.

**Discussion**

1.  In collaboration with participants, defining the scope of the discus-sion, and modifying the agenda.

2.   Have initial general discussion (about one hour), facilitated by the moderator. During this time, the secretary recorded statements that seemed to be agreed on by several participants.
3.   Have a break during which the secretary transcribed those statements onto large sheets of paper.

**Consensus**

1.   Each statement in turn was discussed, reworded if necessary, and voted on, first for clarity. Statements that were clear to all participants were then voted on for agreement. Statements that were not clear to everybody were discussed further, and reworded – often radically changed.

When more than three-quarters of participants voted in favour of a statement, the final version of the wording was retained. (This was the case for most statements). In addition, when less than one-quarter of participants voted in favour of a statement, this was a clearly expressed rejection of the statement, so this wording was also retained.
2.   When between one-quarter and three-quarters agreed, the reasons for lack of consensus were explored. Often, an attempt was made to split the statement into two, or to retain its purpose but completely reword it. Following this process, very few statements (generally less than 10 per cent of them) do not reach consensus.
3.   Typically, a two-hour group meeting produced around 40 agreed statements, most of which were normative forecasts, or plans for programming or management.

**Summarizing**

1.   The final stage, using the statements produced by all groups, was to align the statements to search for common themes. This was done with a small working party of the moderators and secretaries who had been trained to run the groups. Where necessary, tape recordings of the group proceedings were reviewed, to confirm the meanings and intents of similar statements produced by different groups.
2.   In this alignment process, many statements were found to be common to two or three groups; this overlap increased confidence in the trustworthiness of the findings.
3.   Statements were graphed as points in an 'idea space' (Figure 4.1): a two-dimensional chart of difficulty of execution against breadth of application. Thus one corner of the graph contained statements with a narrow focus which were easy to carry out (e.g. A 'move the daily

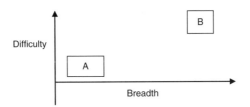

*Figure 4.1 Idea space*

traffic report from 8.15 to 8.25 a.m.'), while the other corner contained statements with a broad focus which were difficult to carry out (e.g. B 'replace the entire management of RRI with local staff'). The size of each point on the graph reflected the strength of consensus on that statement (or one with almost identical wording).

4. Since a real idea-space graph can include 50 or so points, colour coding by topic area can be used to enable the graph to be understood more easily, or a set of different layers can be used, effectively creating a third dimension. The above example is only one of several possible idea-space graphs; another dimension would be that of importance of the statement – in the view of the management and/or the users. Plotting difficulty against importance would enable the identification of some activities that would return high social dividends.

Though the above example used a sample of the general population of Indonesia, it is also possible for consensus groups to include expert analysts. In fact, the training of moderators and secretaries in Indonesia began by moderating consensus groups with senior RRI staff, to both demonstrate the technique and gather information from these professional experts on further ways in which democracy could be strengthened through radio.

## REFLECTIONS

There are often a few problems of organization, particularly when communication must be done mostly through interpreters. Yet, the participants appear to have learned a lot from every consensus group organized. Staff participants have learned a lot about their audience, and gained a sense of empowerment about improving their broadcasting relevance and their work environment. Audience participants become less passive, and can become ambassadors for the radio network, with their new enthusiasm helping to build the size and quality of the audience. Because participants tend to tell their friends about their experience, and because many participants tend to have wide networks of relationships, the meeting acts as a catalyst for another form of dissemination that may be (when second-hand, third-hand and later retellings are taken into account) almost as widespread as a radio broadcast itself. The message disseminated through this verbal network is that RRI is taking its audience seriously and may no longer be a government mouthpiece. So, as well as helping broadcasters forecast the development of their audiences, the technique is also a method of building audiences.

The selection of the participants seems critical to the success of the consensus group approach if used for problem-solving. Getting the right people into the group with the right background offering a wide range of insight may be logistically difficult. Armstrong's (2000) research suggests reasonable outcomes can be achieved by asking some of those who can come to role think. By this it is meant ask them to act out a role such as of a competitor, regulator, someone living overseas or a powerful supplier. One way to imagine who these roles need to include is to think of stakeholders (supportive and antagonistic) who represent the political, economic, social and technological (PEST) factors impinging on the situation. So, for example, under political would be the powerful stakeholders due to their wealth, knowledge or alliances. Under economic factors would be the stakeholders who want to develop new markets and products, including those who want to commodify everything. Under social would be those stakeholders with strong ideological or religious beliefs. Under technological would be those stakeholders who see technological threats or opportunities, including the need for instrument-based measurement and monitoring.

## CONCLUSION

This chapter has argued that group-based dialectic argument can be redesigned to provide a consensus-seeking group facilitation approach that will provide justified concern statements. The stakeholders and analysts' input was sought in an example using the development of a problem solution for instructional radio from an ex-government-controlled radio station given the emergence of democracy in Indonesia. An inverted form of facilitated argument was developed whereby depersonalized statements were openly debated and edited until a recorded degree of consensus was reached.

No attempt was made to prove that the method 'works', beyond providing reasons and demonstrating its use as a method that still used dialectic tension as the guarantor of justified knowledge but with the minimum of confrontation. It is believed that a practical, non-antagonistic group facilitation method was developed by combining the ground experience with this well-developed theory of knowledge creation. The guarantor of truth in this case was the competition of ideas.

## APPLICATION

You might now try and source concern statements from the stakeholders. This may involve meetings, interviews, the Internet, websites, blogs, discussion boards and newspapers. Try to get the concern statements drafted in the form of conjectures. This might include using the form that 'X is A rather than B because . . .'.

For example in the US Ambassador example, this might be redrafted as: 'That Australia should not favour its commercial relationships over its historical ones because it may need its friends if conflict breaks out.' In the fracturing example: 'That gas should not be mined over seeking renewable energy because gas can run out and releases carbon when burned.'

Propositions have two or more concepts in tension.

## NOTE

1. This chapter is based on List and Metcalfe (2004).

# 5. Idea networking

## OVERVIEW

Stakeholders' and analysts' concerns need to be clustered into a handful of meta concerns or organizing principles. Agility, equity, innovation, globalization, expediency, networking, cultural sensitivity or sustainability, are examples of these meta concerns or concepts. This chapter presents a method for emerging these collective concerns or concepts from participant's individual concerns. It draws on the work of Christopher Alexander and his notion of networking ideas. The Small Worlds phenomenon suggests that this network will not be uniform but rather result in a number of clusters (Small Worlds). This means networking concern statements will result in clusters of concerns that can be generalized into meta or solution concerns (priorities or concepts). Having identified these concepts, they can be more easily discussed and contrasted with alternatives.[1]

## CONCERN STATEMENTS

It is repeated throughout this book that pragmatic problem-solving (later called 'messy' by Ackoff 2007, 'wicked' by Rittel and Webber 1973, 'swampy' by Checkland 2000; and ill-defined by others), needs to start in earnest from the identification of the concepts that will be used to make sense of the problem situation. Therefore, some method is required to identify these concepts. The visualization method used here is called idea networking. Assuming informal awareness of a problem starts from someone feeling concerned about some situation. Typically, this concerned person will start talking to others about the situation and thereby start a series of discussions drawing on past experiences. For example, a community might be concerned about the lack of plans in place to deal with the annual threat of wildfires to their town community. They will talk about the situation, perhaps asking the community administration what they think should be done. In response, they might receive a wide range of concern statements back. One of which may be something like, 'Do not worry, we have not had a wildfire go through near here in my lifetime'; another statement might be, 'When it gets chaotic around here, you cannot rely on the state emergency services because they lack enough local knowledge.'

Each concern statement collected, be it from a document or personal comment, presents in isolation, not clearly connected to any other. On first impressions, these statements do not form any sort of coherent whole, rather they are like the pieces of a jigsaw puzzle. So, the first task faced in problem conceptualization is to identify the underlying concepts being used to generate the statements, to find some patterns in them, to identify what concepts they have in common. To do this, to conceptualize the inquiry responses, a networking technique is being suggested; a visualization mapping technique. The process of emerging concepts needs to be done in a collaborative manner else there is a risk of the concepts being rejected. That said, the conceptualization also needs to be creative, to surprise and challenge stakeholders. An uncreative conceptualization is expected to lead to an uncreative solution.

Whether assuming social issues are real or socially constructed, no method for creative thinking should take us beyond rationality (Dennett 1989). An attempt has to be made to explain how to conceptualize problems creatively from the jumble of starting statements. Bailin (2003) argues that those who claim to be rational are accepting that there is a method that can at least assist in thinking creatively. She recommends a semi-structured method, rather than a strict algorithmic process, to create ideas and surface the planners' unconscious self. The pragmatic systems thinking literature (Ackoff 1994a, 1994b) suggests a further important element of this rational creativity. It is to include a process of switching between analysis (picking apart) and synthesis (analogy). This can serve to generate ideas aligned to the conceptual frame of those involved, even if they are initially unaware of that frame.

Dewey sees 'analysis' as reductionism (zoom in); looking inwardly at the problem, not outwardly, dividing the problem into elements (variables) and studying these separately. This is the preferred approach of scientific thinking. By 'synthesize', he appears to mean standing outside the problem, seeing the problem as an example or subset of some wider problem (zoom out). Put another way, what else has the same characteristics as your problem? Think of analogies to your problem. Dewey uses the historical example of water pumps which would only pump water to a particular height. Analysis means looking at the parts of the water pump, the water and the vacuum involved in detail, perhaps even at a chemical level. Synthesis means asking what a tube full of unsupported water is analogous to. Dewey argues that synthesis led to understanding that there must be some force pushing down on the water to force it up so high. This image was then used to design a series of detailed logical laboratory experiments (picking apart) which in turn led to the creative jump of appreciating the presence of atmospheric pressure. The synthesis aims to bring different perspectives to bear, and therefore generate a different set of questions about the problem. Put another way, creativity is thought to be generated by encouraging the problem-solver to 'zoom' in and out on a problem, to change perspectives. Both analysis and synthesis are thought required for creative thinking. The method for problem conceptualization suggested here intentionally uses this approach through the work of Alexander in conjunction with the Small Worlds phenomenon.

The chapter will first briefly discuss the Small Worlds phenomenon and then Alexander's work in *Notes on the Synthesis of Form* (1964). It will then demonstrate how the clusters predicted to emerge from inquiry statements as networks can be used to identify solution concepts or organizing principles. Therefore, the argument of this chapter is that Alexander's suggestions and the Small Worlds phenomenon can be used to network ideas.

## SMALL WORLDS

Simply put, the Small Worlds phenomenon is that social, indeed biological, networks adopt a particular pattern. They usually turn out to not be totally random, but rather turn out to display as a collection of small clusters (worlds). See Figure 5.1.

In Figure 5.1, solid lines represent knowledge sharing between people who talk to each other frequently, and dotted lines are between people who converse infrequently. If one person (node) wants to send a message to someone they do not know in another cluster, it is usually possible for us to

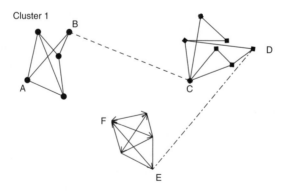

*Figure 5.1   Clustered network showing 'Small Worlds'*

find a 'weak tie' between the clusters, someone who knows someone, who can carry a message through these clusters. For example, if A wants to send a message to F, whom they do not know, then first they would ask friends in cluster 1. B says they know someone C in cluster 2 who may be able to pass the message on. When C gets the message she asks her friends and D suggests E who does know F. A cluster may be created from any connected activity such as a committee, task force, group of residents, professional body, departments, skills, or it may purposely be multidisciplined. A node may also be anything that has a relationship with another node. It may be a person, a web page, city, power station or idea. The clusters identified depend on the problem definer's overall problem. If I were interested in university research, then I would see different clusters compared to someone interested in designing a website.

The Small Worlds phenomenon was exposed by Milgram (1992) in his letter experiments, and later popularized in a play and film, *Six Degrees of Separation* (Watts 1999). The phenomenon means that any two people picked at random usually turn out to be connected via a chain of not more than six intermediate acquaintances. This seems counter-intuitive given that, for most of us, frequent direct two-way conversation occurs with less than 20 people – our Small Worlds cluster. However, each node in that cluster is part of a slightly different cluster or has been in the past. These different acquaintances' clusters are linked, albeit not as strongly as the links within our everyday cluster. This suggests we have adopted an overall population network which is neither 'everyone knows everyone else', nor one where local clusters of socially interactive persons (cliques) have no means of contacting other clusters. Rather what seems to naturally occur is a mix of the two: clusters that are weak-tied.

There is now a reasonable amount of empirical evidence supporting the Small Worlds phenomenon from a range of natural situations (Buchanan 2002; Killworth and Bernard 1979; Matsuo et al. 2001; Richardson and Lissack 2001; Watts 1999). Much of it extends the social network research (e.g. Borgatti 2002; Scott 1996).

That we should arrange ourselves socially into clusters can also be explained by knowledge sharing theory (Hare 1976). This highlights that we can have direct two-way knowledge sharing with only a limited number of people due to the exponential growth of knowledge sharing channels given an increase in people numbers. With three people wishing to communicate with each other freely, there are only three knowledge sharing channels that have to be kept open (A to/from B, A to/from C, and B to/from C). For four people there are six, and for five there are ten channels that have to be serviced. The number of channels grows exponentially. For people, that means sharing pleasantries, as well as being able to physically get to and from them (same time, same place). Having to service a lot of channels becomes very time-consuming. But channels once opened can be left inactive for considerable time and only used as the occasional need arises.

As mentioned, the Small Worlds phenomenon has been found to apply not only to human relationships but also to food chains, ant nests and biological cell structures. This chapter uses the assumption that it will also apply to a network of inquiry statements. But first, Alexander's argument that idea statements can be thought of as being networked needs to be explained.

## ALEXANDER'S SYNTHESIS

Alexander (1964), in the context of being interested in designing a new village for people being relocated in a developing nation, suggested that it is useful to think about ideas as being networked. This is a simple concept but powerful in that it allows us to analyse ideas, using what had been learnt in social network theory. For example, the idea of 'we need our livestock to be well protected' may be seen to be connected to the idea of 'we need good-quality water', 'the cows must be fenced from the bulls', 'our health and the health of our livestock are woven together', and so on. As a network this may be drawn as Figure 5.2, an ideas network which shows that the idea of fences may also be connected to the idea of communal property.

The ideas expressed as statements are nodes on the network. If the synthesis sees two idea statement nodes as being connected then a line is drawn between them. Seeing idea statements as being in a network enables many to be connected together in a network ever increasing in size, and then allows analysts to set to work looking at some emerging patterns of characteristics of the network. For an example of a larger network, see Figure 5.3.

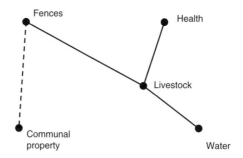

*Figure 5.2    Simple ideas network*

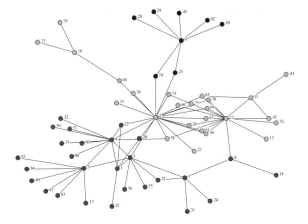

*Figure 5.3   The network diagram*

Clearly, the source from which the idea statements are extracted can be anything deemed relevant to a particular problem situation. It may be the transcript of an interview, a community meeting, remembered comment from a conversation or statements in corporate documents. The statements are about anything thought important or interesting, be they factual points, knowledge claims, recommendations, summations or ideas. It is better that they be conditional statements[2] because the condition can be used to provide a richer set of links between the statements.

So, the statements can be seen as nodes in a network, with the connections between them represented by the lines between the nodes. The Small Worlds phenomenon predicts that if this is done, the resulting network will display a clustered pattern (this will be illustrated next). After this, how the clusters are useful for conceptualizing problems will be explained.

## AN ILLUSTRATION

Moving away from Alexander's village example, let us return to the wildfire example used earlier. Assume you have been asked to suggest how a community structures its thinking about the problem of the wildfires that threaten to sweep through their region each summer. They need help in conceptualizing the problem to enable them to start thinking in more detail about the myriad of different issues involved.

Assuming you also decide to use Alexander's suggestions and want to draw a network of stakeholders' idea statements, then the first task would be to collect a large number of conditional statements. One of these may be, 'The community's ability to self-organize depends on the services offered by the local radio station.' If considered a useful idea, then it can be numbered and recorded; for example conditional statement number 29. Through a series of meetings and from the documents of other affected communities, numerous other conditional statements can be identified, recorded and numbered.

Next, these statements need to be linked. This is a synthesis, which will use the implicit conceptual frame of those doing the linking. This suggests that a group of stakeholders should debate these connections. This has the added advantage of encouraging them to become involved in the problem conceptualization. While labour-intensive, this connecting debate is also thought important to surface assumptions and to force some intense consideration of the statements. It may also generate further statements. This provides thought about the statements in a rich context with shared understanding.

So the statement, 'The town has not experienced a wildfire but the risks seem to be increasing' might be seen to be linked to the statement, 'The establishment of new parklands to the north increases fire risk because of increased density of vegetation'. While many statements might be thought to be linked remotely, only the strong links need to be recorded. The author's experience is that for this exercise there needs to be only about 10–15 per cent of connections compared to nodes, else the resulting network becomes too cluttered.

Moving back to analysis, the statements as numbered nodes and the connections (links) between these nodes can now be diagrammed in a network. The mechanics of doing this using modern computer software is first to draft an interaction matrix (see Table 5.1). This is the required input format for the software to draft the network diagram. The numbered statement nodes make up the top and side headings of the matrix. The connections between the nodes decided upon (e.g. that statement 2 is connected to statement 5 and 74) make up the contents of the matrix.

The matrix can be used to calculate the network diagram using one of a number of computer algorithms as reported in the network analysis literature (Scott 1996). Such programs help draft a diagram (graph) of the statements networked, by first calculating for all the connections together and then locating the nodes in the diagram as if the line connections were 'elastic'. Clearly, this would be rather hard to do by hand.

Returning in more detail to the illustration of a community wanting to conceptualize the problem of wildfires, assume that 91 conditional statements have been identified, recorded and numbered. Two examples of these statements (numbers 2 and 5) are:

*(Statement 2) Presentations of new ideas for protecting the town will always include some language games to persuade an audience, who in turn will appreciate that the presenter's choice of language will not be completely neutral. (Statement 5) Good ideas to protect the community cannot speak for themself; rather they have to be passionately argued for.*

I have chosen these two because, to me, the two statements are about persuasion or advocacy. So, I think statement 2 is connected to statement 5. The task is to find other statements thought to be connected to either 2 or 5, again either in terms of advocacy or some other basis. For example:

*(74) There needs to be recognition that discontinuous innovations of town management are hard to justify compared to incremental improvements.*

The three statements may be recorded as connected because they are all about advocacy. However if the person linking the statements had the issue of 'protection' foremost on their mind, they might say statement 74 is not connected to 2 or 5. Deciding what is connected is intended to be very subjective. This may allow the problem definer's deep underlying assumptions or conceptual frame to make the connections. This is especially so when only a low number of connections are sought. The connections can be drafted into a matrix (spreadsheet) which has the numbers of the statements (1 to 91) as both the left-hand labels and along the top.

Table 5.1, the interaction matrix, therefore shows the statement numbers as column and row headings and the decision that certain statements are connected as 1s in the body of the matrix. For convenience, the interaction matrix presented here is a very cut-down version of the overall 91 x 91. It shows only that statement 2 was considered to be connected to 5 and to 74, but 5 was not thought connected to 74. If only 10–15 per cent of the statements are deemed connected then the matrix is going to be sparse. No connection is recorded as a blank cell (or zero), meaning there is no connection (line) between the row number statement and the column number statement.

This matrix can then be used as input for network analysis software to draft the network diagram. Figure 5.3 shows the network diagram that resulted from the complete illustration interaction matrix. It was drawn by entering the matrix into a piece of standard network analysis software called UCINET6 written by Analytic Technologies. The software has an advantage over a manual drafting of the network, because it has all the connections before calculating the layout of the network. The number of connections, and which connections, determines where nodes (statements) appear in the network diagram. The software allows for later

*Table 5.1   The interaction matrix*

|     | 1 | 2 | 3 | 4 | 5 | 6 | 7 | ... | 20 | 21 | ... | 30 | ... | ... | 74 | ... | 89 | 90 | 91 |
|-----|---|---|---|---|---|---|---|-----|----|----|-----|----|-----|-----|----|-----|----|----|----|
| 1   |   |   |   |   |   |   |   |     |    |    |     |    |     |     |    |     |    |    |    |
| 2   |   |   |   |   | 1 |   |   |     |    |    |     |    |     |     | 1  |     |    |    |    |
| 3   |   |   |   |   |   |   |   |     |    |    |     |    |     |     |    |     |    |    |    |
| 4   |   |   |   |   |   |   |   |     |    |    |     |    |     |     |    |     |    |    |    |
| 5   |   | 1 |   |   |   |   |   |     |    |    |     |    |     |     |    |     |    |    |    |
| 6   |   |   |   |   |   |   |   |     |    |    |     |    |     |     |    |     |    |    |    |
| ... |   |   |   |   |   |   |   |     |    |    |     |    |     |     |    |     |    |    |    |
| 20  |   |   |   |   |   |   |   |     |    |    |     |    |     |     |    |     |    |    |    |
| 21  |   |   |   |   |   |   |   |     |    |    |     |    |     |     |    |     |    |    |    |
| ... |   |   |   |   |   |   |   |     |    |    |     |    |     |     |    |     |    |    |    |
| 30  |   |   |   |   |   |   |   |     |    |    |     |    |     |     |    |     |    |    |    |
| ... |   |   |   |   |   |   |   |     |    |    |     |    |     |     |    |     |    |    |    |
| 74  |   | 1 |   |   |   |   |   |     |    |    |     |    |     |     |    |     |    |    |    |
| ... |   |   |   |   |   |   |   |     |    |    |     |    |     |     |    |     |    |    |    |

manipulations of the network diagram, such as 3D rotation, identification of cliques and changes in the appearance. In the network diagram presented in Figure 5.3, the numbers are the statement numbers and the lines show which statements were said in the matrix to be connected. For example, from the network diagram you can see that statements 6 and 28, 6 and 74 and 6 and 89 were recorded as being connected.

As predicted by the Small Worlds phenomenon, the network turns out to have 'clusters'; it is not evenly distributed. My interpretation is that there are three main clusters of statement numbers. One might be called 'top centre' and has statement numbers 28, 29, 45, 82, 89, 6, 74, 23. There is another which might be called 'bottom left' which includes 52, 55, 21, 4 and 5. The third might be called 'centre right' which includes statements 65, 43, 13, 34 and 26. These three clusters can be thought of as a generalization of the statements that make it up. For example, consider the 'top centre' cluster made up of statements 74, 23, 28, 29, 45, 82, 89 and 6.

It is hoped that these emergent clusters are not as expected from the connections debated by the stakeholders. The original example used was that 2 and 5 are connected, and that 2 and 74 were connected. In the resulting network, due to many other connections suggested, statement 5 has appeared in the 'bottom left' cluster, statement 2 is rather central to the 'centre right' cluster and statement 74 is in the 'top centre' cluster. Moreover, the 'top centre' cluster is suggesting that 28, 29, 45 and so on are connected to 74 through 6, even though this connection was not explicitly entered into the interaction matrix.

## NAMING CONCERN-CLUSTERS AS CONCEPTS

Once the clusters of concern statements have been identified from the network diagram – and it may not need to be too exact a process – they need to be named. This stage moves back again to synthesis. It requires creative thinking about what statements make up the cluster. It can be seen as synthesis because of the need to struggle to understand why the diagramming algorithm resulted in the particular clusters that emerged. Importantly, although the process can be seen as creative, it occurs in an informed way, reducing a complex task to a handful of issues that emerged as clusters. By trying to envision what is suggested by the statements that make up each cluster, you are forced to think synthetically about the cluster. What does it remind you of?

In the wildfire illustration, the statements in the 'top centre' cluster included (in no particular order) the following:

*(6) Have I got it right?: self-organization means each of the community sub-groups has to think up its own reaction, being aware of what other subgroups are doing?*

*(23) Why did it go wrong last time? Because we were all waiting for each other to act. Electricity was needed to pump water, and the electricity utility were waiting for vets to clear wild animals from the area, while the vets needed water and electricity. The town administration was overwhelmed.*

*(74) There needs to be recognition that discontinuous innovations are hard for the town management to justify, compared to incremental improvements.*

*(28) The town administration, not the radio stations as a subgroup, will be a special subgroup responsible for the communications between all the other community subgroups.*

*(29) The community's ability to self-organize depends on the services offered by the local radio station.*

*(45) Self-organization does allow for the input of suggested changes by the appropriate people after the appropriate processes have been followed; it is a complex process.*

*(82) The subgroups each say what they will do, not what needs to be done by others.*

*(89) We are the only ones with the skill to repair high-tension cables and*

*we are not going to do that unless we have clear contracts with the town management.*

Reading this passage over a few times, not paying too much attention to particulars and inevitably drawing on my own past experiences, I start to think about the power struggle between the community subgroups – or at least the radio stations – and the town administration. This suggests to me that the whole wildfire planning problem situation may need to be thought about, brought into existence and conceptualized, using the concept of 'power tensions'.

The same sort of synthetic thinking is also needed for the 'bottom left' cluster and the 'centre right' cluster. Let us assume for brevity that these are interpreted as being something about 'legal' issues and something about the 'empowerment' of specialists. This suggests that the overall wildfire problem also needs to be conceptualized using the three concepts of power, legalities and empowerment. Doing this will conceptualize the problem in a particular way, one recognizable to the stakeholders involved in this whole process. Sense is being made from the original maze of often conflicting statements. Hopefully, it is a conceptualization that was unexpected and one that decentres those involved a little, so they are forced to see the problem somewhat anew.

## CONCLUSION

This chapter has attempted to introduce a method for networking stakeholders' concerns as means of identifying the meta concerns, priorities or concepts. The intent of this chapter was to demonstrate a rational method for revealing appropriate collaborative concerns or concepts from prior concerns of participants. Stakeholder discussions often result in an extensive array of disjointed concern statements, be they the result of interview transcripts, organizational documents or from group meetings. Idea networking gives structure to these concern statements.

The creativity in the method outlined comes from mixing the analysis needed to draft a network from the creative selection of conditional concern or idea statements, and deciding which are connected. The Small Worlds phenomenon predicts that this network will display clusters that would not have been easy to predict without the statements being entered into network graphing software. This creation of an unexpected cluster provides the opportunity to make another creative leap by naming these clusters. These names provide the start in providing the 'solution concepts' to be used to coordinate stakeholders' thinking.

The chapter has suggested the use of networking software to link concern statements and to map them. UCINET6 was the software used. Many other alternative network diagramming software programs are available. NodeXL has many attractive features. Perhaps a more important comparison is between using diagramming software and the other options for collating concern statements. Many planning sessions put the concern statements on sticky notes and participants are asked to stick those they think are similar together on the wall. This is a group version of someone just putting the statements into piles. Doing it this way runs the risk of the statements being clustered into preconceived piles or groups. The networking approach allows statements to be linked to several others with no notion of how the clusters will come out, thus the clusters are not deductive but rather inductive. The networking diagram also allows the relationship between clusters to be seen and statements to be associated with more than one cluster. The relationships between the clusters say something about the dependence or interdependence of the concepts. On a computer, the network can be viewed in 3D and many network metrics can be used to indentify clusters. Also you end up with an easy to show and use graphic when those involved ask where their statement went and how it related to the clusters. Perhaps most important though is that the networking process provides an audit trail of the statements of how they were linked, and which cluster they ended up within. This can be useful for those asking to replicate the process for validation processes. Networking also provides a useful link between qualitative methods such as Post-It notes and quantitative methods such as cluster analysis, multidimensional scaling, factor analysis, principal components and so on.

For more detail on networking statements see the Appendix at the end of the book.

## APPLICATION

You have at least 80 numbered concern statements which first need to be networked (linked, grouped, related) together to produce the network or concept map. That is, you need to record which concern statements are similar with other concern statements. For example, you might feel statements 12, 27 and 37 below are about the need for appropriate innovation, but statement 21 is not. This means 12, 27 and 37 are considered to be linked. In practice this job is best done by the analyst or a very small group tracking through each statement, comparing it with all those below it. One of the skills of an analyst is to be insightful about identifying similar underlying assumptions (root cause analysis) to link sets of statements creatively.

*No 12: We do not encourage out-of-the-box science by funding a wide range of research and development (R&D) organizations doing pure research.*
*No 21: If we do not make a concentrated effort to improve the health of the South Australian Aboriginal population then we will be seen as racist or elitist.*
*No 27: We need to find ways to encourage patients to exercise properly, to distinguish ourselves from other allied health services.*
*No 37: We need innovation from the shop floor, bottom-up continuous improvements in a controlled way, else we will never compete internationally.*

You should aim for all of your statements to be linked to between one to five other statements. There needs to be a fairly strong connection between two statements in your mind for two statements to be recorded as linked. A common mistake is to have too many links.

This linking can be summarized:

1: 6, 13, 22, 34, 41 (statement 1 is linked to statements 6, 13, 22 etc.)
2: 7, 14, 30, 39, 43
3: 23, 34, 36, 41, 43
Etc
12: 27, 37
Etc to 80+

Underline any links you are not sure about so that they can be removed easily later if required.

Next you need to download the UCINET6 software onto your computer and then enter these links in the spreadsheet matrix it provides. This will then generate the right file format for drawing the concept map from your linkages matrix. For more on how to use UCINET6 see the Appendix. Mac users might want to use NodeXL.

The endpoint of task is to produce a jpeg file of your network map. If it has no clear clusters, think about removing some links.

## NOTES

1.  This chapter is based on Metcalfe (2007c).
2.  A statement containing words such as 'if', 'where', 'when', 'while' or 'because'.

# 6.   Solution concepts

## OVERVIEW

Problem-solving is being explained as first agreeing and enacting an appropriate set of organizing principles or solution concepts. The previous chapter explained how these concepts might be emerged from consultation. This chapter will explain what organizing or solution concepts are, and why and how they can provide creative order. Examples of useful concepts will be discussed, as will how and why they might be drafted into a Statement of Intent.[1]

## CALCULATION CONCEPTS

The use of maths, algebra, models, and quantifications generally, has historically been iconic to problem-solving. It has been extremely effective in structuring problems, making solutions appear obvious. For the example of a plane crash, the computation conception would make the drafting of flight or stress models seem reasonable. For the problem of whether to go to war it would suggest building a decision or logistics model. Despite the usefulness of this conception of how to solve a problem, this computational or analytical philosophy of problem-solving has been shown to be riddled with hidden internal inconsistencies, paradox and leaps of faith. It does not provide a solid bedrock source of knowing; rather, it is idealistic.

If an analyst believes a computation provides a true, accurate, context free abstraction of relationships between measureable events and objects, then he or she is assuming idealism. Plato thought mathematics was a particularly excellent ideal form, pure, untainted by the earth – an ideal means of explaining the ideal world. Plato's writings provided the Abraham religions with its pure forms, and science with its great quest for an algebraic theory of everything. Theoretical science, with the aid of mathematics, was set on a course to expose these ideal forms from a dissection of the messy, imperfect real world, which hides some ideal abstraction. Ideal forms provided the social elite with the right to claim that their vision of the world order and what problems should be solved, and why their utopia was the correct one. Their world order was universal (placeless), hierarchical, abstract, static, timeless and coherent, without contradiction, conflict, or need for change. The Marxist and anti-Imperial literature works to expose this oppression.

Rorty (1982) and many others have argued that ideal forms, including computations, are merely words, metaphors, concepts, forms or patterns which we use to interpret, structure or make sense of the world. They only provide recognizable patterns that can be used to reflect on a problem. For example, historically the ideal forms, metaphor or concepts of simple geometric shapes (circle, ellipse etc.) were used to recognize patterns in the movement of the planets. The one that most closely matched their actual paths was used. The metaphor of attraction was then used to explain the deviations in these elliptical patterns as inter-planetary gravitational pull. Newton also used the concept of attraction (flowing towards) to give structure to calculus. Another example of the use of a recognizable pattern to think about a problem is that of 'balance' (harmony). This has been used to find patterns in the movement of forces, energy and gases. Balance has also been used to find patterns in the environment, assuming that nature left alone will return to its ideal state or natural balance. Evolution, progress and competition are more modern metaphors or concepts that can be used in place of balance to design environmental models. The concept of feedback loops provides very different patterns that have been used to display nature's shapes as fractals or chaotic. The concept of organic growth has been used to give pattern in linear programming and life-cycle models. Many models assume the hard systems mechanistic metaphor of their problem having machine- or organism-like parts, with hierarchical, relatively critical roles.

So computation can be seen to start from some conception of the problem, where a conception is a metaphor, form or pattern used to reflect a problem. Using the concepts of feedback, organic systems, attractions, evolution, competition and life cycles would result in very different computations of a plane crash or whether to go to war. Computations provide one perspective, one dependent on the underlying concept assumed.

## OBSERVATION CONCEPTS

Observation is a cornerstone of scientific problem-solving. Scientific attempts to solve the problem of a plane crash would have to include careful observation of the crash site. Scientific attempts to decide whether to go to war would have to include the collection of intelligence on the enemy. Observation, or more generally empirics, evidence collected through the senses via the eyes, nose, ears and skin, appears to offer first-hand, unbiased evidence that can form a solid reliable basis of problem-solving; seeing is believing. However, observation appears to be an act of comparison, if only the comparison of light, motion or colour. Similar terms are 'difference' and 'reflection'. Bateson (1972), the biologist, reminds us that the brain and senses are difference detection devices, comparing millions of input senses to some norm, only becoming explicit to their owner when a significant difference is detected. Counting what is seen is a comparison, this time with an international numbering system, typically to a base of ten. To measure the length of something is to compare it to an internationally agreed measurement standard. Laboratory experiments are logical comparisons. Science wants repeatable findings, that is, comparison. Truth is a comparison to the known. Maps, graphs, drawings, pictures, writing and recordings are comparison to something physical.

We think by comparing our sensory input to our prior conceptions. What is selected out of the massive inputs to our senses depends on what our brains are concerned about. Experienced crash investigators will see different things to a novice. Experience means having particular prior conceptions with which to reflect on what our eyes see. For example, to describe significant plane wreckage as dull speckled grey or cracked requires knowledge of the importance of the concepts of speckled grey or cracks. The choice of these conceptions considerably changes what is observed. Further critical analysis requires that particular or insightful concepts be used to interpret what is seen at the crash site. Are just cracks to be looked for, or cracks with discolouration? What is significant cracking, or dangerous discolouration? Should the search look at the depth of cracks, the length or the location? Experience and professional norms determine which of these are the most appropriate concepts with which to make sense of the mess of a crash. All of which demonstrates the dependence of observation on prior concepts learnt from talking with others.

Observations also need to be explained. What caused it, what does it do, and why is it like that? These definitely need language. Observation without explanation is as incomplete as explanation without observation. They are a joined pair. Some problem-solvers, typically critical social theorists, prefer to focus on the explanations rather than the observations. Karl Marx was not interested in the 'mere appearance' of things. Rather, he thought it was important to understand why an observation existed, the underlying 'processes in tension' that cause an appearance to occur. For example, a married couple can be living, eating and sleeping together but not be happy with their relationship. The appearance is of a compatible couple, but to really understand marriage you need to understand the underlying tensions that result in the state of marriage. Mere observation of their relationship might not reveal very much. Marx used the example of the caterpillar. You cannot really understand the caterpillar by merely observing and measuring it. You need to also understand the underlying evolutionary forces driving its butterfly life cycle. What appears in the physical form for us to observe is the result of some underlying forces. The concept of evolution, for example, so powerfully explains the physical appearance of every living thing. The concept determining what we see may be more insightful than the observation itself.

One role claimed for observation is that it identifies cause and effect. For example you may observe a cracked door lock on a crashed plane and induce that it caused the crash. However, as Hume pointed out, you cannot actually see a cause and effect even in an example as simple as turning on a light. Rather you induce that the switch turned on the light. Perhaps more importantly, it was not just the switch that caused the light to go on. Electricity, wiring, light bulbs and generators also caused the light to go on. To say you saw the switch cause the light to go on is to use the concept of switches to interpret the situation. Someone interested in light bulbs might say it was this invention that enabled light to be controlled so easily. Your prior conceptions choose the causes and effects you use to reflect on an observation.

Cause and effect is a prior concept so entrenched in our thinking that Kant thought it, along with time and space, to be hardwired in our minds. Today he might have claimed it is in our genes. However, it may just be another concept from our childhood. What we see is a pattern of activities, a sequence where one thing comes before another. We are told this has a name: cause and effect. If our profession is very interested in causes, rather than say consequences, then the concept of cause and effect will become second nature to our thinking. But really we are just selecting one particular concept or criteria to reflect on the situation.

The concept of objects is another so entrenched in our thinking that we often fail to appreciate that it is interpreting what we see in a particular manner. Objects have attributes or properties. Alternative concepts with which to see the mess of a crash site, or interpret the intelligence of a war threat, are process, underlying tensions, interconnection, betweeness, becoming or actions. Each will make us see different things. To use the concept of objects with the assumption that their properties are independent of the observer has been a cornerstone of science since Galileo. He focused scientists on picking apart objects to understand their often hidden properties. Heidegger was not happy with the notion that objects had properties separate from the observer. To him, we give things their properties depending on the use we want to put them to. If, for example, we were concerned about rigidness, we would use this concept to think about things that come to our attention. Previously the pragmatists Peirce, James and Dewey had similar concerns. They argued that something is what we think it does, not what it is. It does not have properties, but rather perceived patterns of activity. Mangled metal at a crash site is what metal does: its pattern of activity. Seeing something as what we think it does, rather that what it is, changes what is thought and the consequences that follow. So more generally, what is observed depends on what conceptions are used to reflect. Using the concept of objects with attributes is a choice among many others.

## PROBLEM-SOLVING CONCEPTS

The critique of strategic thinking by Mintzberg (1994) and Weick (2006) is that organizations need more thinking before analysis. The pragmatic, or concept-driven, approach to problem-solving suggested in this book makes sense of this critique. It explains thinking as reflecting off an agreed set of explicit prior conceptions (Baggini 2005). This suggests that problem-solving is a process of stakeholders agreeing on an appropriate set of concepts as criteria that they will all use to make future decisions. This agreed set of concepts therefore has the potential to organize, coordinate or make consistent the thinking and conduct of those involved. The concepts will determine everyone's interpretation even of what the problem is, and thus what is interpreted to be a reasonable response. They should provide a coordinated sense of direction and identity.

The selection of different concepts makes different future actions seem reasonable. For example, Ackoff (cited in Jacques 2003) and Wenger and Snyder (2000) suggest we use the concept of communities rather than organizations. They therefore suggest action be taken to loosen controls and hierarchy. Schumpeter (1942) uses the concept of evolution to think about products and services. He therefore sees a need for governments to act to create effective marketplaces to enable this evolution to occur. An organization might use idea networking to reveal 'agility' as a cluster of stakeholder concerns suggesting the organization needs to be more agile. This raises questions such as: how are they to become more agile? what impact will new federal legislation have on their agility? Other concepts might conflict or set the limits of this agility concept. Using more than five concepts might be reaching the limits of our brains to 'chunk' information (Miller 1956); using less may exclude the opportunity for a creative dialectic between the concepts.

A concepts approach to problem-solving places goals (targets, objectives) in a secondary position: they come later (Drucker 1973; Locke and Latham 1990; Ordonez et al. 2009). Goals contain inherent concepts. For example, a goal to be ranked in the top ten providers of a business service in the Pacific region is based on the concept of 'comparative ranking'. Identifying and agreeing that the concept of comparative ranking be used to guide those involved comes before setting goals. Identifying the concept first is also justified by not wanting to predict exactly how the future will unfold. Setting goals requires prediction of the end state of disturbances in large, competitive, complex and chaotic systems. However, those involved may be more concerned about maintaining some particular characteristics during change rather than about these end states. For example, it may be more important to an organization to maintain its quality identity rather than whether its Atlantic or Pacific operations are more successful. The concept-setting approach also differs from goal theory in that it provides the explanation for why particular goals are thought useful. The goal sets the 'what needs to be done', for example 'we need to be ranked in the top ten'; while the concept provides the 'why' (motive), for example 'position in the rankings determines the ease of securing new clients' (Ulrich 2002).

As discussed in more detail later, the interrogative pronouns and adverbs in the English language are systemized into the six Wh's: why, when, where, who, what and how. Planning has been explained (Mintzberg 1994) as providing the 'what' that needs to be done and 'why' (motive), rather than planning, which is assumed to be the 'how', 'when', 'where' and 'by whom'. The interrogative of interest is the motivational 'why' question. This can be understood as the motive for acting in a particular way, as used in detective stories: 'why did the murderer do it?'. Put another way, what was the reason (the reasoning), that is, the thinking driving this action? Dennett (1989) calls this the murderer's intentional stance. Ulrich (1983) describes purposeful action as an intrinsic motivation; there is a reason why action is being undertaken. This suggests that the 'why' question comes before the 'what needs to be done' statement. What needs to be done is an interpretation derived from the motive. For example, a proclaimed activity might be that an organization needs to expand into India. That this is a reasonable action stems from understanding the motive behind proclaiming the activity – the 'why'. The organization may need access to somewhere with a population with high software skills evenly spread throughout the entire country, which also has a complementary time zone. This makes India more reasonable than other locations. The concepts of software skills, expansion and time zones are being used to make sense of a location strategy.

# PRAGMATIC CONCEPTS

It may be useful to elaborate even further on exactly what is meant by a pragmatic concept. As mentioned, the term 'concept' has been chosen over similar words such as concern, priority, frame, idea, vision, issue, stance, perspective and metaphor, to align with the language of the original pragmatists. Peirce (1878) used the word 'conception' perhaps partly to distinguish from generalizations or universals. Some of the modern management pragmatists use words such as conceptual frame(work). The 'idea', as praised by Piaget (as cited in Gruber and Voneche 1995) and Nietzsche (1979 [1873]) seems to refer to what here is being called concepts; ideas such as empathy and justice. However, in popular usage the word 'idea' carries connotations of invention or entrepreneurship, a novel action, so it will be defined here as suggesting an action, as 'what might be done'. The related word of 'ideology' has a very different meaning, derived from Plato's ideal. It clashes with pragmatism. Ideal managers, like ideal women, seems to be a very dangerous universal. It contrasts with the evolutionary or contingencies concepts of being appropriate to an environment. Vision-driven or scenario-driven problem-solving has some similarities to concepts-driven, but concepts cannot be visualized whereas examples can. Mintzberg and Westley (2001) talk about digging up ideas that provide vision. Concepts provide the drivers for (action) ideas, and evaluating action ideas. Visions are out there, to be strived for like goals, while concepts are drivers of behaviour, avoiding the need to construct a single-scenario endgame. The future is thought too unpredictable to produce accurate future scenarios. However, these future guesses might help an organization think about suitable collaborative concepts. Moreover, many vision statements demonstrate a poor understanding of vision-driven problem-solving. Their visions often cannot be visualized, so fail to provide guidance on day-to-day decision-making (O'Brien and Meadows 2007a, 2007b). Issue-driven management is a very similar term (Liebl 2002), like concern-driven change. The term 'policy-driven problem-solving' sounds like a confusion of terminology. Gustavsen et al. (1996) argues that the terms 'expert-driven problem-solving', and 'communications-driven problem-solving' are not similar to concepts-driven collaboration but rather competitors. They sound more hierarchical.

The use of metaphoric analysis is very pervasive in the modern management, philosophy and humanities literature (Lakoff 1993). However, among many people, it still carries connotations of flowery artistic language more appropriate to poetry than serious thinking. Metaphor differs from concept in that a metaphor usually draws on a noun which can be visualized; concepts cannot be imagined – examples can. The pragmatist

Schon (1963), while arguing that creativity is about displacing concepts with alternatives, argues that metaphors are not concepts but they can be turned into concepts. To use a classic example, the machine metaphor has been used to think about organizations (Morgan 1986). This can be turned into the concepts of mechanization or automation.

Concepts would appear not to be as abstract as values, but more abstract than words and ideas. This is what makes them attractive to those interested in designing problem solutions – flexibility within limits. James (1890) explains why concepts cannot be imagined, although examples can be. For example, there is no mental image of agility, but it is possible to think of agile things. New concepts are derived from the three steps of compare, reflect and abstract. The example James uses is the concept of leaves, suggesting a process of comparing a wide range of leaves from different plants, reflecting on their similarity and abstracting the concept of a leaf as a generic term. This perhaps does not use Hegel's concept of the dialectic. How does 'leaf' differ from other concepts such as 'flower'? Some leaves are mistaken for flowers, the distinction not being their colour or shape but that flowers have pollen-shedding anthers and/or the pollen-receiving stigmas. James's explanation of how to generate concepts suggests the would-be strategist look through the activities of organizations thought successful. First, similarities between the organizations may be sought, then reflection on the desirable attributes and then abstracting commonality. Concepts such as transparency or agility might emerge in this way.

Continuing with the task of trying to understand pragmatic concepts, James also writes that a concept ought to be proposed by the consequences of it not being there. In his examples of freedom and God there is a contraction: the concept is being defined in terms of an opposite (antonym). A possible antonym of organizational agility might be documented accountability. This can be generalized. For example, the proposition that 'all men are mortal' contains two concepts in contraction. In this case, living beings are being defined as having to die. This provides a link with how setting collaborative concepts can be both rational and creative. Creativity can be defined as bringing together two or more concepts not previously combined. Bringing together biology and chemistry created the biotechnology industry. The coming together of calculating machines with typewriters and telephones created the Internet. Having a set of dialectic concepts might mean something like making one concept, 'documented-agility'. Alternatively, it may mean simply that the concepts used to guide the problem solution include agility and being well documented.

If the set of solutions concepts is carefully chosen, after an analysis of the organization and environment, then they can result in developing the organization's unique identity and intrinsic motivation (Mintzberg 1987).

For example, a research organization might draft a Statement of Intent or purpose which uses the following set of concepts: elite, rigorous, scholarly, nationalistic and conservative. Meanwhile another research organization might draft a Statement of Intent using the concepts of equity, problem-solving, scholarly, international and opportunity. If these concepts were fully internalized by the participants of the two universities so that they intuitively used them to make sense of their day-to-day problems and solutions, then these concepts would eventually drive the creation of institutions with very different identities. This aligns problem-solving with the collaborative, interorganizational networked or communities of practice view of problem-solving which aims to bond those involved by its identity (Wenger and Snyder 2000).

## CREATIVITY

As was mentioned above, Mintzberg (1994) and Weick (2006) call for there to be more creativity or imagination invested in complex collaborative thinking before any detailed analysis. Evidence in support of the creative opportunities of using dialectic concepts for creative problem-solving comes, perhaps strangely, from argumentation theory (Bailin 2003). Bailin points out that if you believe in reasoning, then creativity cannot be written off as being some mysterious inspirational act only available to gifted individuals. There is a need to explain creativity in terms of reasoning, where reasoning is the process of justifying propositions (knowledge claims) by providing convincing supporting evidence. The tension between contradictory concepts within a proposition provides the catalyst for this synthesis. This contradictory tension can also be between two or more propositions (dialectic argument). For example, arguing that the future cannot be forecast sets up in tension the concepts of future and forecasting. These concept(ion)s can then also be set up in tension with the other concept(ion)s. It may be claimed that the future is deterministic or that it is unknowable. A plurality of concept(ion)s are now in tension: future, forecasting, determinism and unknowable. The outcome of discussing these may be the creation of a new idea: a synthesis. This explains the creative potential of reasoning. This is seen as being analogous to using a set of dialectic concepts in problem-solving. Reasoning is clearly our most successful method for generating creative, yet well-justified knowledge. Hopefully the same can be said of concepts-driven problem-solving. The creative dialectic can also be seen in the evolution of science (Kuhn 1970 [1962]), species (Darwin 1859), products (Schumpeter 1942) and ideas (Dawkins 1989).

Creativity can also be achieved through the selection of concepts. Some concepts, such as evolution (Foster 2000) and social power (Habermas 1984), are very powerful, offering creativity through how they are interpreted. Evolution has been used to make sense of species, capitalism, ideas, antibodies, brain neurons, organizational structures, social habits such as cooperation and empathy, as well as the survival of small companies. Once adopted, it is hard not to think of any problem situation without the use of the concept of power. It raises issues of types of power and the responsibilities of power. Concepts such as mimicry (Brower 1988) have been used to make sense of organizational structures and people's actions but still seem underdeveloped as a concept, given the centrality of mimicry to our lives. In management generally, the concepts of efficiency and effectiveness have almost become endemic, leaving little chance to use them creatively. Creativity might also be measured in terms of usefulness or number of uses. A concept that makes sense of more of an organization's problems will be more useful to that organization, more creative. The concept of transparency might be full of uses through many levels and areas of an organization. It might refer to participants, promotion, product selection and customer relations decisions. Put another way, the usefulness of a concept may be said to be how creative it is, how many activities it suggests across a whole organization.

Another means of finding creative concepts, apart from holding brainstorming sessions with participants, is to look for concepts advocated to be used by others. Below is the author's quick attempt to identify some concepts from a random volume (40) of the journal *Long Range Planning*. It is possible to interpret articles to be calling for strategists to think about the dialectic concepts of:

- sophistication versus fit (alignment or appropriateness);
- process agreement versus outcome agreement;
- profitability versus sustainability;
- European versus US identity;
- intuition versus rigorous process;
- independence versus networked;
- managed versus egalitarian networks.

Chief executives' comments in annual reports also provide use of some concepts:

- A taxation department's report includes use of the concepts:
  - ease of compliance;
  - inside-out systems development;
  - enabling clients to do the right thing.

- A university's report includes the concepts of:
  - innovative products;
  - agility;
  - family-friendly.
- A large mining company's report also includes the concepts of:
  - courage;
  - urbanization in developing countries;
  - pipelining new projects.

Social theory can also be thought of as another source of creative concepts. For example, the concepts of visualization, contradiction, time-positioning and systems come to mind.

**Visualization**

An organization might use the concept of visualization as part of its problem solution. The concept of visualization has been well discussed by Latour (1986). He uses it in the context of the social development of science over the last 500 years. Star charts, maps, mathematics, graphs, writing and technical drawings are all examples of how thinking was assisted by making ideas visual. This asynchronous form of mass communication assisted in enabling a community of scientists to work collaboratively and incrementally on complex ideas. In the form of documentation, visualization has also allowed large organizations to function, especially the legal fraternity in the form of accountability. Vision statements and scenarios would appear to come from the same genus (O'Brien and Meadows 2007a, 2007b). Logos, corporate architecture, corporate image and vision statements start to suggest how visualization might be used as a solution concept. Alternatively, organizations may want to use the concept of visualization to mean transparency of their expertise, knowledge or core competency either within the organization or to potential customers. The concept of visualization has also been used by logistics organizations in the form of visible supply chains, knowing where everything is all the time.

**Contradiction**

Some communities might want to use the creativity of contradiction as a solution concept. The history of the concept of contradiction is that of the political history of the twentieth century (Mao 1967; Seo and Creed 2002). It was to politics what evolution was to religion. Perhaps this concept is now better understood as seeing the world as it appears to us as the result of numerous underlying tensions. In evolution, these tensions are between reproduction rates and competition for food, resulting in the physical form of species. In manufacturing, these tensions include creativity, costs, science and connectivity. The tension between these results in the particular design of products as they appear in the marketplace. In the economy, these tensions are between things such as the means of production, constitutional power, and cultural attitudes towards justice and innovation. This results in a particular design of the economy. As a solution concept, contradiction can be used in a way reminiscent of the concepts of balance, recursion or interdependence. Appropriate pay schemes can be seen as a tension between incentive schemes and recruiting self-motivated participants. Organizational structure can be seen as a tension between the need for constant change and the need for stability. Participants' profiles can be seen as a tension between outsourcing and developing an independent capability. Dealing with the future can be seen as a tension between planning and being responsive. The opposite of contradiction would be something like ordered hierarchy.

**Progressive**

Iyer (2004) uses the concept of time to explain the global struggles of capitalism and religion going on at the beginning of the twentieth century. He sees religious and indigenous cultures as wanting to look back to tradition for guidance on how to act in the future. The alternative is to look forward in time, to want to be innovative or progressive. The imagined future is better than now. This forward-looking attitude is typified by the cultures of the information technology (IT) industry, Silicon Valley and California generally. The assumption of progressivism can be seen in different cultural celebrations. Some cultural groups present figures of historic nostalgia, while others present futuristic science fiction characters. Some communities present a marketing image of tradition, while others present themselves as futuristic or innovative. This concept of being progressive can be used by communities to suggest continuous improvement, of growth or enlightened leadership, of innovation and creativity. This may be either in products and services or in organization routines.

**Systems**

The concept of systems (Ackoff 1971) plants in the mind the idea that objects can be thought of in terms of their relationships, connectivity or betweeness. A product or service can be thought of as being one element in a marketplace, an industry, a livelihood, a scientific specialism, a customer convenience system or an organizational image. Organizations might use the concept of systems as a solution concept, as many do, to suggest an attitude to problem-solving or project management that takes a more holistic perspective, that thinks about the interconnections between things when making changes and how those changes affect other things. Problems are therefore to be looked at in terms of processes, not individuals. It would encourage consideration of things such as how new products and services fit into identifiable systems.

**Financial Instrument**

A very popular concept for thinking about organizations nowadays is that of the financial instrument. This draws on the analogy of equity shares or a bank loan to see an organization as an inflow and outflow of cash. A factory is not seen as supplying a service to customers but as a financial bundle with a history of cash flows which can be bought and sold as a package in the financial marketplace. The staff, products and processes of the organization are merely attributes of the financial package, like inter-est terms and repayment dates in a bank loan. Using this concept can help owners make the organization more attractive to the financial marketplace either to attract senior staff, to raise future investment money at cheaper repayment rates, or when preparing to sell the organization. It becomes problematic when it results in dismissing the needs of staff and the mar-ketplace or when used to think about organizations such as universities and the provision of essential services such as health and water. It has been used to think about parks, lakes and fire prevention.

Concept-driven or pragmatic thinking differs from science in being about how things ought to be rather than how they are. However, failure to use the generic epistemology of science for designing public policy has led historically to massive loss of life (Lysenko 1948). Pragmatism attempts to foil this by requiring the justification of knowledge claims (Rorty 1989). This is partly done by encouraging more interpretations of phenomena from a wide range of participants – pluralism. This proliferates the para-digms, or schools of thought, mentioned by Kuhn (1970 [1962]).

The challenges of using dialectic argument to assist small groups to seek creative concepts in a non-confrontational manner have been addressed by both the argument mappers (van Gelder 2003), the judgemental forecast-ers (Armstrong 2000), the electronic Delphi designers (Grohowski et al. 1990) and the community consultation designers (List and Metcalfe 2004). Argument includes making justifications to the evidence-based sceptics. This means attempts to collect evidence on the effectiveness of concepts used, implicitly or explicitly, in the past. This might also include reflec-tion on what actions or investments have been made against the solution concepts articulated historically. Pragmatic thinking is very much about learning from explicit reflection on consequences, intended or not.

### Participatory

The concepts-driven approach to problem-solving outlined here, however, carries implicit assumptions that may clash with centralized planning practices. First, setting a set of solution concepts does not assume there is a centralized problem analysis team which prepares detailed 'what needs to be done' action plans. There is need for a leadership group to agree and explain the solution concepts. It, or another group, may generate activities to achieve those concepts. However, a key part of the concepts-driven approach is thought to be the coordination of decentralized planning and decision-making activities by, for example, requiring use of the solution concepts as performance evaluation criteria. This coordinated decentralization allows the opportunity for minority voice, creativity, tolerance, difference – pluralist solutions, pragmatic morality, within limits. Second, setting solution concepts is about aligning all members to respond as agreed to day-to-day events, rather than being a decision-making method. Chia (1994) summarizes the arguments against the notion of decision-making. These include its assumption that decisions are one-off events made at a certain point in time. Third, setting solution concepts requires any later goals set to be allocated under whichever concept they serve. For example, in the Statement of Intent outlined in Appendix 6.1 to this chapter, goals might be set under each of the concepts of agile, precise, transparent, and so on. Last, as mentioned, the solution concepts approach provides the 'why' an action is appropriate, not what needs to be done, or how. This leaves any planning meeting free to concentrate on these latter two interrogatives.

Perhaps more complex is the issue of who decides which solution concepts ought to represent the identity of concerned community. It has been hinted through the chapter that it would be nice if justified usefulness or creativity determined which solution concepts were selected. This could perhaps be informed by a careful analysis of intended and unintended consequences. Given the politics and public relations realities of most communities, this suggestion displays an optimism bias. Concepts such as documented accountability, obedience and risk mitigation are often clear organizational realities but not articulated as organizational concepts. Culture, legislation and personal values would suggest mitigation against the selection of certain concepts. But the Milgram (1992) and Standford prison experiments, to say nothing of the popularity of Nazism, Stalinism, neo-conservativism, spiritualism and fundamentalism, demonstrate how quickly most of us are willing to accept even extreme concepts to make sense of our lives. Habermas (1984, 1990) suggests the need for a healthy balanced dialectic argumentative process, many other Continental philosophers suggest a historical critique of conceptual ideas now deeply embedded in society – deconstruction. Secret ballots and/or independent arbitration may be the only realistic way to maintain balanced input in an organization. Hopefully this process will somehow be informed by synthesis, creativity and imagination.

## REINFORCING

Regardless of what concepts are selected, concepts-driven problem-solving works by ensuring the desired concepts dominate the default concepts controlling the thinking of participants. Once the solution set of concepts have been documented, and briefly scoped in the Statement of Intent, the usual organizational 'carrot and stick' motivation and influence methods can be used to ensure the concepts are applied. Problem-solving meetings might advocate, explain and contrast the concepts. Selection criteria for promotion, for new participants, for project funding and for performance evaluation can be aligned with the solution concepts. For example, if the Statement of Intent concepts include that the organization intends to become more scholarly, then the performance and budget allocation needs to be determined in terms of how participants have made the organization more scholarly. The opposite is also true: there also needs to be some disincentive for participants to make choices that will make the organization less scholarly. The intent is to get participants to make their day-to-day choices so that each one improves the scholarship of the organization. To back this up, a number of activities that are explicitly designed to improve scholarship can be initiated. Examples include a review of capital equipment, training and culture for ways of increasing the organization's overall scholarship. This is discussed more in later chapters.

## STATEMENT OF INTENT (PURPOSE)

Having agreed on a set of solution concepts they need to be documented so as to provide what Latour (1986) calls an 'immutable mobile'. The obvious name for this document is a Statement of Solution Concepts; however there is an overlapping literature that can be used here. This is the intent and/or purpose literature which is reasonably well established. Solution concepts provide an intended solution. For example, to have the solution concept of wanting to mimic a particular successful outcome elsewhere is to have this intent. Purpose is in the present, intent in the future; both are the means to an end, drivers, only available to self-conscious beings. It is a conviction to achieve a future state of affairs. So strictly speaking, a solutions document would be a Statement of Intent, not a Statement of Purpose. However, in the literature and in practice, there is a lot of confusion between the uses of these words. The important distinction may be with the words 'vision' and 'goal', as these require forecasting, an ability to see into the future and a belief in Utopias – ideal forms. Purpose and intent are drivers of action, intrinsic motivations, providing the justification for why particular actions are appropriate or about to be undertaken. Using the example above, actions can be coordinated as being because the organization wants to mimic another organization.

There has been an extensive literature calling for project managers to start with being clear about their purpose or intent. The pragmatic systems thinkers (Ackoff 1994a; Churchman 1971) were among the first saying that any system is defined by its purpose. The purpose of a health system is to deliver health. The early management writers, such as Bernard and Drucker, talked about corporate purpose. Drucker (1973), for example, in defining management tasks and responsibilities, has an early chapter calling for a clear statement of purpose but he explains it as deciding 'what business are we in?' The term 'corporate purpose' tended to get replaced with 'vision and goals' in the 1980 and 1990s. More recently it has received more attention (Ellsworth 2002), now back to encouraging managers to ask: 'why does the organization exist, what is its reason for existence?' Ellsworth (2002), for example, argues that a vision statement is only an attempt to visualize purpose. His book *Leading With Purpose* makes a strong case for organizations having a clear statement of purpose which provides the 'guiding concepts'. However, the concept-driven approach to problem-solving does not concern itself with asking why an organization or concerned community exists. Rather, because it is pragmatic, it focuses on the concepts which are defined as providing alternative future actions. This reinforces the preferred use of the term 'intent' rather than 'purpose'.

Strategic intent is a term usually associated with Hamel and Prahalad's (2005) *Harvard Business Review* oft-cited article. They explain strategic intent as having three attributes: (1) of giving a unified sense of direction; (2) of discovery; and (3) of destiny (worthwhile-ness) by setting challenges and empowering. This provides a useful description of the Statement of Intent document suggested in this book; the collection of solution concepts. Hamel and Prahalad's examples of organizations that succeeded by having such set of concepts in a Statement of Intent include Komatsu including the strategic concept (intent) of beating Caterpillar, and of Honda including the concept of small engine technology dominance. They argue that the use of a Statement of Intent containing clear drivers or concepts is a preferable approach to the problem of strategy. It is preferable to the oft-used alternatives of: (1) relying on extensive analysis, assuming it is possible to collect enough information to give clear foresight; and (2) the resources-first approach of blindly investing in the best technology and people and waiting to see what they invent. The former is identified by those who ask questions such as: 'what will happen differently in the future?' that is, they assume useful information about how the future will exist. The latter resources approach is often used in research and development strategies. Other examples include many national government research and innovation polices which consist of funding bodies such as universities and other research institutions trusting the researchers to select what research is done. They assume these approaches would be better done if fronted by a Statement of Intent.

Bartlett and Ghoshal (1994) call for a statement of purpose but it may preferably be called 'intent'. They say it should reflect the competencies and the related concerns of all staff. They argue for this because the chief executive cannot be the only strategist in a modern dynamic and complex environment. The expertise is to be found with local or frontline managers who cannot relay strategic information back to the chief executive effectively enough for him or her to be sufficiently informed on all issues. This justifies why the solution concepts are mapped from the concerns of local managers, although this needs to include senior managers and industry experts to ensure a broad range of externally aware concerns. Hopefully, the solutions concepts as summarized in the Statement of Intent will reflect the competency and related concerns of all managers in a coherent, summary (soundbite) manner.

Saku and Sillance (2007) remind us that there is no guarantee that a Statement of Intent will include everyone's intent. They ask who possesses the intent. They agree that a Statement of Intent provides a mechanism for ensuring a continuity of goals, and a means of adapting to internal and external developmental pressures. They add that the role of the Statement of Intent is to precede analysis and planning to address that for which one cannot plan or does not want to plan, to represent a proactive mode of problem-solving, to provide a means to evaluate bottom-up ideas, and to provide a symbol of a concerned community's will about the future. It precedes or is superordinate to goals, uncertain in its achievability, of high significance, prospective and inspirational. It has the potential to energize all those concerned to a collective purpose. But this has to be managed. They ask how a Statement of Intent results in a collective mind (Weick 1995), a collective consciousness, distributed cognition or a virtual role set. I use the term 'aligned'. They suggest having a small succinct set of high-level solution concepts (rhetorical device) is a start. But these need to be sub-divided into a coordinated hierarchy of intents that are more relevant to local managers. They are not, however, assuming that the Statement of Intent contains the solution concepts agreed on by the process of idea networking and mapping advocated in this book.

## CONCLUSION

Thinking about complex social situations involves others; thinking that is going to lead to coordinated outcomes needs to be collaborative. This chapter has provided an explanation of problem-solving, one that responds to Minzberg's and Weick's call for more collective imagination. It suggested how we might think about creative solutions by drawing on the empirical findings of Gustavsen et al. (1996), pragmatism and the literature on mental states. The design suggested is to negotiate an agreed set of conceptions to be used by participants. Problem-solving would then be the use of a set of agreed concepts used by participants when they make day-to-day decisions. If collaboratively constructed, these concepts would also act to provide the future identity of those involved. Correctly chosen and applied, this set of concepts will act to reconstruct the physical form, identity and culture of those involved. They could provide the criteria for evaluating all their activities while allowing individuals the right to apply concepts drawing on their own private thoughts and ideas.

This concepts-driven approach to problem-solving concentrates first on the drivers of change, rather than the goals (targets, objectives). For example, agreeing to use the concept of agility to sense-make future choices is determining why one action is to be preferred over another; that is, determining purpose, intent. Agility is driving change down one path over another. This is thought to be particularly relevant when dealing with large, complex, dynamic environments. The setting of objectives or assum-ing future scenarios may turn out to be limiting, quickly outdated, con-straining, and turn out to be only one of a number of acceptable futures. The concept-setting approach assumes that the task of problem-solving in a dynamic environment should be limited to only trying to coordinate some of the conceptions used by participants to interpret future events, rather than planning specific actions based on having to say what will unfold in the future. Setting the broad concepts by which future choices are to be evaluated still allows the inclusion of local expertise. The shared conceptions provide the coordination of these local activities. Micro-management can be avoided; rather, the opportunity exists for an effective mix of centralized direction and individual imagination.

In this way, concept-driven problem-solving also provides a means of alignment, of 'staying on message'. Having collectively constructed the set of identity-giving concepts, everything done by those involved can be aligned by using them. There is no point in having a solution concept of agility of visible suppliers and then rewarding participants who make choices that restrict supply chain visibility. The money needs to follow the concepts, but they may need to be broad enough not to restrict imaginative initiation. Having around five concepts means there are not too many to remember and apply, but enough to allow creative dialectic with a directed balance.

## APPLICATION

Draw a line around the different clusters in your network diagram (concept map). Try to find about five clusters in your map. Figure 6.1 has been divided into six concepts.

List separately the statements that make up each cluster (that is, sort your 80+ statement list into the five or so clusters). Look for patterns through each cluster of statements: what are they about, what makes them a distinct cluster?

Think up a summary name for each of your clusters of statements, a

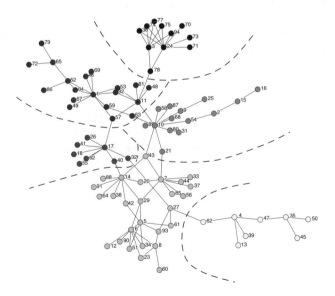

*Figure 6.1    Idea statements network*

name that reflects what they have in common, a meta concern or strategic concept name that summarizes and describes the concern statements in the cluster. This is an important task in need of some very careful creative thinking. Choose the concern or concept names carefully, be imaginative. They should be intriguing and motivational.

Remember, a concept is a pattern of activity that might be used to solve your problem. Usually it is an adjective or adverb, for example, 'agility': the need to be able to respond rapidly to change.

List the five or so clusters of statements separately, provide examples of individual concern statements that made you think of the name of your strategic concern or concepts (cluster) and explain in a sentence or two why you chose that name for that collection of statements.

## APPENDIX 6.1: STATEMENT OF INTENT

This Statement of Intent provides the set of concepts (priorities, concerns) by which this logistics organization intends to guide its future decision-making and so develop its own distinctive identity. This organization intends to become more:

- Agile: able to change processes, strategies, tasks and relationships more rapidly, and able to respond to a wider range of operations in a wider variety of locations.
- Transparent: able to visualize the location and details of products, orders and equipment at all times.
- Precise: able to deliver the right stuff to the right place at the right time more often.
- Interoperable: able to interact with suppliers, customers, competitors and emergency services equipment more easily.
- Distributed networked: have a physical depot or node and transport network which is neither centralized or decentralized, but rather conceptually like the Internet, not single-node dependent.

These concepts will be implemented through the Action Plans.

## APPENDIX 6.2: CONCEPTS – A SUMMARY

A concept is defined by the pragmatists as a recognized pattern of activity. It is evaluated by its usefulness, its consequences (uses). For example, see Table 6.1.

*Table 6.1   Examples of pragmatic concepts*

| Concept | Activity | Consequences/uses |
|---------|----------|-------------------|
| Running | Running | Move fast, get tired, get fit |
| Agility | Being agile | Avoid things, not solid |
| God | God worship, parent substitute | Less fear of death, not empirical |
| Freedom | Being free | Choice, understand confinement and responsibility |
| Justice | Being just | Less aggression, hard to administer |
| Leaf | Photosynthesis, evaporation | Provides sugar/energy and pumps water through plant, food for seed dispersers |
| Absorptive capacity | Ability to recognize the value of new information, assimilate it and apply it to commercial ends | Innovation, wealth, change fatigue |
| System | Think about the relationship between elements, including why it exists | Anticipate consequences, more complexity, consider collective purpose, boundary, transformation etc. |

Concepts can be intuitive, implicit, unappreciated and unnamed (see *The Meaning of Liff* by Douglas Adams and John Lloyd 1983). For example, a young child can recognize and respond to the pattern called 'friendly' without being able to name it.

When named concepts can be shared with others, they point out patterns of activity. Named concepts cannot be imagined, but examples can; for example, agility. This is because concepts are patterns. Images are understood to be visual memories which can be recombined purposefully, as in visualizing the solution to a problem. Dreams may be examples of when visual memories are recombined intuitively.

## APPENDIX 6.3: VISION STATEMENTS

Many readers will have noticed that this book has not recommended the oft-quoted problem-solving process of starting with a vision. It is thought that humans do not think with visions, although they remember experiences as visual memories. This section will argue that vision statements be thought of as primary concept statements. Vision statements need to be read for the concepts they contain.[2]

**Idealism Versus Purpose**

Visions are said to provide an idealistic, inspirational, intellectual coherence for a problem solution, one that conflicting stakeholders can use to address the turbulent complexity (O'Brien and Meadows 2007b; Raynor 2007, 1998; Westley and Mintzberg 1989). The visual turn is argued to provide a common or coordinated mindset, mental model, knowledge structure, schema, prior conception, perspective, world-view, lens, belief structure, map, cognitions or underlying conceptions (Mason and Mitroff 1981; Kaplan 2011; Walsh 1995).

However, it has been known philosophically for hundreds of years, and confirmed by modern neuroscience and psychology empirics, that we humans do not reason in visions. Consider mathematics, logic, and calls to 'create customers', for example. These cannot be pictured in our head, although remembered examples might. In scientific cognition terms, the pictures we imagine in our mind's eye are a remix of our visual memories (Rorty 1989; Rosenfield 1988; Toulmin 1972; Vygotsky 1986; Wittgenstein 2001 [1953]).

The vision turn (Densten 2005; Malaska and Holstius 1999; Raynor 2007, 1998) is not well integrated with the problem-solving cognition literature (Chaston and Sadler-Smith 2011; Daniels et al. 1994; Kaplan 2011; Sillince 1995), yet visions must be cognitions. This cognition literature has focused on the consequences of stakeholders having differing frames, schemas, cognitions, perspectives or conceptions of the same situation, rather than trying to explain what a cognition is (Kaplan 2011; Walsh 1995). Deciding what cognition is, assists in developing an integrated means of formulating, analysing and talking about problem-solving. A dominant modern explanation of cognition takes the linguistic turn; we think with words, so planning needs to be a process of analysing and prioritizing words (Rorty 1989; Rosenfield 1988; Toulmin 1972). Words represent our conceptions or concepts which can be exposed using concept mapping (Clarke et al. 2011; Jenkins and Johnson 1997; Novak and Cañas 2009; Swan 1997; Wilhelm and Bort 2012). Visions, usually communicated as a statement, do not provide a systematic process of problem-solving.

The call for visions to be articulated seems to follow from Drucker's (1973) call for problem-solvers to word a purpose and mission statement. Those calling for vision statements (Cummings and Davies 1994; El-Namaki 1992; Gratton 1996; Lissack and Roos 2001; Raynor 1998) seem to have turned his call for a purpose statement into a vision statement. Drucker's purpose statement was intended to answer the philosophical question of why an organization exists, which was pluralized in Hamel and Prahalad's (2005) call for a Statement of Intent. Drucker goes on to say that the answer to this question for commercial organizations is usually to create customers. This, rather than involving visions, simply calls for pragmatic linguistic reflection using the concept of 'customer creation'. Other writers have argued that this one concept of the purpose be pluralized to include other concepts such as shareholder wealth, workers' rights and environmental footprint (Ellsworth 2002). However, making the vision turn on Drucker's purpose statement was a turn to motivation theory and away from the provision of a linguistic reasoned explanation why.

The vision turn is perhaps concerned more about providing inspiration and creativity rather than being scientifically correct about how we think. Having visions is presented as being spiritual, creative or imaginative, providing images of utopias; a role most visionary statements have failed to deliver (O'Brien and Meadows 2007a). The ability to have these utopian visions is sometimes portrayed as being a mystical gift only available to the inspirational (Bailin 2003). However, stakeholders do need to be motivated, and problem solutions do need to be imaginative if change champions are not to become idea-dead (Weick 2006). Rather than using idealistic utopias, the more recent creativity literature draws on the dialectic of concepts, a participatory, interpersonal interaction of language-based concepts, as providing new ideas (Bailin 2003; Perry-Smith and Shalley 2003; Unsworth 2001). Creativity and motivation are provided by having the right mix of conceptions or concepts. The linguistic turn can therefore also provide an equitable approach which gives voice to all stakeholders' concerns. For projects managed out of Western cultures which expect this sort of social equity, using the linguistic turn has the potential to reduce complexities caused by disgruntled stakeholders (Fischer 2012).

## Visions as Containing Linguistic Concepts

A considerable amount of literature has emerged in the last four decades supporting the call for problems to be solved by a vision statement (Westley and Mintzberg 1989). Writers such as Tichy and Sherman (1994) support this notion of vision by depicting public figures such as Winston Churchill, Abraham Lincoln and Jack Welch as visionary, able to make big bold changes by generating emotional energy and spirit from a vision. This has been very appealing to problem-solvers (Westley and Mintzberg 1989). However, the reality has been less than encouraging. Rather, vision statements seem to have become ritualistic (Raynor 1998).

Part of the problem is that the definition of a vision is largely ambiguous. Lissack and Roos (2001) suggest that vision includes goal-setting, team orientation and a futuristic orientation. El-Namaki (1992) prefers to describe visions as a mental perception of the kind of environment someone aspires to create. Pratt (1996) provides a typical description of a vision as being the concept of where those involved are going: a dream of what they might be. However, this defines visions as concepts, not as pictures. The vague definitions of visions often mention dreams, which ironically questions whether they are realistic (Hatch 1997). All this definitional confusion leads to little or no commonality as to how to write a vision statement (O'Brien and Mathews 2007; O'Brien and Meadows 2007b). Many problem solutions have the same vision: to improve the worlds or to be the best, the highest-quality, most highly ranked, or simply to offer more (O'Brien and Mathews 2007; O'Brien and Meadows 2007b). These are not visions because they cannot be visualized. Rather they are a call to use the concepts of bestness, quality and rankings to evaluate what needs to be done. One of the most famous vision statements (and note, it is a statement) is Martin Luther King's 'I have a dream' speech. It calls for an end to the use of colour to evaluate people, calling rather for the use of the concept of character. Inspiring as it was, it cannot be said to be painting a picture, or providing a detailed image of the future of the US.

Numerous benefits have been advocated for the vision-led approach. For example, vision statements claim to play a vital coordinating role (Larwood et al. 1995). However, as Gratton (1996) and others (Brabetm and Klemm 1994) point out, this assumes the audience can and want to deal with the long-term consequences, identify the actions required to bridge into the future, and act to overcome the likely blocks to change. Visions are also claimed to be an attribute of leadership (Westley and Mintzberg 1989). For example, Morden (1997) contends that leadership is vision. This rather masks the other theories of leadership such as leadership as facilitator, exemplar or servant (Knowles 2002; Price 2000). Another assumed benefit of visions is that they provide a helicopter or God's-eye view of an organization and its marketplace. The bounded rationality literature (Simon 1975) and the pluralist literature contest this hierarchical metaphor of insight (Rorty 1989). Rather, it has been argued that those involved use different concepts to interpret different events as they occur. Typically these draw strongly on their professional training (e.g., finance, marketing) or are mimics of those perceived to be used by the successful (Price 2000; Toulmin 1972).

It is also claimed that visions are important for motivating change (Larwood et al. 1995; Malaska and Holstius 1999). Visions apparently explain the need for change, rejecting the world as static. But they do assume that the world is ordered, coherent and hierarchical, able to be expressed in a static picture (Thornberry 1997). This is counter to other world-views. For example, the contradictions literature sees the world as an endless mix of irresolvable but creative tensions, as with species evolution, Marx's political economics and Schumpeter's creative capitalism (Schumpeter 1942; Sowell 1985). Having visions depicts an ideology and epistemology. It draws on Plato's ideal forms, or 'ideals' (Rorty 1989), 'the sacred' (Margolis and Stephen 2010) or 'dreams' (Morden 1997); something that is 'not real' (Toulmin 1972) and which looks towards new 'constellations' (Malaska and Holstius 1999) for a perfect utopian future (Cummings and Davies 1994). This has hints of spirituality which runs counter to the pragmatism of secular scientific management. So perhaps understandably, the empirical research to date has not been able to produce any solid evidence to support a relationship between visions and perform-ance (Larwood et al. 1995).

As an agent of change, the ideology of unitary vision statements may encourage overlooking the present needs or experiences of other influential stakeholders. In a globalized multicultural economy, stakeholders are likely to have a very different conception of what the vision means anyway, and therefore of what needs to be done in the future. As the 'wisdom of crowds' literature suggests, their collective conception may be more informed and insightful than that of the formal leadership, especially in organizations involving experts, such as in the design of hospitals and research institu-tions (Surowiecki 2005). Much of the vision turn supports the notion that the vision is not a collective process but rather comes from one gifted person in authority having a brilliant insight that will be enthusiastically understood and adopted by all stakeholders (Cummings and Davies 1994). This does not align with the innovation and creativity literature, which argues for decentralization, social interaction, dialogue and stories (Bailin 2003; Keeney 1994; Perry-Smith and Shalley 2003): a language approach.

As mentioned, modern neuroscience argues against our brains even being able to think in pictures (Dennett 1996; Humphrey 2006; Rosenfield 1988; Vygotsky 1986). The long-standing assumption that we have a mind's eye seems to be a confusion between how we think and our ability to remix visual memories as in dreams, imagining and synectics (Gordon 1961). Our brains remember experiences, most likely in the form of patterns of activ-ity with associated sensations (De Martino et al. 2006; Rosenfield 1988). This includes eye sensations which can be replayed in different sequences. Scientifically speaking, visions, especially of the future, are just not physically possible. We can only remember mutated, analogous, historical, visual experiences. We seem to think, in the full meaning of how humans uniquely problem-solve, using words or concepts: using language (Rorty 1982; Toulmin 1972). For example, we cannot visualize predatory capital-ism. We can, however, reflect on the concept of predatory capitalism using the concept of control, or any other concept (Dewey 1982 [1910]; James 1996 [1911]).

## CONCLUSION

In summary, there are reservations about using unitary visions for solving problems. These include that this is not how we think; they are not easily translated into internal and external alignment; stakeholders' concerns are often not well aligned to the vision, that it restricts stakeholder creativity, does not allow for unexpected opportunities, assumes external motivation is sufficient, does not address intrinsic motivation, and is often poorly done (Beer and Eisenstat 2000; Hutzschenreuter and Kleindienst 2006; Jarzabkowski and Spee 2009; Larwood et al. 1995; Raynor 2007; Sminia 2009). It is thought that visions are about the words they contain. They are a source of linguistic concepts. For example, the vision to be the best in the world is to use the concept of 'bestness'.

## NOTES

1. The first part of this chapter is based on Lynch and Metcalfe (2006).
2. Appendix 6.3 was originally written as an as yet unpublished article with Allen McKenna.

# 7.  Concepts as dialectic decision criteria

## OVERVIEW

Enacting solutions will involve coordinating numerous tasks over time. The solution concepts can be used to coordinate these activities, but also to suggest new ones. That is, the set of solution concepts can be used as dialectic decision criteria. This means they will be under tension and therefore contain the possibility of being creative. This chapter will explain why and how this might be done.[1]

## IDEAL CRITERIA

Many decisions have to be made in an environment of multiple conflicting stakeholders, continuous change, and demand for creative solutions. People are asked to make decisions about complex socio-technical problems which have more than one reasonable solution. Typically this decision-making process starts by designing a system of evaluation criteria which can be used to evaluate anything considered prior to the decision being made. Obvious examples of these decision criteria systems are personnel and capital project tender selection criteria. There are two main philosophies used, usually implicitly, to design this system. The first and most common is that these criteria might be thought of as the attributes of an ideal solution state. For example, when recruiting new staff, the selection criteria might be drafted as providing the attributes of an ideal candidate. The decision process then becomes one of attempting to match the actual to this ideal form. To do so is to adopt Plato's ideal forms; we know by comparing to an ideal form.

Ideal forms suggest an impeccable, hierarchical oneness, against which all imperfect forms can be compared. This, therefore, encourages solutions fixed in time acting to close down alternative solutions as incorrect. It seems imposing, overconfident and arrogant in our multicultural world to suggest that there is one ideal set of attributes of appropriate social behaviour. Who is to determine this ideal form? The suggestion of ideal forms encourages power elites to decide what these ideal, context-free, universal criteria should be. Insisting on 'ideal oneism', the need to find the one true set of criteria, can therefore act to restrict the opportunity for ongoing creative insights. This includes alternative perspectives from those expected to act on the outcome.

The pragmatists thought Plato's ideal-forms approach was not the most ideal for encouraging a tolerant, diverse, empowered and creative society. They developed a pluralistic alternative based on Aristotle's dialectic and Hegel's inclusion of time in the definition of knowing (Churchman 1971; Dewey 1982 [1910]; James 1910 [1907]; Rorty 1982, 1989). They suggested the need for a system of decision criteria, that is, that decisions be evaluated using an ecology of concepts (criteria), each providing an alternative perspective or interpretation of the problem domain. Knowing involves awareness of more interpretations. This mix of perspectives allows in opposing views, but more importantly it draws on a dynamic interaction or dialectic between the concepts as an explanation of how human inquiry be designed.

One of science's most useful concepts, evolution, presents species creativity as dialectic. The selection of species by food availability, co-competitive species, sexual selection and designed artefacts presents a turbulent, chaotic, dynamic, interdependent and competitive process, which is not a comparison with ideals or a search for one perfect form. Rather, it is creative, pluralistic and expansive. Plato's and Aristotle's contrasting epistemologies have been around for over 2000 years. However, perhaps due to its association with Marx and critical social theory, dialectic has been confusing to those nurtured on the ideal forms which were used to design the Abraham religions and the scientific method. Rorty's (1989) pluralist pragmatism modernizes dialectic to make it more reasonable to scientists as a competing hypothesis or the description of the behaviour of any community of rational sceptics concerned about more than economics and politics. Rorty was concerned with how pragmatism might be used to design a democracy. Here I am concerned with how pragmatism might be used to design a system for decision-making.

Chapter 7 will address this somewhat by explaining why and how this thread of pragmatism can be used to design decision criteria. In the way that pragmatism places heavy emphasis on comparison, Rorty's pragmatism needs some explanation, which will be attempted in comparison to Plato's ideal form. This aligns to Rorty's preference for the use of the concept of comparison over the concept of truth-seeking. It is argued that his pragmatism suggests the use of an ecology of opposing concepts in creative contradiction. These have the potential to provide a more tolerant, useful and insightful decision-making process. Why and how opposing concepts can be used to design and justify decision criteria, as a system, will therefore be explained. Towards the end of the chapter, examples from rapid decisions are used to illustrate the difference between the two philosophies in action.

## IDEAL FORMS

The assumption of ideal forms is usually sourced to Plato. To him, beyond heaven was a spiritual place where ideal forms exist, as in ideal people, governments, forces and physical objects. What we see around us on earth are merely imperfect forms. Seeking knowledge meant seeking to understand what something is, in its perfect form. Gods, mathematics and theory are examples of ideal forms that have been discovered (James 1996 [1911]; Nietzsche 1979 [1873]; Rorty 1989). Plato thought mathematics was a particularly excellent ideal form: pure, untainted by the earth – an ideal means of explaining the ideal world. Plato's writings provided the Abraham religions with its pure forms, and science with its great quest for an algebraic theory of everything. Theoretical science, with the aid of mathematics, was set on a course to expose these ideal forms from a dissection of the messy, imperfect real world, which hides some ideal abstraction.

Although two-way struggles are often a dangerous simplification, our intellectual history can be introduced tentatively as a power struggle between Plato's ideal forms and Aristotle's less spiritual dialectic which developed into justified pluralism (James 1996 [1911]; Nietzsche 1979 [1873]; Rorty 1989). Ideal forms encourage the dominance of an elite's perfection, as order, brought about by knowing their one correct interpretation, universal (placeless), hierarchical, abstract, static, timeless and coherent, without contradiction, conflict or need for change. For Christianity, this truth is revealed by God. For science, truth itself is an ideal form, revealed by reasoning; empiricism directed by the ideal form of theory. Thus, for the Church this perfection or order starts with God at the top, then the Church, then states, then the aristocracy, and under these, traders and farmers. Perfection reduces as you come down the hierarchy. For science, this order means foundations of knowledge; universal theories heading a hierarchy of lesser theories. The physical world is a messiness which has to be untangled to reveal the pure forms of abstract theory. This ideal-form assumption can be applied not only to the physical world, but also to concepts such as justice and research. They have ideal forms which provide ideal solutions, truths, that resolve complex issues.

If solutions reveal a lack of order or alternative ideal forms, then further explanation is required until order is returned. Analysis into conflicts, contradiction or paradox, assuming ideal forms, will seek for these to be resolved and order again to be returned. The use of ideal forms includes the use of theory, believing in one correct solution, and in the presence of objective facts. It does not recognize these as just the outcome of a power play against legitimate alternatives in a dynamic of socio-technical forces capable of providing alternative insights if allowed to be exposed.

Ideal forms may not be what make science so creative. Its quest for one perfect theory can act to restrict creativity by restricting diversity. Once an explanatory theory is agreed upon by an elite, then the ideal form insists that further analysis is unnecessary; further explanation is only sought for apparent abnormalities generated by the theory. Ideal forms imply seeking an ordered ascension to the one best explanation; new discoveries have to be explained in the context of old discoveries. So again, ironically, Kuhn's (1970 [1962]) paradigms, the multiple parallel universes of quantum mechanics, and the presence of hundreds of research methodologies represent the unresolved rather than being seen as an opportunity for creativity. The same is true for having relativity as a universal law for large things, and string theory as a universal law for small things. This divergence is seen as a temporary inconvenience that will be resolved as knowledge converges to the one true explanation. However, the search for the ideal forms seems to always end with the unexpected generation of viable alternatives

## DIALECTIC

Aristotle suggested a different approach to Plato's ideal forms: that of dialectic (Richards 1936), the use of dynamic, competitive, continuous processes intended to expose and compare alternatives. It is this method that has made science creative (Bailin 2003; Latour and Woolgar 1986; Rorty 1989). Dialectic argument between two or more interlocutors requires the presence of multiple interpretations each evolving over time while using competitive, evidence-based reasoning. Hegel (1956) and other Continental philosophers (Rescher 1979) abstracted dialectic from the ideal-forms view of it being an irritant, tolerable only if the arguers emerged an improved understanding of the ideal forms. For example, Popper's *Conjectures and Refutations* (1972) can be read as encouraging dialectic between scientific conjectures or theses, but Popper was very intolerant of the unresolved. For Hegel, one of the early process theorists, dialectic represented a non-static conception of knowledge, which needed to be in constant struggle. He moved dialectic from people arguing, to the struggle of knowledge claims, propositions or theses; thesis against antithesis to synthesis. Any new synthesis, over time, became the next thesis against a new antithesis. Knowledge was a historical argument between theses, a struggle between what communities thought they knew. Modern examples of the struggle between theses include the struggle between the creationist and the evolutionist, between imperialist and indigenous cultures, between relativity and quantum mechanics, and between postmodern romanticism and the need to justify knowledge claims to a sceptical audience. Ironically the person who most advocated this dialectic understanding of research in modern times, Hegel, still saw this struggle as working towards an absolute (ideal form). Later writers saw the struggle as the end form.

Marx (1992) and Engels (1964) drew on Hegel but concerned themselves with using it as a means of assisting in the practical struggle between alternative ideas or theses about the structure of society (Ormerod 2006; Shields 2005). This included the struggle for who ought to determine the allocation of material excess generated by an economy. More recently this has been developed into a struggle between alternative theses (arguments, propositions) about the relationship between individuals and the social order. The presence of a struggle between different theses over long periods of time means there were alternative historical possibilities (deconstruction) to the interpretations we assume today; alternatives of how social issues could be interpreted. Foucault's research into the social construction of madness and sexuality are classic examples. He exposed the historical struggle of these, of how society might have interpreted madness and sexuality differently given the long struggle between social, political, economic and technological forces (Flyvbjerg 2000).

One very relevant way to understand this struggle of theses, dialectic, is to draw on an analogy with natural selection: evolution. Darwin's (1859) evolution theory clearly influenced Marx (1992), Engels (1964), Schumpeter (1942), James (1996 [1911]) and Dewey (1958 [1929]). *Das Capital* was dedicated to Darwin; Schumpeter explains capitalism as the evolution of products and services. Natural selection is the never-ending struggle of multiple species against each other in the context of a complex dynamic environment, all of which acts to creatively generate increasing diversity. Dialectic replaces species with theses (memes) (Dawkins 1989; Blackmore 1998). Dialectic can therefore also be seen to have creative potential, to generate an increasing diversity of knowledge claims (thesis) partly by not allowing any one to dominate. The domination of theses is achieved by discouraging historical analysis to expose alternatives and by talk of objective facts as if they cannot be debated, claiming they are resolved and need not be reinterpreted. A third way of discouraging fair competition between theses is to accuse those seeking well-justified alternatives of relativism (Rorty 1989; Stove 1998). Our present knowing is the result of ongoing historical, political, social, economic and technological process of struggle.

Dialectic suggests an ever-changing, complex, ironic, paradoxical, physical world, where mentions of ideals sounds like someone trying to impose a preference (Chanin and Shapiro 1985; Lewis 2000; Nielsen 1996; Walton 1998; Zeitz 1980). However, the presence of multiple contradictory interpretations alone does not distinguish dialectic from idealist. Both can see problem situations as messy. Idealists will slip back to assuming ideal forms and feel that the mess can and should be tidied up, paradoxes resolved and disputes settled. The dialectic analyst sees the mess as realistic, rich, wonderful, educational, creative, and that encouraging it provides a means of encouraging diversity. Idealistic analysts will recommend one preferred approach or system, intended to tidy up a sadly chaotic situation. Doing so is like calling for the standardization of species, elimination of those that presently do not seem ideal. It would remove the diversity – competition among which was the very thing that generated the species in the first place. The dialectic analyst intends to expose a dialectical world, an ecosystem, and make recommendations for encouraging that diversity. For example, dialectic problem-solving involves seeking out alternative plans and interpretations of the world. This enables debate from which a richer understanding can be developed (Mitroff and Emshoff 1979).

## PRAGMATIC DIALECTIC

Pragmatism gives us one of the better interpretations of diversity of thought with its use of our conceptions or concepts (James 1996 [1911]), but it does come in numerous streams (Haack 2006; Menand 2002; Rescher 2005; Rorty 1989). The James Dewey–Rorty stream has much in common with Hegel, Marx and Engels and therefore with dynamic contradiction (dialectic) (Rytina and Loomis 1970). They all wish to use the actions of humans to define knowledge and to bring repressed assumptions to the surface. Epistemology is to resolve human problems, including changing what is into what ought to be. Thought and action are combined, as thought is a reflection on action. The conceptual apparatus between the observed and the observer is developed through action and experience (experimentation), not ideals determined by authority or tradition. The pragmatists are against a static conception of knowledge, seeing knowledge as needing to be useful, judged by its consequences and not by its causes (Rytina and Loomis 1970). However, the pragmatists are also concerned with explaining why we act as we do: why logical people can go to war against each other. They explain our actions as being due to the concepts (criteria) we use to interpret our world, concepts such as nationalism, religion, peace, diversity, tolerance and equity. These concepts and many others help us make justified choices of how to act. The pragmatists therefore replace the search for Plato's ideal forms with the exposure and counter-positioning of concepts: why we are choosing alternative actions. Pragmatic pluralists explore the usefulness of an ecosystem of interpretations of the world revealed by us through the use of multiple concepts. Miller's (1956) $7\pm2$ research on human information processing, refined by Cowan (2001) for different categories, suggests not using more than around five concepts (as words) to think about anything.

The pragmatists' argument, to recap, is that we interpret the world through a handful of concepts, implicitly or explicitly. The war in Afghanistan can be interpreted using any concept, but examples include revenge, imperialism and terrorism. Pragmatic conceptions, cognitive ideas or concepts are named abstractions of recognized patterns of activity. Other examples include running, nationalism, tolerance and mathematics. We recognize particular activities which we abstract together as similar. These patterns of activity, concepts, may not be articulated, named, but when named they can be shared with others and used to interpret the world. Klein's (1999) patterned recognized or naturalistic decision seems to be about implicit or unnamed concepts. He writes of experienced firemen able to recognize patterns in the fires they attend, patterns that signal danger which are often hard to articulate. It appears as though Klein is referring to their use of implicit concepts: unnamed patterns or concerns, learnt or innate. We have, for example, innate concerns over eating, reproduction and of being attacked. These are patterns of activity and therefore concepts are used to interpret different events as they occur to us, each promoting different responses.

The pragmatist recognition of concepts in explaining our behaviour may have been inspired by Kant's concepts but the pragmatists evolved them into something quite different. Toulmin (1972) and Rorty (1989) draw on Heidegger (Dreyfus 2007a, 2007b) to justify James and Dewey's non-Kantian understanding of concepts. They do not see them as structures in a mind, an ideal form for the brain, but rather as recognized patterns of activity. However, since James, much of modern psychology has assumed the Kantian and Cartesian meaning of concepts (Mareschal et al. 2010). Pragmatic concepts are not, but are similar to, mental models, rules, frames, representations, or anything Cartesian providing images in an abstract mind (Lakoff 1993; Morgan 1986; Schon 1963). They are patterns remembered in a brain which, when named, are simply words which remind us of a pattern of activity. The term 'frame', although very similar in consequence to concepts, is avoided because of its Cartesian associations. Concepts, as rationalizing our actions, join together theory and practice. They are derived from experience yet they are logical and so also join together logic and empirics (Rytina and Loomis 1970).

Concepts provide an explanation as to 'why'. Darwin used the concepts of natural selection and sexual selection to explain why new species evolve. Einstein used the concept of relativity to explain why light bends when it passes a planet. Analysis can be interpreted as a search for the most useful concept to explain whatever is under study. The study of why some analysts are more creative than others might find the concept of mimicking more useful than the concept of personality. It has more uses, it explains more, it provides preferable ways of acting in the future. Baggini (2005) discusses the usefulness of seeking alternative concepts using the classic example of whether the earth is flat or round:

> if we treat the world as if these concepts do exist then we find we can manipulate the world and make things work much better. The point about this is that you cannot just choose any concept. What is useful is not just on our whim to choose. [A concept is] a better concept for looking at the world because it works much better than others. You don't have to worry, as some British philosophers have thought that if you go down the pragmatic route that you might believe the world is flat because [that fits best with our sensory input]. Ultimately it isn't useful to believe that the world is flat. All sorts of things won't work if you construct your view in that way. These concepts are tools for helping us manipulate the world and some work better than others. (Baggini 2005)

Dialectic analysis, therefore, can be seen as setting up a contradiction of concepts in tension with each other to learn which is more useful in which situation. So, the intent is not to find the one best concept but rather the generation of competitive alternatives, to set up dialectic. James's *Pluralistic Universe* (1996 [1909]), Dewey's (1982 [1910]) reflections, Mason's (1969) use of the dialectic to surface assumptions and Rorty's (1989) irony can also be seen to further refine the meaning of dialectic. They move it from the struggle between theses to the struggle between concepts. All propositions contain a struggle of concepts (Toulmin 1972).

For the James–Dewey–Rorty stream of pragmatism (Haack 2006) this struggle is not intended to produce the one, single, most useful, survival of the fittest. Rather, it is intended to encourage further diversity, an ecosystem, the struggle between which generates knowing, which is defined as an act of interpreting. The choice and use of concepts to provide an interpretation does need, in the way of Aristotle's argumentation, to be justified to a sceptical audience. A dynamic contradictory or dialectic view of concepts or interpretations suggests recognition of an ongoing struggle that needs to continue. It would be limiting to analyse any complex situation by assuming one concept in isolation, given that concepts depend so much on their relationship to other concepts. You cannot understand eucalyptus trees without understanding their relationship to fire. What is preferable for analysis is an interrelated contradictory set of conceptions understood to be changing over time: an opposition of concepts. These concepts provide an interpretation of how to design a system of criteria for making decisions

## DEMONSTRATION EXAMPLES

Consider the situation researched by Dodd et al. (2006) where soldiers were perceived to be making battlefield decisions which did not align with what higher command wanted. Using ideal forms, a reasonable solution would be to implement some form of improved communication systems so that the higher command could better communicate instructions to the soldiers. This would correct an imperfection. Improvement suggests moving towards an ideal state. Ideally there would be perfect communications and understanding. The decision criteria using idealism would provide the attributes of this ideal state.

The opposing concepts approach is to assume that perfect understanding will never occur; assuming that it will occur may suppress the opportunity for dynamic and creative learning. The solution would then be to agree a dialectic of concepts (requirements, criteria, principles) that everyone would use to make decisions. This would provide alternative, but coordinated, interpretations of any unexpected future situation that local and higher commanders find themselves grappling to understand. For example, the concepts (criteria) those involved might use to evaluate their future action might be:

- Communication: let everyone on your side know where you are, what you are doing and why.
- Agility: be ready and able to change what you are doing quickly.
- Sustained strike: all attacks should be capable of being sustained over the long term using all taskforce resources in a coordinated manner.
- Protection: protect your fighting ability and that of the taskforce.

These agreed concepts could also be used to justify and anticipate the actions of others. Clues from the battlefield by either local or higher commanders will be interpreted (sense-made) and acted upon using these agreed concepts. This means there is then some chance of coordination and prediction by all involved but with room for creative and rapid independence.

As mentioned previously, the set of concepts needs to be contradictory, not ideal; to be in competition with each other – irresolvable and evolving, thus realistic. For example, the need to communicate exposes local forces, reducing their protection while being a time-consuming task that reduces agility. The use of sustained strikes might also reduce agility and protection. This contraction encourages both sets of commanders to appreciate that all their decisions require creative balancing between opposing alternatives. This is a more adaptive attitude to decision-making, encouraged by not searching for ideal states.

The opposing concepts approach enriches understanding by requiring an appreciation and balance of the internal tensions or contradictions inherent between the concepts. This is also true of the tensions within the concepts. For example, the concept of communication may be understood to be made up of the subconcepts of authority, completeness, medium, detection and reciprocality. Communication runs the risk of being ignored, of being misleading, of detection, of being dependent on how it is communicated and of causing offence by not being reciprocated. Balancing these internal tensions or contradictions also means evolving and adapting to the situation. Put another way, Wheeler (2006) suggests that combat teams are self-adapting, agile and reconfigurable teams. This then determines the selection of evaluation concepts.

A second, shorter example of how using a dialectic of concepts may be preferable to trying to build an idyllic utopia involves forecasting the outcome of conflicts. Green and Armstrong (2011) research the accuracy of alternative methods for forecasting the outcome of allocation disputes between countries. The idyllic approach to forecast the outcome of this conflict might be to build a comprehensive computer simulation model. This model might use input from interviewing experts, from scientific geographic data about rainfall, estimated population growth, potential land use, the concerns of those directly involved, and from noting the aggressive capability of each nation involved.

Green and Armstrong's research finds that more accuracy can be achieved, especially in a realistic time frame, by the use of role thinking. This allocates roles to semi-experts which mirror those involved in the negotiations. These semi-experts are asked to think how their role would respond to what is said by other participants during the role-playing exercise. The roles represent a system of concepts that will be used to think about the conflict. For example, one participant may be asked to use the role of the treasurer of one of the countries. This role would use concepts such as economic development, debt levels, exchange rates and employment statistics to think about the conflict situation. Another role might be as a United Nations environmental protection officer, who may use concepts such as land degradation, species diversity, pollution and river flows to think about what is said during the mock conflict negotiations. The roles provide the dialectic of concepts that can be applied in an interactive and dynamic manner during the process of the mock negotiations. Green and Armstrong obtain the forecast by asking those involved to make a forecast using what they observed after hearing the mock negotiations play out.

## CONCLUSION

This chapter has explained why and how pragmatic dialectic might be used to justify and design a creative system of decision criteria. The pragmatists' approach was presented in contrast to using the ideal forms approach which interprets decision criteria as attributes of a perfect solution. Contradictions, paradoxes or underlying tensions, as in evolution, are seen as creative, the driving force of adaption. This endless process view contrasts with the optimism of imagining some fully resolved utopian future. Seeing decision criteria as dialectic or an ecosystem of concepts in creative contradiction encourages pluralistic understandings through evolving and competing perspectives that do not need resolution. Two examples of the difference this makes to decisions were discussed.

This stream of pragmatism provides an alternative epistemology to underpin the practice of how to design any solution system, one that offers an alternative to idealistic theory building (Rorty 1989; Shields 2005). System elements need to be seen to be in creative tension. This approach aligns with wanting to design a better world, rather than just observe it (James 1910 [1907]), and with evolution (selection) theory (Darwin 1859; Dewey 1958 [1929]; Dennett 1996; Marx 1992; Schumpeter 1942; Van de Ven and Poole 1995). It provides an approach to designing systems that rationalizes pluralism (Metcalfe 2007a), sees knowledge as a process, and aligns with the emacipatory intent of critical social theory (Engels 1964; Rytina and Loomis 1970; Shields 1998).

## APPLICATION

Draft a Statement of Intent, remembering that it will be used to provide the criteria for making future decisions. Statements of Intent from the running examples include the following.

**Organization Mindset: Statement of Intent**

This organization intends to give priority to:

1. The post-global financial crisis (GFC): the market is slowly recovering from the GFC, which has a significant impact on the housing and loan sectors.
2. Expertise: the market needs more world-quality designers and installers.
3. Sustainability: the market is demanding more consideration of carbon footprint and careful water use.
4. Labour cost: the struggle between unions and shareholders continues, with a risk of high labour costs forcing operations offshore.
5. International tastes: with TV, films, international travel and high levels of immigration, customer tastes are getting more discerning and cosmopolitan.

**Cultural Tourism: Statement of Intent**

This emergent accommodations industry intends to become:

1. Sufficiently legitimate: a balance needs to be maintained between interaction of operators and government bureaucracy.
2. A selected market: consciously selecting those tourists or guests who cause less harm and damage to these operators and to the local community.
3. An inclusive local experience: needing to involve locals in offering primarily a home-oriented cultural experience.
4. Appropriately financially structured: looking to sources of funding which will not distract from the intent of the industry.
5. Collaboratively empowered: developing a collective decision-making identity for the local cultural accommodation network which empowers its members.

**Social Enterprise Business Models: Statement of Intent**

This caring industry intends to develop its trading activities through:

1. Safety nests: to provide a safe place overnight for anyone, and their belongings.
2. Social expertise: to develop income earning expertise and skills that address gaps for people with special needs through either a product or a service.

3.  Activity coaching: to provide people with disabilities or a disadvantage with supported employment opportunities and leisure activities, to help them work, learn and live independently.
4.  Mission engagement: to engage clients, members or supporters to interact directly with a cause to motivate them to get involved or provide other support such as time, skills or money.
5.  Needs distribution: to source, reuse or distribute physical goods that help address a social need or gap.

## NOTE

1.  This chapter is based on Metcalfe (forthcoming).

# 8.   Solution action plans

## OVERVIEW

Solution concepts (criteria) need to be turned into appropriate actions. This chapter will provide generalized suggestions for what those action plans might be. It broadly divides them into two. The first is to suggest possible organizational action plans, including changing the financial reward systems to encourage enactment of the concepts. The second is to suggest possible investment projects or initiatives that will also help to enact the solution concepts. For example, new equipment, markets or alliances might be used to enact a concept.[1]

## ORGANIZATIONAL ALIGNMENT

Solution concepts have the potential to provide a common sense of intent for those involved in solving a problem. This will only happen if these stakeholders are aligned mentally with the solution concepts. Therefore, the issue of how to achieve mindset, frame or conceptual alignment is of importance.

Following on from the spirit of the previous chapter's discussion on contraction, it may be consistent to start thinking about alignment by looking for its internal tensions, its contradictions. It is an engineering or geometric metaphor, suggesting being able to draw a straight line between two elements, as in wheel alignment or in lining up paintings hanging on a wall. Comparative words include fit, harmony or bricolage; bringing together diversity. Its darker side suggests control, centralized order and conformity. The balance sought from these tensions is between some sense of common purpose for members of an organization, and allowing room for questioning, constructive dissent and innovation. It is usually assumed that there is some competitive advantage in getting this balance right. The skill of selecting, naming and defining the solution concepts will have some bearing here. The concepts need to be explicit enough to offer a common sense of intent, but abstract enough to allow for local creativity: variation on the theme, harmony as in jazz.

There are numerous structural and process approaches to gaining alignment, the usefulness of which will depend on the circumstances of the organization. First, the solution concepts can be used to structure all relevant documents including plans, budgets, value statements, vision and mission statements, internal and external marketing slogans, procedure manuals or contracts. For example, there is no point is saying that the solution is to be more agile and this not being a distinct issue (or section) in any budget or planning documents.

Enacting the solution concepts may also require a restructure of those involved. There needs to be a name and department responsible for each concept. Someone needs to be responsible for each concept being enacted. Having leadership roles of accounting, internationalization or knowledge management is saying that the group wants more accountability, internationalization or knowledge management. These departments, and their priorities, are the implicit solution concepts, the unwritten statement of purpose of the group looking to solve the problem. The same can be said of job and department descriptions, committee constitutions and reporting hierarchies. These should not be at odds with the espoused or professed solution concepts.

To be relevant to all levels and functions of the solution group there will need to be some elaboration of the concepts into a hierarchy of subconcepts. For example, the concept of wanting to be more agile would need to be made operational as work practices through all levels of whatever organizational structure is being used. For example, how will intending to be more agile impact on the job description of maintenance engineers, marketing, accounting, human resources controls, and so on.

As discussed in the previous chapter, the solution concepts, in an appropriate form, need to be used as evaluation criteria. This includes for new staff appointments, projects, budget allocations, promotion requirements, and incentive, reward or innovative idea generation schemes. An example here would be that if innovation or an enthusiasm for change was a solution concept, then appointing or promoting staff who take pride in being very conservative, preferring tradition and stability over change, would be inappropriate.

The role of the leadership in securing long-term alignment is to reinforce the solution concepts in their own actions. They need to stay on-message, ensure 'their feet follow their mouth', 'walk the talk', and not ask for X while rewarding Y. If the leadership profess that those involved need to be more agile, then they need to say so repeatedly in speeches, as feedback to staff, and in issuing rewards and discouragements in line with everyone becoming more agile. They need to act agilely. If those involved see that successful requests for resources, or personal advancement, are genuinely dependent on advancing the solution concepts, then they will do so for as long as those in whose control of the resources require it.

## INTRINSIC CHANGE

It has been argued that the use of new solution concepts as criteria to evaluate day-to-day decisions can lead to an evolutionary significant change in the solution group. Alignment of these changes can be encouraged with the structural and external motivation measures just mentioned. However, inevitably there will need to be some social persuasion processes put in place to win over the hearts and minds of stakeholders. This is particularly necessary when the expertise and insight of specialist local officers are genuinely sought-after. Preferably the local officers will use the concepts willingly to improve the functions they control. It is easy to underestimate the problems of effectively changing, or adapting, the routines, implicit concepts (concerns, interests) and mood of stakeholders (Francis et al. 2003; Palmer and Dunford 2008; Schwarz and Huber 2008; Seo and Creed 2002). This social re-engineering is necessary if those involved are going to capture the full benefits of the new solution concepts.

The research into social change in organizations is extensive and long-lived (Churchman and Schainblatt 1965; Desombre et al. 2006; Van de Ven and Poole 1995). The tribalism, politics (Butcher and Atkinson 2001), insecurities and engagement needs of those affected by the change, coupled with the complexity of modern organizations, means that any change is likely to be threatening to someone. Managers can use their technical power (Markus and Bjorn-Andersen 1987) to resist change, while excessive enforcement by change agents can demotivate and kill creativity (Weick 2006). Many organizations are communities (Wenger and Snyder 2000), globalized, dispersed, reliant on powerful stakeholders, in partnerships and/ or operating in difficult labour markets. The costs of demanding conformity in these communities can make enforced changes counterproductive.

For most changes to be creatively enacted there is a need to win over the intrinsic motivators of the new users in both the intent and the technicalities of the solution concepts. Complex changes usually involve significant adaptation of adjacent routines, systems and policies before they are fully integrated with the new routines and mood required of the new concept. Researchers such as Barley (1986) have long shown how proposed changes can be adopted very differently by groups, depending on existing routines, personalities and hierarchies. This may not be a problem so long as the overall intent of the solution concepts is not compromised. Indeed it may encourage innovative adaption of the concepts.

There is now also considerable literature on the use of alternative socialization processes for encouraging change (Tidd et al. 2001; Todorova and Dirism 2007). This is supported by a formidable philosophy literature including Heidegger, in *Being and Time* (2008), and Rene Girard, in *Violence and the Sacred* (1977). They present a comprehensive argument for how we learn, how norms are established, arguing that it is a process of imitating others, which starts in the womb. This works through talking to, working with, observing and then imitating respected peers. This conception of learning can be used to start thinking about social change. But the problem remains as to how exactly this socialization process is to be operationalized as a series of social activities, most of which can be seen to involve an imitation process. Van de Ven and Poole's (1995) review of the management literature found four main conceptions of organizational change: teleology, evolution, dialectic and life cycles (growth stages). They recommended that all be present for a successful change.

Much of the organizational change literature refers to organizational learning (Brown and Duguid 2000). Organizational learning is an extension of individual learning where organizational routines, norms and systems also need to learn. Research by Aiman-Smith (2002) demonstrated the problems of trying to encourage this type of learning assuming only formal individual learning. Both new systems and their intellectual property can be hard to document – to make explicit. Organizational learning often requires all users to go through similar experiences (Tidd et al. 2001; Kluge et al. 2001). Tidd et al. (2001) argue that the ability of an organization to make the best use of new equipment, or to produce products or skills with novelty in design, quality or performance, depends largely on the skills of those involved in adopting the new systems to an organization's particular and present needs. Further, they argue that the training that implementers receive needs to provide not only the 'know-how' but also the important 'know-why'. This suggests the need for learning by doing (experiential learning), which in a community setting means learning apprenticeship style: watching, talking with peers, imitating and adopting through experimentation (Tyre and von Hippel 1997). Focusing on what needs to be known (instructional learning) rather than the socialization processes in learning may be problematic.

## LEARNING AS SOCIALIZATION

Heidegger (2008) provides an ontological basis for focusing on the socialization processes involved in social learning, providing a view of community learning that minimizes the emphasis on learning as acquiring objective facts. He goes behind any distinction between explicit and tacit knowledge (Polanyi 1966), learning by doing, or classroom learning versus apprenticeship learning. Whether we learn and what we learn depends on the mood of those around us. In *Being and Time*, Heidegger (2008) distinguishes natural entities (present to hand) from entities designed by people (ready to hand). Things move from being around but not appreciated (present to hand) to being used (ready to hand) by coming to our attention due to some concern (disturbance). What comes to our attention is a socialization learning process involving beings who have the ability to inquire about their own thinking (*dasein*; mainly humans). This moves what we often call objects from our unappreciated surroundings into being something useful. He extensively uses the example of hammers as a process technology. A socialization process teaches us what hammers are and how they are to be used. Rejecting the subject–object Cartesian divide, including mind and body and thus the unconscious, Heidegger sees our behaviours as being the result of mimicking the behaviours of those around us – our parents, our teachers and those we respect – as our means of making sense of the universe and our social world. There are not really any objects out there, rather mimicked classifications. We emerge out of the behaviour of particular others; individual difference might be explained by the combination of whom we copy. Knowledge is knowing 'how', not 'what': we are how we do what we do, which we get from a socialization process that itself is changing. For example, gravity is knowing how to explain falling objects, but understandings of gravity as knowledge can be expected to change. Heidegger is using the perspective of time to think about these things, so socialization is a changing process. Everything is process; seeing so-called objects as static is only because they are changing at a slower rate than actions taken on those objects. What we think of technology is a process – changing. The rate of perceived change is a socialization process, itself changing. This all strongly suggests a social process view of organizational learning around the change of using new solution concepts. Learning cannot be seen as accumulating objective facts that aim to instruct the correct way to operate or implement a change. Potential users need to be placed with those they respect; people who exhibit an appropriate mood around the new technology. These respected members of society will pass on their mood to newcomers, determining whether the change is adopted or not, how and why.

Many of the socialization processes discussed in the management literature are about how staff of a similar personality tend to collect together. This is very much a psychological view of socialization. It is thought that Heidegger is thinking of a much more sociological view where mood, norms and identity are formed by the group onto the individual. This socialization process of how groups determine individual behaviour was classically studied by Milgram (1992) and in the Stanford prison experiments (Haney et al. 1973). The group situation seemed much stronger than personalities. The Milgram and prison experiments seem aligned to the biological studies showing how social insects such as ants and wasps are able to provide significant responses to environmental disasters without any leadership structure (Camazine et al. 2001). Socialization processes in the more recent management literature (e.g. Todorova and Dirisin 2007) has focused on networking structures with an interest in the knowledge-sharing capacity of weak ties and Small Worlds. All the socialization processes mentioned here can usefully be seen as networking. However, this tends to recognize only relationships; it does not place emphasis on how these relationships determine our behaviour.

## PROCESS (BUILDING RELATIONSHIPS, CONNECTIVITY)

Martin et al. (2009) identified four social learning processes to map onto Van de Ven and Poole's (1995) four conceptions of change; job rotation particularly through the supply chain; benchmarking with continuous improvement; debate and competition; and the use of champions. These provide some practical means of altering the concepts being used by those involved from their implicit ones to the new solution concepts.

Job rotation can be seen to provide a strong relationship-building or socialization process where a newcomer is totally immersed in the mood of the new work group. A Heideggerian interpretation of what would make for successful job rotation would be that the newcomer has or develops respect for the mood of the new group over whatever mood they had from previous experiences. This respect would then encourage the newcomer to imitate the new group's mood. This situation could be manipulated by those wishing to implement a new solution concept. Once one respected group uses a new concept, others could be job-rotated into the group to pick up the mood of the committed group. Job rotation through supply chains is thought particularly useful for encouraging change. This is easy to imagine in terms of gaining a better understanding of the systems used to support professional practices.

## BENCHMARKING AND CONTINUOUS IMPROVEMENT (CI)

Francis and Holloway (2007) warn that there has been more rhetoric than evidence supporting the usefulness of benchmarking. It has been used as a label for a range of organizational learning programmes intended to assist changing work practices. Under the change conception of evolution, benchmarking with CI is meant as incremental change encouraged by continuous comparison with respected rivals. In Heideggerian terms, benchmarking would seem to work as people implicitly or explicitly imitating whoever is identified as using best practice. If the 'best-practice people' use a new concept, then the learners will respect it.

## CHAMPIONS

Kanter (1983) coined the term 'change masters', referring to those persons and organizations adept at the art of anticipating the need for and of leading productive change. If these people are admired by others then they can become change champions: those who act to promote a change by altering the mindset of others. To achieve this, the champion needs some sort of personal appeal, some charismatic attributes (Weber 1997), which act to encourage mimicking by others. This is very much in line with Heidegger's views. We seek the respect of someone, be it loved ones, mythical characters, colleagues, publishers or the powerful: those whom we respect. This is akin to what Adam Smith (2006) was referring to in his *Wealth of Nations*, when he talked of self-interest driving innovation in trade.

To be mimicked, or listened to, a champion needs to be credible in the mind of whoever is going to be influenced. For encouraging a new concept, this may mean the champion being seen as an exemplar of how to act in response to the solution. This credibility might rely on many things, including past implementation success, monetary rewards or having a particular ethical stance.

Past change success means proven success in dealing with the political processes, resource allocation and technical issues around making changes, and having effectively solved the everyday problems generated by any organizational change. Rost et al. (2007) report that it is a German tradition to say that new projects need at least an idea champion operating at a senior level in the organization, plus a technical champion who deals with the technical issues required to make the project work. Thus, there can be a champion team, dealing with ideas, power, process and relationships. There may be some overlap here with the usefulness of self-managed teams.

## DEBATE OR COMPETITION?

A little rivalry between groups is thought to be very creative; too much or too little can be problematic (Girard 1977). This can be a rivalry of conceptual ideas as well as of actions. Rivalry is a process of difference, contrast, distinguishing one from another. Within social groups, this 'them and us' conception can drive issues of identity, inclusion needs and internal imitation. Reasoning rivalry or debate (argumentation) is considered the cornerstone of objective rationality, very distinct from social imitation. However, socially it is an act of engagement, or respect to some extent for the opinions of others. Walking away from debate is the more aggressive act. The opposing groups' debating skills, if not their reasons, can be imitated. The rules of debate counter physical aggression.

As mentioned, Heidegger argues that knowledge is not the rational collection of facts, but rather it is imitating how to do things. For encouraging the use of solution concepts, rivalry offers a powerful socialization process. If effective, then the new system can be shown to offer one group an advantage which the other group will need to imitate or exceed.

## SELF-MANAGED PROBLEM-SOLVING TEAMS

The use of setting up new relationships or connectivity through a dedicated small group to drive the use of a new solution concept appears to be a common practice. Following their review of the survey research on teamwork, Delarue et al. (2007) found that teamwork has a positive impact on group performance. Katzenbach and Smith (1993) distinguish groups from teams in that teams require both individual and mutual accountability. Self-managed problem-solving teams do not simply recommend, they assist, argues Sexton (1994). The self-managed, multidisciplined, autonomous, problem-solving team idea developed as an outcome of the socio-technical system theory in the 1960s and 1970s. This specifically focuses upon the group rather than the individual; on sociology not psychology. Its operating mechanism is socialization processes within the team. Small teams develop much stronger social bonds than larger teams. Sexton points out that for effective self-managed problem-solving teams, the team members and those setting up the teams need an imitated mindset, benefits, managerial faith and a risk-taking attitude (Sexton 1994).

It is not clear, using Heidegger's ideas, why self-managed teams would necessarily mimic appropriate acceptance behaviours and become committed to encouraging the new concept. If the team was already committed then it could be used to champion it. Martin et al. (2009) saw teams as representing a teleological conception of change; change occurs because of internally generated goals developed by a socialization process within the group. Martin et al. suggest it may be necessary to have two self-managed teams, one to implement the new concept and another to audit their success, each aware of the presence of the other. With rivalry, a dialectic conception, change is driven by underlying tensions. Competition is also an evolutionary concept, so teams may therefore be seen as making operational more than one conception of change.

In summary, there is going to be a need for social learning changes if those involved in a problem are expected to enact the solution concepts. The problems of getting those involved to change their thinking and habits can be enormous. However, ensuring their work practices and reward systems are aligned with the solution concepts would be a good start. A new concept for thinking about how to design social learning change is that of computer gaming. These games have prizes, scores, assistance, layered challenges, collaborations, and so on. This provides a way of thinking about what has to be done to persuade staff to behave in a manner consistent with the solution concepts.

## SOLUTION PROJECTS

As well as aligning its social learning processes with the solution concepts, an solution group might also choose to invest in a particular set of projects or initiatives to further enact its concepts. For example, what investments in new skills, equipment, processes or collaborations might be undertaken to make the situation more agile or innovative? The concern statements may have some ideas for these activities but the planners may need to imagine more. A solution is only as good as the ideas it contains.

Pragmatism explains creative ideas as reflecting on the problem situation using a novel or unusual concept. For example, every year the *Harvard Business Review* journal publishes a list of what its sources claim are commercial opportunities. It calls these 'Breakthrough Ideas'. In one year these were:

- Mobile Heath Care – monitoring and drug delivery;
- Financial Instruments Public R&D (research and development) – a Central Science Investigation and Research Organisation (CSIRO)

or Department of Education, Science and Technology (DEST) for finance (Australian government);

- Standard Drug Database Structures – to enable sharing;
- Green Loans repaid through Land Tax Increases – global warming opportunities;
- Staff R&D Reward Opportunities – entrepreneur spin-offs;
- Hacking Work – systemize work-arounds;
- Spotting Bubbles – reporting systems;
- Hong Kong for China – autonomous development units;
- Independent Diplomacy – talk to the invisible and your enemies;
- Progress Pleases – assist staff to achieve things.

In an earlier year the list was:

- P2P – Internet shopping, social networking, Wikipedia, virtual supply chains;
- Tasks Not Time – output measurements;
- Opposition Planning – dealing with lobby groups;
- Lies and Security – cybercrime, identity theft;
- Gamer Disposition – it's just a game;
- Virtual Worlds – media, entertainment, music, fashion, sport;
- Metadata Trends – marketing from Internet tracking;
- Crossover Adoption of IT – social use of work IT and work use of social IT;
- Multi Home – home as office, shop, cinema and gym;
- Social Lobbying – social mobbing;
- China's Second Cities;
- Islam – finance, food, alternative to the West.

These might be used to think about specific action plans a solution group might take to enact its concepts. For example, a situation requiring more agility might reflect on the role of mobile technologies and the impact of Islam as a means of becoming more agile, and so on.

## TECHNOLOGY TO CHANGE BEHAVIOUR

New equipment, processes and technologies can be used to implement a solution concept, one the use of which will require adopting the new behaviours sought. For example, if more networking is sought then implementing social media, Skype or blogging technology may help. By 'technology' is meant man-made, not in nature, not just digital information technologies. Art, tools, cultures, religions, clothes, writing, buildings, manufacturing, processes, equipment, machinery and diagrams are all technologies. So, if a solution has an intent to increase its operational capacity in hot weather, then installing more air conditioning may be the relevant technology.

Many organizations have implemented large computerized enterprise resource planning systems to improve their financial control. Many have also implemented electronic communications to allow 24/7 global communications, virtual team projects, and generally to improve levels of innovation. Automatic teller machines (ATMs), self-service and self-checkout in supermarkets and petrol stations has acted to reduce and standardize customer service costs plus pass more control to the customer. Prisons try to use appropriate building technology to reduce crime. Improving product quality in manufacturing often requires investment in improved machinery. Improved agility often means moving to Wiki documents, iPads, and multimedia communications for quicker updating and reorganizations. Improvement in visibility in logistics may mean improved radio frequency identification device (RFID) and geographic information system (GIS) tracking. Podcasting and Internet talkback radio may be used to improve mobile staff training during travelling times. Implementing a solution often means thinking of a technology which will help.

Creative ideas often follow from trying to improve something, to improve what it does. So, alternatively, all the technologies, elements or things that make up a solution effort can be reviewed for what they do and how that could be continuously improved, where improvement is defined by achieving the solutions concepts. For example, how might skills, equipment, processes, departments, products or relationships be continuously improved to make the situation more agile, if agility is a solution concept?

## ACTIVITY TABLES

In summation, the problem solution needs to include exactly how the solution concepts are to be enacted. The action plans do this. These plans need to include a remix of social learning processes, including the changing of performance measures and evaluation criteria. These change plans will also usually include processes where champions, job rotation, benchmarking and problem-solving teams are used to tacitly influence stakeholders to start using the new solution concepts in their day-to-day decisions. These might be summarized using an actions table such as Table 8.1.

The action plans also need to include the provision of new equipment, markets, collaborations, supply chains, products and/or services. A similar

*Table 8.1   Actions table*

| Solution concept | Organiza-tion structure | Perfor-mance measures | Com-mittee structure | Job selection criteria | Socializa-tion training | Budget alloca-tions |
|---|---|---|---|---|---|---|
| Agile | *Put actions here* | | | | | |
| Innovative | | | | | | |
| Precise | | | | | | |
| Secure | | | | | | |
| Distributed | | | | | | |
| Overall | | | | | | |

table to Table 8.1 can be drafted to show how these projects will enact what solution concept.

## APPLICATION

Draft activity tables showing what might be done to achieve your Statement of Intent. These are basically incentives or constraints to encourage enactment of your concepts.

The stakeholders' concerns might contain some suggestions for what might be done, as might the list of concepts. For example, for the social enterprise problem, an organization that assists African immigrants arriving in a new country may use these concepts to inspire new revenue-generating opportunities. Possible options triggered by thinking about each of the concepts for this organization may include drawing on their knowledge of African cultures to develop training courses and workshops for schools to educate young people about the value of other cultures and illustrate how Africans and other immigrants contribute to society ('social expertise'), or to establish a restaurant or cafe that sells African food, and provides African cooking classes delivered by immigrants ('mission engagement' and 'activity coaching').

New social enterprise activities might also be generated by combining two or more of the trading concepts. For example, by reflecting upon the combination of 'mission engagement' and 'social expertise', a social enterprise may coordinate holiday packages to visit conflict areas in Africa. In this way, potential sponsors may gain more empathy for African immigrants. Or by combining the concepts of 'mission engagement' and 'needs distribution', a social enterprise may charge a fee for tours of organic farms that encourage participants to establish their own organic gardens, and provide a venue for excess produce to be swapped.

## NOTE

1.   This chapter is based on: Martin et al. (2009).

# 9.   Paradoxical consequences

## OVERVIEW

Change often has paradoxical consequences. Before the solutions concepts, and related action plans, are made operational they need to be cri-
tiqued, especially for paradoxes that might arise from enacting them. This
might be done by the experienced problem-solver simply using his or her
imagination. However, the classic aid to thinking about paradoxical consequences is feedback loop diagramming. This chapter will discuss paradox
and provide an example of how to use feedback loops to think about a
solution concept. It will discuss a variant of multiple cause diagramming,
one in line with pragmatism, which is called consequences networking.

## PROBLEM STATEMENT

Paradox, and its related concepts of irony, contradictions, underlying
tensions and perspective clashes, offers particular insights (Muecke 1982;
Quine 1961). When combined with consequences, paradoxical consequences can be used to think about the emergence of apparently contradictory, and unexpected, outcomes occurring from our actions. For
example, counter to the original intent of introducing carbon taxes, enforc-
ing Treasury departments can end up wanting increases in emissions to
provide funding for popular alternative social programmes. A retaliation
policy to counter suicide bombing can result in providing increased means
and motive to the bomber community. Patent law and requiring evidence-
based research can inadvertently act to restrict innovation. Analysts need
to anticipate unexpected consequences either from their projects or from
their actions within projects. Why paradox and consequences offer useful
insights is reviewed, but to be of use they do need to be made operational
as an auditable method.

Luscher and Lewis (2008) provide a case study showing the mechanics of how the literary concept of paradox was used to analyse change at
the Lego Company. They use action research to look for Quine's (1961)
paradoxes of organizing, belonging, learning and performing. However,

identifying paradoxes in a situation without an auditable analysis tool is demanding. Consideration of the consequences of any actions taken to resolve a problem situation is also a useful analytical tool (Suddaby 2006). Combining paradox and consequences offers a reinforcing analysis method, but one that provides a method for systematically identifying paradoxical consequences

The problem situation used as an example in this chapter is that of wanting to promote innovation in a localized private physical therapy clinic industry. A means was sought of improving commercial innovation, while still operating under an evidenced-based ideology. Generally, the medical industry has a significant reputation for being innovative. Yet, the medical science-based physical therapy clinic industry in Australia has been urged to be more innovative (Australian Bureau of Statistics Report 2010, at http://www.abs.gov.au/). That it is not innovative is something of a mystery. The clinics are staffed by well-qualified, often young, intelligent, motivated, caring, medically trained staff operating in a commercial marketplace. This chapter will therefore use paradoxical consequences made operational by networking consequences to analyse this industrial problem and make suggestions for change.

Consequence networking provides an alternative use of loops. Loops have long been mentioned in the paradox literature (Smith and Lewis 2011). The long-established means of identifying feedback loops is multiple-cause diagrams (Daellenbach 2003). Multiple-cause diagrams offer a well-established formal quantitative method which sets the network nodes as variables and positive or negative causal pressures as the links. This form of mapping is used to identify feedback loops, often after an extensive quantitative model has been built. While a formidable analysis tool, this method can be daunting to many managers. Consequence networking offers a softer, more qualitative alternative in the cognitive and networking mapping tradition, one that can be used to make operational both paradox and consequences theory. It uses feedback loops in a different manner to traditional multiple-cause diagramming, using instead the comparison of pairs of loops. Pairs of contradictory loops are interpreted as paradoxes.

This chapter will therefore first review the explanations of why paradox and consequence are useful ways to think about problem situations. Then it will explain how consequences be used to identify paradox using network mapping, remembering the dynamic and dual nature of paradox. This is followed by an application of consequence networking in the search for innovation paradoxes in the physiotherapy clinic industry in Australia. Four paradoxes were identified through a grounded process of discussing the problem with those involved. It was then possible to make suggestions as to how innovation might be encouraged, bearing in mind the inherent underlying tensions.

## PARADOX

Paradox is increasingly being used to analyse management problems (Lewis 2000; Lusher and Lewis 2008; Smith and Lewis 2011). Given that the terms 'paradox' and 'irony' are used interchangeably in much of the management literature, the distinction will not be explored here (Muecke 1982). Both have been found to provide unique, creative and particular insights into both problems and how we think (Miron-Spektor et al. 2011a). However, how paradoxes are identified has been largely undefined. Quine (1961) defines a (logical) paradox as a conclusion that at first sounds absurd, but later a reasonable argument can be presented to sustain it. Lewis (2000) provides numerous examples arguing that paradox denotes contradiction as interrelated elements that seem logical in isolation but absurd when appearing simultaneously. She goes on to define it more carefully as: (1) opposing interpretations of particular phenomena; (2) oppositional thinking; (3) aids to understanding divergent interpretations; (4) perceptual; (5) becoming apparent through social interaction; (6) denoting a variety of viewpoints; (7) residing in the observer not the observed; and (8) being a possible outcome of using negatives to define something. Poole and Van de Ven (1989) represent the classical examples of paradox, suggesting that organizations (like rivers) are at the same time both constant and constantly changing, and how people are both independent and yet dependent on others. Arnold (2003) in his discussion on the paradoxical nature of mobile phones opts to use the term 'Janus-faced' after the Roman deity with two faces, cursed and blessed with the necessity of facing two directions at once. Miron-Spektor et al. (2011a) provide some empirical basis by finding, in laboratory experiments, that the presence of paradoxical frames makes for more creative solutions.

When Hatch (1997) discusses the humour generated by paradox, she sees it as a particular cognitive construction where what is said is different from what is meant; the use of opposite frames. Oswick et al. (2002) contrast this form of analysis with the use of metaphor, arguing that it is more stimulating. As an example, they revisit Willmott's exposure of social empowerment where those chosen to be empowered through promotion are often those who have so far exhibited the highest degree of conformity. This form of analysis provides something he calls a double exposure: on one plate, co-existing, irreconcilable, irrelatable realities.

Lewis (2000) and Smith and Lewis (2011) argue that managers are increasingly learning to accept paradox in their work. Rather than trying to resolve tensions, they are using them to provide alternative sources of analysis. Poole and Van de Ven (1989) in contrast recommend ways of working through paradoxes which include distinguishing levels of analysis, synthesizing new conceptions and using the concept of time. Luscher and Lewis (2008) also provide advice on how to work with or through paradoxes. This involves sense-making (Weick 1995), which can be interpreted as needing to identify the conceptions (frames, perspectives, interpretations) involved in our thinking processes. With paradox this invokes the pragmatist William James's (1910 [1907]) advice, that when faced with a contradiction one should make a distinction: a distinction between the concepts or frames in use. So, for example, in Willmott's example, the distinction is between social empowerment and conformity. The paradox is not resolved but seen as the consequence of thinking about promotion using this particular pair of opposing concepts (frames or interpretations).

## CONTRADICTION AND DIALECTIC

Paradox exposes dialectic, the result of a dynamic contradiction of processes (Muecke 1982; Quine 1961). Smith and Lewis use Quine's examples of learning, belonging, organizing and performing, to emphasize the dynamic nature or paradox which results from numerous organizational processes being under tension with each other. For example, Quine's learning paradox can be explained as being a consequence of at once wanting change, and also wanting a standardized product. The paradox of belonging can be explained as at least a consequence of wanting tolerance of others, and also wanting strong group norms. However, it is easy to lose sight of this dynamic aspect and to think of paradox as mysterious, locked and therefore static. This distracts from identifying and working through paradox in terms of processes under tension with each other. Talk about paradoxical outcomes, or paradoxical consequences, might assist in emphasizing the dynamics at play (Mohr 1982; Poole and Van de Ven 1989; Van de Ven and Poole 1995).

As Lewis (2000) points out, what we emphasize by using the term 'paradoxical consequences' is dialectic contradictions. A deeper understanding of paradox requires using this particular way of seeing the world. One of science's most useful concepts, evolution, also requires use of the dialectic or contradiction world-view. Natural selection is seen as a never-ending struggle of multiple species against each other in the context of a complex dynamic environment, all of which acts to creatively generate increasing diversity. It is ironic: the beauty of all living species is created by a bitter life-and-death struggle. Talk of resolving the dialectic tension between species is meaningless as it would destroy the process of evolution. Rather, dialectic provides a means of understanding. The selection of species by food availability, co-competitive species, sexual selection and designed artefacts presents a turbulent, chaotic, dynamic, interdependent and competitive process. Occasionally, however, this dialectic process has the consequence of paradoxes, such as excessive courtship plumage and birds that cannot fly.

Dialectic, or the contradictory world-view, is usually credited to Aristotle who saw evidence-based and reasoned argumentation between interlocutors as the basis of creative scientific method. While very effective generally, this dialectic occasionally generates paradoxical consequences such as scientists blocking debate by claiming they are the only ones informed enough to understand the problem. Aristotle's dialectic is in contrast to Plato's notion of knowledge coming from comparing what we see with imagined ideal forms (Bailin 2003; Rorty 1989). Hegel and other later Continental philosophers (Rorty 1989) moved dialectic from people arguing to the struggle between community beliefs. Modern examples include the struggle between imperialist and indigenous cultures, and between relativity and quantum mechanics. The latter results in the consequence of the paradox that relativity provides a universal theory of large things, and quantum mechanics a universal theory of small things. Darwin's (1859) evolution theory clearly influenced Schumpeter, and Marx's *Das Capital*, where capitalism includes the evolution of new competitive products and services (Engels 1964; Marx 1992; Rescher 1979). Marx saw dialectic between capital and labour, the exposure of which has considerably improved the life of countless millions, but also resulted in our identifying consequences such as the paradox that capital is now largely the savings of workers, and that the empowered oppressed have sometimes turned into aggressive oppressors. Dialectic has also attracted the attention of numerous writers interested in explaining organizational behaviour (Benson 1977; Mason 1996; Nielsen 1996; Seo and Creed 2002).

This section has addressed the question of: why use paradox to think about problem situations? In summary, paradox, in all its related forms, opens up our thinking to dialectic. This in turn offers unique and particular insights into apparent problem situations. These include that contradictory, unexpected consequences can occur from our well-intended actions. This is partly the result of how we think, and how we should think about problem situations. Paradox opens us to the advantages of alternative perspectives. However, how we might identify paradox, beyond by being imaginative, remains something of a mystery.

## CONSEQUENCES

Being dynamic, paradox will have consequences. Consequence is therefore an obvious partner concept to use with paradox when analysing problem situations. The use of consequences, rather than causes, to explain anything is to take the pragmatic turn (James 1910 [1907]; Rorty 1989). James (1910 [1907]) understood that tolerance for pluralism, or multiple perspectives, would sometimes result in paradox. The pragmatists argued that we do and should interpret everything in terms of consequences (James 1910 [1907]). Peirce's (1878) initial pragmatist maxim was: 'Consider what effects . . . we conceive the object of our conception to have. Then, our conception of these effects is the whole of our conception of the object'. This might be colloquially put as: a thing is what it does, or we know a thing as what it does – the consequences of its being. Freedom is the consequence of what freedom does, a policy is what that policy does, its consequences of existing. Occasionally, these consequences are seen to be paradoxical.

The use of consequences, the actions subsequent to an event, was a deliberate move by the pragmatists to overcome some of the shortcomings of thinking about science as a study of inherent properties or in terms of cause and effect. Nietzsche (1979 [1873]) seems to have started the modern concern over causes as being the basic study of science when he noticed that causes suggest prediction, but could only be recalled as an *ex post* experienced pattern of activity, a historic sequence of events. This suggests that causes be thought of historically, as consequences. Much of science drew on Kant's (1974 [1781]) arguments that cause and effect is hardwired into our illusive minds, along with the concept of time and space. These were therefore obvious concepts to use as the basis of scientific investigation. Nietzsche saw this as a circular argument. The pragmatists (James 1910 [1907]) took up this disagreement with Kant, wanting rather to use past experience, and thus also consequences, as the basis of all thinking. Even prediction can be interpreted as anticipating the future from reflection on past experiences. They used Hume's (1975 [1777]) point that causes are not directly observable, only effects: outcomes or consequences. This made causes unscientific. The preferred alternative was to argue that science is about the study of effects, outcomes or consequences. This had the added advantage of also providing a method of ethics: consequentialism.

Strong support for the use of consequences over causes also comes from the empirics of Darwin (1859) and Skinner (1981) who found that biological species learn by the consequences of their actions: feedback loops. We do something and what happens next determines whether we are encouraged or not to do it again. Darwin observed this in the young when learning both actions and language. Skinner's box for training pigeons with food rewards can be seen as their using consequences to learn. This connects consequences with responses and reactions. Consequences, including what leads to rewards, can be seen to be feedback patterns of activities. Our brains have been described as feedback pattern recognition systems (Juarrero 2002; Simon 1975). Some of these feedback patterns or consequences can be recognized as favourable and others as paradoxical. All of which provides further support for the use of consequences to think about paradox. Combining paradox and consequences, as paradoxical consequences, offers a reinforcing way of thinking about problems. It also offers a method for identifying paradox.

## CONSEQUENCE NETWORKING

A diagram or picture is said to be worth a thousand words, but only when it would take a thousand words to explain the relationships between the objects in a picture (Larkin and Simon 1987). The problem-solving, systems, operational research and systems dynamics literature has long advocated the use of diagrams as a particular means of seeing complex situations (Axlerod 1976; Bryson and Ackerman 2004; Coyle 2000; Forrester 1994; Sterman 2000). Latour (1986) argues that visualization methods are critical to the development of the sciences, which now use an extensive range of visualization including graphs, electron traces, oscilloscopes, maps, technical drawings and X-rays. He calls them 'immutable mobiles', stable over time and able to be easily shared asynchronously. But as with maps, they can be edited when new evidence comes to hand. Maps, technical drawings and pictures are about relative positioning or connectivity. In this chapter the interest is in the relative positioning of successive consequences on consequences. Consequences networking can make alternative, successive consequences visible. This provides a means of assisting in identifying paradox.

Consequences networking can only be thought of as assisting with the identification of paradox. It is not an algorithm. Some assistance, by drafting and interpreting consequence networks, including the use of diagramming software, has been found useful. However, too much process does run the risk of closing down some of their opportunity for creative thinking. Too little structure, and the old problem of merely relying on intuitive insight returns. As a mainly qualitative analysis, consequence networking does provide a simple analysis method that allows untrained individuals and management groups to make some attempt at indentifying paradox. However, there is still room for the skill of the analyst, as the final consequence network will still need some imaginative interpretation if it is to be used to identify dynamic tensions or paradox.

Consequence networking is a particular form of networking. Networks show any form of connection, including tensions, between any elements of a system. Computer, social and ideas networking are well-known examples linking things, people and ideas (Borgatti 2002; Burt 2002). Critical path analysis, flowcharts, process maps, fishbone diagrams, multiple-cause diagramming, matrix analysis and input–output analysis can be seen to be network diagrams, most of which emphasize flow, usually physical flows. Consequence networks have successive consequences as the nodes (vertices). The arrows (edges) represent 'leads to' statements. Consequences can be sourced directly from the analyst, a panel of experts, or a community of stakeholders by asking them to list one or a handful of events and their consequences. Consequences are events, which have consequences. Experience stories might also be used to identify consequences. However done, it may be useful to first draft a consequences tree and then input this into network software like UCINET6 or NODEXL. Pairs of converging but contradictory loops in the resultant network diagram can be studied to assist in indentifying paradoxes.

Numerous forms of 'loops' have been identified in the literature (Argyris 1977; Sterman 2000). Hofstadter (1979) identified the presence of strange or recursive loops in numerous activities from music to maths to the behaviour of insects. The neuroscientists, and Murphy and Brown (2007), use feedback loops to provide a systems explanation of how our brains work, and therefore how we think, make judgements and act. They see our brain's neuron connections as being in a feedback loop diagram layout. Systems writers such as Churchman (1971) and Ackoff (1971), as second-generation pragmatists, suggested using the concept of a system to represent dialectic social ecologies. The interconnected dynamic non-linear tension of the elements in any system is perhaps best demonstrated by feedback loop diagramming (Juarrero 2002). This systems dynamics version of loops identifies and allocates polarities to feedback loops, often adding stock functions to allow for flow timing differences. Loop maps have also been advocated in the related sense-making and managerial cognition literature (Huff and Jenkins 2002; Kaplan 2011). The economist Hayden, when discussing social fabric matrix diagramming, refers to all these loops as cumulative circular causes (Hayden 1982). The dominant management theory writers on paradox, Lewis (2000) and Smith and Lewis (2011), advise the identification of paradox using loops. They reference Hofstadter's *Eternal Golden Braid* (1979) recursive loops, and positive and negative loops of systems dynamics, using the language of virtuous (favourable) and vicious (detrimental) cycles. To align with the dialectic mentioned earlier, paradoxical feedback loops must come in pairs: pairs in tension, two events being true at the same time yet contradictory. Mapping of sequences of consequences as flows is expected to result in identifiable pairs of paradoxical loops.

## AN ILLUSTRATION

This section will explain how consequence networks were used to study a paradoxical situation in a physical therapy clinic industry. These small clinics provide scientific evidence-based medical services and yet need to be commercially viable. Comparable doctors' clinics and surgical clinics offer a financially rewarding and sustainable career, but the physical therapists struggle. Physiotherapy clinics provide a medical science service aimed at the recovery of muscle, tendon and joint function without medication or surgery. It is arguably how medical intervention started. Discovery of drugs, germs and surgical techniques spawned innovative practices off this foundational physical therapy. These new medical practices, such as surgery and drug treatments, have often been more rewarding, financially and socially, than just offering physical therapies. So nowadays, physical therapy sometimes does not hold the prestige of drug or surgical interventions. The solution recommended by industry, professional and government reports is that physiotherapy clinics needed to be more innovative. After all, the medical industry generally is renowned for its innovation. For the low-technology therapy industry, this innovation is limited to not using innovative drugs or surgical interventions. However, physical therapy innovation may include novel treatments, novel equipment and improvements in what and how services are offered. Use of the term 'innovation', rather than the more common medical research terms of 'discovery' or 'invention', is used to emphasize the need for a commercial outcome for practicing clinic therapists.

Prior to starting a project of helping those in the therapy industry to think about why these enthusiastic, well-educated therapists were paradoxically not as innovative as they might be, my researcher interviewed or surveyed more than 140 clinic principals operating in one metropolitan region. They were asked about their innovations and why they were, or were not, innovative. Statements gathered by this process were used to construct the diagrams that follow.

The networking started with the practitioner researcher, who had worked as a clinic principal, undertaking a literature review on the sources of innovation, and then recording and analysing the survey and interview data. The researcher then selected an example of an innovation that had the potential to be of commercial and treatment significance to clinics. The innovation was a electrical sensor gadget that therapists could use to

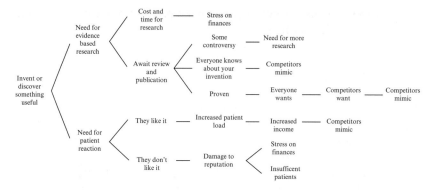

*Figure 9.1    Consequences tree*

relax or stimulate particular muscle groups. The event of imagining this gadget was used as the starting event or node in a feedback loop diagram. Next, the researcher compiled a consequences tree, as shown in Figure 9.1. She used comments from participants as to what did, or would need to, happen next as a consequence of this invention occurring. For example, one stakeholder argued that the consequence of inventing this gadget was the need for clinical trials. Another commented that any innovation would also need to be acceptable to patients and therapists. The consequence of needing medical trials was the cost and time involved, but this process would most likely require complete exposure of any intellectual property embedded in the innovation. In this simple step-by-step manner, a hierarchy of consequences was identified. Between 20 and 30 events (five consequences, of five consequences – about 5 x 5) was found to be sufficient not to overcrowd the final diagram and yet to provide enough practical content for later identifying loops. The drafting process ended when some repetition of consequences started to occur. In this case, the repetition comes in the form of the consequence mentioning financial stress and competitors' copying. To some extent the analyst has to have the idea of wanting some of the final consequences to sound like the initial consequences. This makes the loops occur. The consequences tree makes no attempt to connect similar consequence boxes, so there will be repetition. Therefore the tree will have numerous boxes which contain the same consequences occurring at different levels of the tree.

The consequences tree was then used as input to networking software. When displayed as a network, these nodes will only appear once, but will have numerous 'leading to' arrows pointing to them. The networking software suggest the best layout, given one node per consequence and numerous paths (links) to and from it. The networking software used

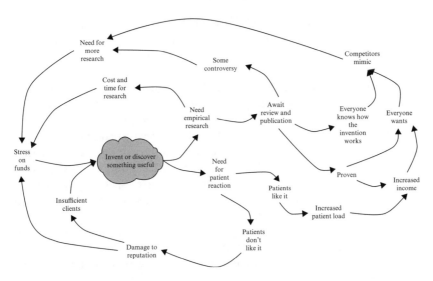

*Figure 9.2    Consequences network diagram*

was UCINET6 (Borgatti et al. 2002), given its accessibility, popularity and high standard of calculative algorithms. Other products, such as NODEXL, offer more scope for editing the appearance of the network but take more set-up time. The consequences network diagram is displayed in Figure 9.2.

## ANALYSIS

The network diagram is interpreted remembering paradox theory. This means identifying pairs of loops that are in tension. This is a very subjective process, but the authors identified the following four loops:

1. Invent or discover something useful; Need empirical research; Cost and time for research; Stress on funds; Need to invent or discover something useful.
2. Invent or discover something useful; Need for patient reaction; Patients don't like it; Damage to reputation; Insufficient clients/patients; Need to invent or discover something useful.
3. Invent or discover something useful; Need empirical research; Await publication and review; Some controversy over findings likely; Need for more research; Stress on funds; Need to invent or discover something useful.

4. Invent or discover something useful; Need empirical research; Await review; Proven; Everyone wants; Competitors mimic; Need more research; Stress on funds; Need to invent or discover something useful.

Comparing loop 1 and 2 suggests the paradox: Spending money on research may result in reduced patient numbers if they don't like it, even if it improves health outcomes (Innovative vs Popular Paradox).

Comparing loop 1 and 3 suggests the paradox: Spending money on research to improve your income can commit you to needing to spend even more, and become a huge drain on resources (Accelerating Costs Paradox).

Comparing loop 3 and 4 suggests the paradox: Spending money on research may be of more benefit to those that copy your findings than to yourself (Innovating for Others Paradox).

Comparing loop 1 and 3 suggests the paradox: Spending money on research may lead to excessive patient demand than is desirable for the clinic owner's lifestyle, facilities and policy of close patient liaison (Over-success Paradox).

## DISCUSSION AND CONCLUSION

Paradox has been a topic of some interest in the arts for a long time. It provides a way of seeing the world that contrasts with that of balance and harmony. It reveals a world of dialectic, of dynamic tensions, of contractions. It is increasingly being used as an analysis tool because it has the potential to offer novel insights. However, it can be demanding to indentify paradoxes without some methodological assistance. This chapter has suggested the use of consequences networking. This started with the drafting of a consequences tree which provides input to network analysis diagramming software. These consequences need to be sourced from in-depth consideration, analysis and prediction of context by experienced practitioners discussing their perception of an issue of some importance for their professional development and livelihood. Once the consequences tree has been drafted, the production of the network is fairly straightforward. Analysing the resultant network diagram then requires identifying pairs of contradictory loops, as illustrated in the case provided in the chapter.

This case involved a physiotherapy clinic industry. The industry was concerned about why it was not more innovative. There has been a lot of theorizing about what paradoxes exist when trying to promote innovation. Examples include: (1) the more a firm pays attention to innovation, the less likely it will be to innovate; (2) whoever makes the most mistakes (takes the most risks) will be the most innovative; (3) most technology firms do not transform their know-how into value; (4) those staff with a creative think-ing style are not the best for implementing ideas; and (5) organizational hierarchy kills innovation (Farson and Keyes 2002; Miron-Spektor et al. 2011a; Raynor 2007). Rather than use these deductively, consequences net-working inductively identified four specific paradoxes from the comments of those involved. These paradoxes were used to help plan how innovation might be encouraged and managed in this industry.

Paradox, consequences and network mapping are powerful analysis tools; used together they are more so. The contradictory dynamic nature of paradox makes it hard to identify without method. It is a specific way of thinking, of seeing the world; one that does not provide problems to be solved, but rather, warns of the need for balance and the dangers of unex-pected consequences. Good examples of paradox stand out when reported from someone's intuition. Merely calling for creative insight is an insuf-ficient analysis method. Analysts need auditable methodological methods which stand up to the scrutiny of sceptical stakeholders. This chapter has offered a practical method for thinking about the almost inevitable paradoxical consequences of any action enacted in our complex socio-technical world. It also offers a reminder of the dialectic or balanced way of seeing the world. It does not offer a crystal ball or algorithmic method, still requiring significant skill by the analyst. However, it does provide a theoretical way forward that is compatible with other systems dynamics, cognitive and network mapping methods.

## APPLICATION

Take time out to reflect on your concepts and action plans. What will others do in reaction to your plans? what will sceptics say? can you overdo things? do you need to be more subtle, more balanced? Perhaps draft a consequences network diagram. You may want to revise some of your ideas.

# 10. Questioning action plans

## OVERVIEW

Action plans need to be thought through and clearly communicated to those expected to enact them. This chapter addresses the problem of how to think systematically about the detail required in action plans. For example, if there is intent to reorganize to enable more innovation, then how exactly is this reorganization to be achieved? Who does what? Elaborating and enacting this detail is going to be the task of a project manager. Using a systematic questioning approach is thought to provide a thinking aid for the problem-solver and to assist in communicating what needs to be done to the project manager. Therefore, this chapter explains why and how systematic questioning might be used to scope the action plans.[1]

## STRUCTURING QUESTIONS

The details of what actions that might be used to enact the solution concepts needs to be thought up, and communicated, to stakeholders, especially the project managers. This presents us with the practical task of suggesting a structure for this generation and communication. Doing so systematically will help everyone think about the task. To some extent, Checkland's (2000) CATWOE root definition provides an example of this, one which has been tested over some 30 years of continuous use. The root definition does provide a 'what needs to be done' statement which includes mention of the:

- Customers (decision-makers);
- Actors (doers);
- What is to be transformed to what;
- World-view action plans to be undertaken;
- Owners (decision-makers); and
- Environment.

Ulrich's *Critical Heuristics* (1983) provides a more elaborate alternative, one that makes more explicit use of a moral imperative: what ought to be done and who ought to do it.

Another alternative and yet still systematic approach to generating and communicating action plans is to use the interrogative pronouns and adverbs of the English language. These are best known as Kipling's (1902) 'six honest serving men', namely, what, where, when, who, why and how. These provide an obvious starting point for English speakers looking for a systematic approach to generating questions from concepts. They are simple enough to prompt thinking, while flexible enough to apply to any concept. The origins of the interrogatives can be traced back to Aristotle, who makes mention of eight interrogates of an act.[2] An act is connected, firstly, with its cause; secondly, with its circumstances; and thirdly, with the effect or results of the act, namely:

- Cause of the act:
  1. Why did it happen?
  2. What made it happen?
  3. Who made it happen?
  4. With what instruments?
- Circumstances of the act:
  5. When did it happen?
  6. Where did it happen?
  7. How did it happen, in what manner?
- Result of the act:
  8. What happened? Quoted from Aristotle, *Nicomachean Ethics* (book 3 section 1):

A man may be ignorant, then, of who he is, what he is doing, what or whom he is acting on, and sometimes also what (e.g. what instrument) he is doing it with, and to what end (e.g. he may think his act will conduce to someone's safety), and how he is doing it (e.g. whether gently or violently).

The interrogatives were further developed by the thirteenth-century Danish theologian Augustine of Dacia, for use as a meditation to analyse the deviation of the soul from the path of righteousness.[3] However, as mentioned, possibly the best known reference to the interrogatives comes from literary Nobel prizewinner Rudyard Kipling's poem (1902) from 'The Elephant's Child' in the *Just So Stories*:

### 'I Keep Six Honest Serving Men'

I keep six honest serving-men (They taught me all I knew);
Their names are What and Why and When, and How and Where and Who.
I send them over land and sea, I send them east and west;
But after they have worked for me, I give them all a rest.
I let them rest from nine till five, for I am busy then.

As well as breakfast, lunch and tea, for they are hungry men.
But different folk have different views; I know a person small –
She keeps ten million serving men, who get no rest at all!
She sends 'em abroad on her own affairs,
from the second she opens her eyes –
One million Hows, two million Wheres, and seven million Whys! (1902)

Unfortunately, the poem does not provide much advice on how to apply the questions in various situations. In the wider problem-solving and project management literature, there seem to be far more cases of these interrogatives being recommended than researched. Yet their application does seem to span many different disciplines, perhaps illustrating the versatility and generalizability of such a simple scheme. A typical example is Purcell (2000), who writes about value engineering, which is a method of determining how to perform a function at the least cost possible, and who suggests the use of Kipling's six honest serving men when evaluating cost–function relationships, citing an example of designing an advanced transponder in an aircraft.

The systematic application of questioning to solution concepts to provide action plans is therefore thought to provide a means of expanding how the concept is to be enacted. Using Hookins's (2005) findings on the six interrogatives in the English language provides a systematic approach to this questioning (see Table 10.1).

## SIX WH'S

Perhaps the keystone of these interrogatives is 'why'. Hookins aligns with Ackoff (2007) and the pragmatic notion of problem-solvers implicitly

*Table 10.1    The Wh's*

| Interrogative | Interpretation |
| --- | --- |
| 1. Why | Reason, intent, concept |
| 2. What | Action |
| 3. Where | Spatial |
| 4. Who | Identity |
| 5. When | Temporal |
| 6. How serious | Qualitative action |
| 7. How much | Quantitative action |
| 8. Which | See: Who or what |

*Note:*    Negatives have been excluded, e.g. why not, who not.

or explicitly using concepts to interpret their world. The 'why' question is asking for reasons, explanations, drivers, intent (Dennett 1995) or, in terms of this book, the concepts that are implicitly (concerns) or explicitly used to interpret a situation as problematic: why particular reactions are thought reasonable.

The conceptual interrogative 'why' is a powerful and perhaps a rather different question from the other five interrogatives. It demands interpretation, reflection and explanation. It drives the answers to all the other interrogatives. Explanations 'why' are the basis of scientific theory and move the respondent from merely repeating sensory input (what is seen, etc.) to interpreting that input with reasoning and insight. Being an eyewitness cannot answer the 'why' question; interpretation requires expertise. Automation may answer many of the other interrogatives but not this one. It requires a reflective, thoughtful person.

Concepts provide explanation as to why particular actions are seen as reasonable. Explanation has been extensively discussed in the epistemology literature (Haack 1993, 2003; Ruben 1993) with the modern consensus seeming to settle on a pragmatic interpretation. This means that explanation is context-specific, needing to transfer specific understanding in a form relevant to specific inquirers. This decentres the suggestions that explanations can use the rigours of pure logic, or focus on causality without first identifying the concepts being used by participants to interpret their world. Understanding occurs when inquirers feel an explanation 'works best' in their paradigm (James 1910 [1907]). For example, a satisfactory explanation of war will differ for a military strategist, a psychologist and a financial investor. Possibly aligned to pragmatism, Walton (2004) argues for rhetoric as a reasonable mechanism for understanding to transfer from the explainer to the explainee, and one that is in a manner that is sensitive to context.

Haack (1993) qualifies the suggestion that the quality of an explanation is solely dependent on its scope, using the example of explaining nature's wonders as all God's creation. She argues that some 'specificity' is required. This can be encouraged by applying the interrogative pronouns and adverbs, especially 'why' or 'how'. They have already been used to challenge the scope of brute empiricism (knowledge only from measurement) by asking for explanations for 'why' particular measurements occur in nature. For example, if we really understood gravity we would understand why masses not in contact with each other can still exert an influence on each other. Also, those interested in how the social world should be rather than how it is are going to be interested in explaining how to change.

Elster (1983) distinguishes three types of explanation. Causal explanations are preferred by physical scientists: why does sunlight bend in gravity?

Biology needs both causal explanations and what he calls functional explanations: why does evolution prefer adaptability over specialization? The study of self-conscious humans requires causal, functional and what he calls intentional explanations: why did he react in that way to that news? Intention is understood to be like concepts, what drives our thinking. Elster's distinction again reinforces the suggestion that the 'why' interrogative be required to explain the concepts being used to interpret the world.

Moving onto the other interrogatives, the action or behavioural interrogative, 'what' appears the most expansive of the interrogatives. As Aristotle notes, you can have, 'to what ends' (cause) or you can have 'what happened' (result); both are about action or conduct. The interrogative has been picked up by logicians in the form 'what if'. This has converse as well as negative converse (mirror image) forms (what would not happen if you did/did not). In all but the basic form of 'what happened', this interrogative also requires some interpretation. It also has the potential to be a perspective-buster as it demands falsification rather than only confirmation thinking, something that the human brain can easily forget unless prompted by questions.

Hookins (2005) goes on to comment that the interrogative 'which' seems to be the least useful, as it immediately leads to 'who' or 'what': which person or which thing. It was not included in the service or communication projects questions and there was little evidence that it was missed.

The temporal interrogative, 'when', seems to have a clear role of introducing the universal concept of time into the discussions. Time coordinates the world's activities; we need it to integrate one task with another. People have a strong sense of time as it underlines their very existence on earth. 'When' therefore seemed very relevant to those focused on operational activities.

The special interrogative 'where' has some similarities with 'when'. It also has a role of connecting the task to another universal, that of geographical location. It is used to co-locate all activities relative to others. Again those interested in operational activities will be interested in 'where'.

The identity interrogative, 'who', seems powerful in subjectifying human activity.

The action interrogative, 'how' quickly needs to be distinguished between 'how serious' (qualitative), and 'how much' (quantitative). The former places activities in order of priority and the latter compares it to another universal, numbers. It is a very attractive interrogative for the functionally minded, the doers. Action research and pragmatism are particularly attracted to this interrogative. How does action tell you what you know?

Hookins (2005) reports that the order in which the interrogatives are presented is important: they interact. Starting with the 'why' interrogative can encourage deep thinking, or interpretations. Starting with 'where' or 'when', on the other hand, may encourage a level of thinking and subsequent conversation more attuned to providing eye-witness reports. When planning, the leadership role may be seen as proving the instruction (what needs to be done), and the 'how' is delegated to operational staff. To improve the communications between the leadership and operators, as well as to maximize flexibility, the 'what needs to be done' instruction is supported with the 'why', the intent, an explanation of the concepts being used to sense-make the situation by the leadership. For example, what needs to be done is to open an operation in India, the 'why' is because we are trying to make our organization more international.

The negative form of the other interrogatives was expected and found to be useful. Questions such as 'why not', do not always solicit a directly matched negative response to the question 'why'. As with the negative forms of 'what if', it can be a perspective-shifter, which seems like a useful attribute of questions. It may be that there is some opportunity to do more research about the converse of interrogatives.

Lastly, the number of the interrogatives fits close enough to Miller's (1956) 'magic number five'. The whole complex situation domain is 'chunked' into about five overall questions. This seems to be very appropriate, providing a flexibility that makes the interrogatives an attractive systematic means of questioning solution concepts as a means of making them operational as useful action plans.

## WHAT AND WHY

So, drawing on Hookin's review, the first question that might be asked is for an explicit statement of: what might be done?

This is the action interrogative; it states the idea as an activity. Asking this first focuses on knowledge being defined by its usefulness in providing alternative ways of acting. Reflective thinking (Dewey 1982 [1910]; Klein 1989, 2009) suggests that this question will be provided by experienced persons intuitively generating action ideas from their sense-making of a problem as presented to them. Example responses to this question may be: to introduce Internet voting; or that to stop global warming we need a global solution. Responses to this question might be elaborated upon using Lewis Carroll's (1939) 'logical box':

- What will happen if this is done?
- What will happen if this is not done?
- What will not happen if this is done?
- What will not happen if this is not done?

One way of reinforcing what needs to be done is to set goals, targets, aims or objectives. There is a quantification movement in management, perhaps a leftover of logical positivism, which suggests that these objectives need to be specific, measureable, achievable, realistic and timed (SMART). This requires complex human activities to be measured. If care is not taken, then the action actually achieved is measurement, not the intent of the objectives. Many organizations, for example, set SMART quality objectives which become an end in themselves; measurement, not quality, becomes the output.

Related to the 'what' question is the 'why' question that both evaluates and justifies the action idea. It is the key to creativity and deep thinking. Justification in pragmatism requires appreciation of the solution concept (idea) that is driving the activity idea. Therefore, the question immediate to the 'what' question is the 'why' question: why did you suggest that activity?

This is the motive, justification or reason for suggesting the action plan. This is the solution concept wanting to be enacted. So, the action plan of introducing Internet voting may be explained ('why') as coming from intending the solution concept of having more e-democracy. The action plan of needing a global warming strategy may be explained ('why') as coming from using the solution concept of intending to be more environmentally responsible.

It was mentioned earlier that actions be evaluated in terms of their consequences, intended or not. These consequences can be divided into two types. The first is consideration of the logical sequence of responses to the action idea, intended or not, from either stakeholders or the physical environment. The second type is the consequences for how the action will advance the recursive concept. Using the examples above, the activity of using Internet voting will have the consequence of encouraging more e-democracy. Likewise, the action of drafting a global warming strategy will have the consequence of encouraging more planning. Are these consequences intended and desired?

The consequences of a solution concept (criteria) are determined by how useful it is, how many possible future actions it generates. Put another way, some actions are thought to be generative; they spawn many other action ideas. The invention of electricity and the Internet are two obvious examples. These ideas have spawned whole industries. The pragmatic response to this is to observe that these are concepts that need to be evaluated in terms of how many possible future activities they generate. The concepts of electricity and the Internet are very useful; they generate many choices of how to act. Numerous actions can be taken to encourage the concepts: more users, more applications, more efficiency.

The novelty or creativity of an action idea is thought to be related to how novel the concept is. The reason the idea of a global strategic plan does not sound novel to deal with global warming is because planning is a well-established concept. The use of Internet voting sounds a little bit more innovative because it uses a more novel concept, that of e-democracy. The action idea of communities buying electricity from each other rather than from a central utility is novel because the concept of peer-to-peer (P2P) electricity networks is novel, as least when coupled with electricity rather than music file-sharing. Traditionally electricity used the concept of centralized utilities. Switching to using the concept of P2P to think of electricity actions is novel. Finding other P2P applications is also likely to be novel, because it is a new concept. Use of a novel concept to generate action ideas provides the intuitive leap present in novel actions.

Moving on from the 'what and why' question combination, the depiction of an action can now be further explored by now asking for details of how the action might be enacted.

The questions that might be asked to elaborate this include who is involved in enacting the action (stakeholders), when, where, with what and how exactly it is to be enacted. The timing question of when can be answered in detail using scheduling techniques such as Gnatt charts. Checkland's CATWOE suggests that the 'who' question (stakeholders) include the decision-makers, affectees and the doers (Bergvall-Kareborn et al. 2004). Similarly, the 'how' can be thought of as analogous to Checkland's transforming: what exactly is to be changed to what.

As explained earlier, pragmatism suggests that the answers generated in response to these six 'Wh' interrogative questions might be clarified if they are contrasted with some alternative. The action is 'to do what' rather than what not to do, why not, who not and so on. Stating the underlying tensions in the situation might also act to highlight the alternatives being made and the environment surrounding those choices. For example, it may be useful to identify the underlying tension in the concept of self-organization as being self-interest versus group interests.

Having at least given some thought to the responses to the interrogative questions, and having considered the consequences and the contradictions, these might be unified into an action plan depiction or one succinct paragraph. The reasoning and comparison tenets of pragmatism suggest that this statement be in the form of a well-argued proposition. Actions need to be justified to a sceptical audience.

## CONCLUSION

This chapter has provided an explanation of how and why systematic questioning might be used to generate and communicate action plans aligned to different solution concepts, as summarized in the Statement of Intent. The solution process thus starts with the solution concepts and progresses on to action plans for enacting those concepts. The two parts need to be aligned, one informing the other. Questions can be used to structure that process. For example:

What needs to be done (action plan)?
*We need to introduce electronic voting.*
Why (because of the solution concept; purpose)?
*We want more e-democracy.*
How (transformation) . . . who, when, where, with what . . . doers' means and motive.

It might be remembered that for action to take place it is necessary for the 'doing' participants to have the means and the motive. Having said what solution activity is required, and why, it is then necessary to provide the doing participants with their means and motive. The means are the resources, including skills, time and equipment. The motive includes the reward system. This means that things such as performance measures, new staff selection criteria, budget allocations and promotion criteria need to be aligned with the solution concepts. There is no point in wanting agility while promoting those who introduce rigid procedures. Solution action plans include providing the means and motive for the participants to enact the solution concepts.

## APPLICATION

Provide more details on your action plans: who exactly would do what, when, where and how?

## NOTES

1. This chapter is based on Hookins and Metcalfe (2005).
2. Aristotle, *Nicomachean Ethics*, book 3, section 1.
3. Walther (1963, Entry 25432, variants at 25428–25432).

# 11. Solutions mapping

## OVERVIEW

A picture can sometimes say a thousand words. It can be hard, especially when working collaboratively, to think about all the elements involved in enacting a set of solution concepts and their subsequent action plans. One tool for thinking about these elements and their interactions is to draw a map (sketch, diagram or picture). This might show the process by which different actions will lead to enacting each solution concept. This can also help with communications between stakeholders. This chapter explains how and why there is advantage in providing a map or picture which might help with problem-solving.[1]

## VISUALIZATION

Latour (1986) argues that knowledge advances considerably when human imagination is augmented by the rigour and reinterpretation made possible by writing and drawing. This seems to be true for art, science and the professions; the act of writing or sketching advances thinking. However, Latour (1986) sees this as particularly powerful when it assists collaboration. The classic example is map-making. When the first navigator sees a new coastline, he makes his images asynchronously and rigorously, with measurements of bearings and soundings. Written down, they allow for reinterpretation by other navigators, who might return to the same area and add more detail and rigour, refining the original map. As the map passes through numerous hands it becomes more and more detailed through each edit, each reinterpretation. The presence of the first sketch saves having to reinvent the information; rather, newcomers build on what has been learnt by those who went before.

Latour's conceptualization has also been extended by numerous other writers. Do (2000) conceives of the language of sketching as being important for ideas generation, because it provides an 'external representation' to facilitate thinking. Newell and Simon (1972) talk about sketching as a way to capture and record ideas, a brainstorming tool for idea generation and a process of reasoning and synthesizing thoughts. The 'learning loops' ideas of Schon and Wiggins (1992) focus on the reiteration of the sketch, which can potentially be perceived in different ways. These reinterpretations can have unintended, as well as intended, consequences. For example, the overview of the implicit interconnections between different entities can only be appreciated after the sketches are done (Purcell and Gero 1998). Communicating, even to oneself, and clarifying these different interpretations, is thought to facilitate ideas generation and clarification. The view of Suwa and Tversky (1996) is that the process of sketching provides visual cues for the revision and refinement of ideas. Tracking visual representations of an idea is thought to allow review through self-reflection. Forbus and Usher (2002) also argue that many abstract concepts and situations are best explained by sketching. The combination of sketching and talking can act to better define vague ideas.

Verstijnen (1997) also claims that the process of sketching can be particularly good for ideas generation. He calls these images 'idea-sketches' and believes that they are important in the creative process because the sketching allows individuals to interact with their mental images; they deliver these images to the physical world, serving the functions of both analysis and synthesis. McKim (1980) tested 'visual thinking' empirically and found that drawing not only helps to bring vague inner images into focus but also provides a record of advancing thought streams. Interestingly, Stanwick (1996) turns this around by showing that when individuals look at sketches, their mental images are much simpler than those in the sketches, even those using cartoon images. Larkin and Simon (1987) align with Latour (1986) by concluding that the use of visual representations in sketching helps the problem-solver draw upon relevant, pre-existing images as representations of prior knowledge. Stylianou (2002) indicates that, for most people, both visual and analytical thinking may need to be present and integrated in order to construct rich understandings of complicated concepts.

That said, the term 'sketching' is preferred over that of 'picturing' because sketching emphasizes the process over the end-product. 'Picture' suggests a snapshot or a final product, and 'picturing' is a clumsy verb. Bloomer (1976) and Rottger and Klante (1976) argue that pictures are similar to sketches in having lines, tones and textures on a surface. However, historically, drawings had a specific role. Clark and Scrivener (1994) and Gombrich (1966) identify that drawings consisted of lines done prior to painting. The drawing process scoped scale onto a surface, usually by pricking out boundaries with a needle. Then colour pigments were blown onto the surface to finish the painting. Hence, the drawer had a vision of the final form before starting – an essential difference to collaborative problem sketching. Clark and Scrivener (1994) and Gombrich (1966) do, however, point out that Leonardo Da Vinci's drawings were quite different, being 'visually indeterminate'. Leonardo's technique allows the drawer to start 'sketching' without the need of a clear idea in mind. The process is intended to serve as a means to stimulate the mind to invent. Hence, the final picture remains mysterious until its completion. This type of drawing is often referred to as 'Leonardo's sketching'. Clark and Scrivener (1994) and Gombrich (1966) conclude that Leonardo's sketching is the originator of the contemporary 'free-flow' or 'free-hand' methods used for creative thinking. This view is supported by many authors, such as Goel (1995), Gombrich (1966), Rodgers et al. (2000) and Tovey et al. (2003). Consequently, by using the word 'sketching', as opposed to 'drawing', it is intended to place a focus on a technique that emphasizes the act of creating. Moreover, sketches are thought to be not of visible objects, but rather of objects recalled from memory, or non-experienced objects constructed by the imagination (Tovey et al. 2003). Kolli et al. (1993) go further, arguing that sketches may include quick documentation, verbal descriptors, squiggles, abstract notations, collages, ideas with a particular focus, storyboards, and representations of activity in context.

## TALKING SKETCHES

While the term 'idea-sketch' is attractive for the purposes of this chapter, another term used by Ferguson (1992) is also attractive because it links sketches to sketching processes in collaborative groups. He uses the term 'talking sketches', which are produced during exchanges between individuals in order to clarify complex and possibly confusing parts of the problem situation. Small-groups literature (e.g. Hare 1976) indicates that small groups are more creative than individuals and make implementation easier. The act of sketching seems to lend itself to this sort of collaborative problem-solving.

Lugt's (2000) four experiments provide some empirical support for collaborative sketching, as the author argues that visual expression may foster a group's ideas-generating process in several ways, including: (1) by providing a collective graphic memory for the group members; and (2) by allowing the group members not only to be involved in conversations with their own drawings, but also to be involved in conversations with each other's drawings. Consequently, during problem-solving meetings, visual expression is thought to stimulate participants into building on each other's ideas. Lugt (2000) shows that early idea generation, including visual expression in creative problem-solving groups, changes the characteristics of the thinking process substantially. There is a high level of correlation between the quantity of useful ideas and the use of graphics in a group setting. Lugt (2000) suggests that focusing on the communication role of collaborative sketching may explain his experimental results.

According to Al-Kodmany (1999), sketching enables all members of a group to play an active role in their problem-solving exercise. He finds that 'in many cases, participants would become so involved in the discussion that they would walk up to the electronic sketch-board and draw their own ideas'. Group members were found to be comfortable with collaborative sketching because it represents a way of working that is not wholly linear. It allows for going back and re-examining given suggestions. The sketching process serves as a 'visual community conversation'. The process of sketching also produces a storyboard that shows the evolution of group understanding. Moreover, when the relationships between drawings and words grow strong, a more sophisticated shared understanding is obtained. Al-Kodmany finds that 'the sketches became guideposts to trace the development of ideas throughout the workshops and they also provided a trail to guide others who were not present'.

Massey and Wallace (1996) also suggest that the most difficult part of modelling an ill-structured problem by a group is establishing a common framework and a relaxed atmosphere to facilitate communication. The author points out that collaborative sketching works by improving communications. The process of group sketching provides ways of visually presenting and manipulating alternatives. For example, even without much explanation, participants can appreciate that the lines in a sketch represent relationships. Larkin and Simon (1987), in their chapter 'Why a diagram is (sometimes) worth ten thousand words', argue that a graphical representation system shortens the time taken for individuals to verbalize their problem interpretation. Moreover, when cartoon-like representations are introduced, the effects of humour will break communication barriers. Thus sketching not only allows each member access to a snapshot of others' mental perspectives, it also allows more time for discussing and building upon on each other's ideas.

## SYSTEMS SKETCHES

Having discussed sketching generally, and argued that problem-solving needs to be systematic, it may be useful to look at some specific example of systems sketched. The most basic form of systems sketch is shown in Figure 11.1.

*Figure 11.1    Basic form of systems sketch*

So if the transform box was a hen, it has inputs such as food and outputs such as eggs. Note: a hen does have the attributes of a system with elements (body parts), transformation (inputs to outputs), it learns, has a boundary (its skin), has connectivity of its body parts and with ecology, and is analogous to other farm animals, or could even represent a cynical person's interpretation of their own organization as a system. The weakness of this representation of a basic systems diagram is that it does not represent flow, sequence or process well.

## FLOW DIAGRAMS

A system is a process or flow, so flow diagrams can be used to represent systems: a start and finish, something transformed, purposeful with a boundary (some things excluded). The classic diagram forms for showing flow or sequence are fishbone diagrams, process mapping, flow charting generally, Gantt charts and critical path analysis diagramming (see Wikipedia).

Figure 11.2 is the classic map of the London Underground; it may be tempting to say that it represents a system. The connection between stations (elements) is shown both in terms of the rail line but also in terms of their geography. However, it does not show flow, a transformation process.

Another classic map that shows flow to some extent is Menard's map (Figure 11.3) showing Napoleon's military campaign to invade Russia. He got to Moscow and then had to retreat through the snow. It shows the number of soldiers diminishing, the temperature, the dates, the major battle towns, and so on.

Figure 11.4 is a Minard map showing the source of cattle consumed in Paris from the nineteenth century.

Leonardo de Vinci invented technical drawing and thus encouraged more functional flow diagrams. Figure 11.5 is the basic form, but they can be extended and used to display complexity, as demonstrated in Figure 11.6 in a modern depiction of the sequence of events in a United States criminal justice system. The arrows depict sequence. Flowcharts tend to be more relevant when dealing with a mechanistic process with a high level of certainty. Flowcharts lack much of the craft of the Minard cattle map, but are a very common means of representing systems.

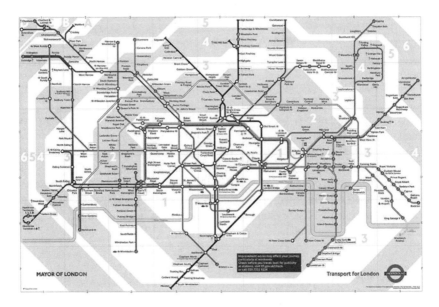

*Source:* Wikipedia.

*Figure 11.2   London Underground map*

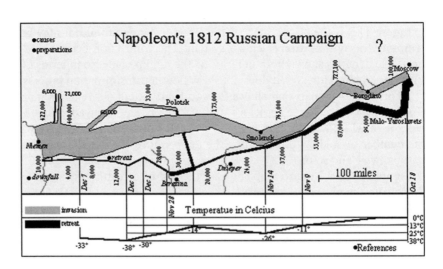

*Source:* Wikipedia.

*Figure 11.3   Menard's Russian campaign map*

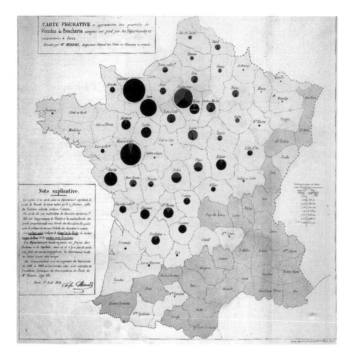

*Figure 11.4    Minard's cattle map*

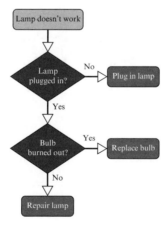

*Source:*    Wikipedia.

*Figure 11.5    Flowchart*

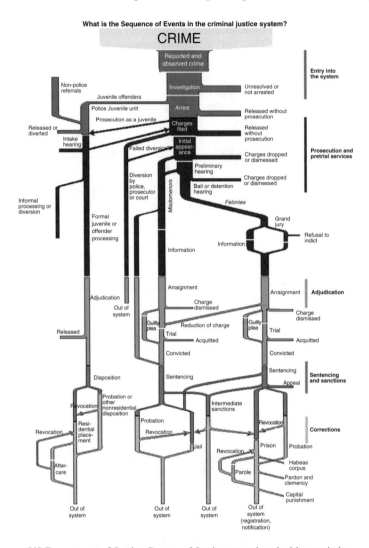

*Source:*   US Department of Justice, Bureau of Justice, reproduced with permission.

*Figure 11.6    Justice flowchart*

Process maps or flow diagrams are an established method of visualizing systems, although it is often not explicit that they are representing a system. The connection is reflected in the wording of the generic advice for how to draw a process map or flowchart, which is:

1. When drafting a process map, try to identify:
   - purpose of process (why process exists; put in heading);
   - main elements (put on post-it notes?):
     - people (who) and things: nouns as nodes
     - actions (how, what), verbs as arrows
   - boundaries: start and stopping points, what is to be excluded;
   - level of detail, audience: who will use the process map for what?
   - icons to symbolise nodes, actions, relationships, tensions and emotions.
2. Start with the trigger (what starts the process).
3. Imagine yourself walking through the process: what would be done next?
4. Stop should link back to the start of the process (circular).
5. When drafted, reflect on the controls used to ensure the process is undertaken to the required quality.
6. Identify positive and negative feedback loops; revise as appropriate.

## PLANNING PICTURES

The classic planning pictures include Gantt charts, fishbone (Ishikawa, spray) diagrams and critical path analysis maps. There is an extensive literature on these. See Wikipedia for examples, explanations and the source literature. For example see the hype cycle diagram, Figure 11.7.

The use of 'icons' to represent elements in flow or process diagrams is elaborated in a popular form of collaborative sketching which comes from the soft systems thinking literature. Checkland (1981) sees the role of his cartoon-like systems sketches as helping in the task of developing the richest possible appreciation of the situation under study: 'as rich as it can be assembled in the time available'. However, there has been considerable variation in the design and application of his so-called rich pictures. Even Checkland does not follow the same symbolic and iconic system all the time (Checkland 2000). Daellenbach (2003) comments that a rich picture may not even be a sketch. A 'rich picture' is simply a more colourful term for 'situation summary'. He does, however, identify three major components:

- elements of structure including all physical aspects such as the materials used in the structure of buildings and equipment, and products involved, as well as logical, functional and intellectual structure aspects and their properties (i.e. organizational power structure);

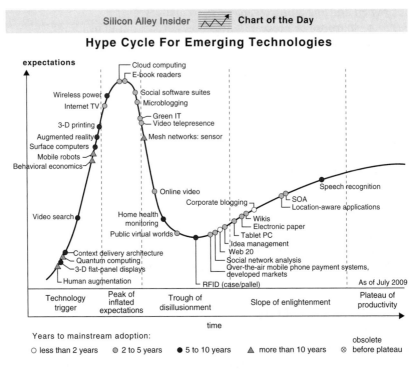

Source: Wikipedia

*Figure 11.7   Hype cycle rich picturing*

- elements of process including all dynamic aspects of the situation, that undergo or are in a state of flux (i.e. activities within the process such as handling enquiries, etc.);
- relationships between structure and process and between processes, which refer to how the structure affects or conditions processes: how does one process affect another?

In addition to these three elements, Daellenbach highlights that, for designing human activity systems, the rich picture should include not only 'hard' aspects (i.e. the physical structure and processes, etc.) of the problem situation, but also the 'soft' aspects. The soft aspects consist of personal opinions, gossip, hunches and interpersonal relationships, or what could broadly be called the concerns of the problem situation. These concerns can be shown as call-outs, balloon symbols, with short slogans, which describe the areas of concern and actual and potential issues.

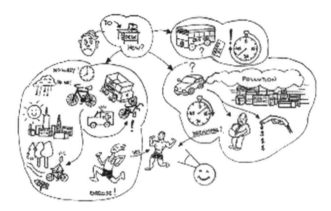

*Source:* Daellenbach (2003). Reproduced with permission of Hans Daellenbach, REA Publications.

*Figure 11.8* *'Getting to work' dilemma*

Those not involved in the drafting of this 'collaborative sketch' may have trouble fully understanding all it represents, even though there are recognizable 'cartoon icons' such as people and crossed swords. Daellenbach provides a 'getting to work' rich picture (Figure 11.8) which is a good example of a collaborative sketch that has been redrafted to a standard where it is now intended to communicate with those not involved in its drafting. It shows the dilemma of getting to work by car, bus or on a bike. But note that it is not clearly a sketch of a system, and it does not have any strong suggestion of flow.

Rich pictures are often explained as a snapshot of the problem (as a system) at one point in time. That is, they are not intended to show flow but it may be preferable for problem-solving sketches to show the flow of transformation.

The impact of cartoon icons in sketches is discussed in the cognitive literature. For example, Murch (1984), Hurvich (1981) and Tullis (1981) discuss the usefulness of colourful icons for attracting attention and making emphases. Arend et al. (1987) and Byrne (1993) find that the icons can represent extra dimensions through the use of different shapes. McDougall et al. (2000) and McDougall et al. (2001) conclude that icons are thought to be effective in sketches because they allow users to draw on correspondences between the real-world objects they depict and the representations of those objects embedded in problem sketches. Drawing on these correspondences often forces users to be explicit in their interpretations of the problem domain objects. Additionally, according to

Eulie (1969), a cartoon icon is a combination of humour, exaggeration and symbols, which presents a point of view in a simple form of drawing. Horn (1980) suggests that cartoons have the ability to make a point without the semantic ambiguities inherent in the written word. Ball (1982) indicates that messages can be easily communicated through the medium of humour. Nelson (1975) highlights that, through humour, the receiver will pay extra attention to the information to be processed. Therefore, the combination of cartoon icons becomes a powerful medium for representation, collaboration and thinking.

Figure 11.9 is a rich picture of strategy formulation using the concept-driven approach outlined in this book. Although included here, many rich pictures do not have icons.

Interestingly, Checkland acknowledges a debt to the American philosophers Churchman, James and Dewey who make the connection between soft systems methodology (SSM), rich picturing and pragmatic thinking. Moreover, as mentioned, there is extensive evidence that the label 'rich picturing' has been liberally applied to a range of collaborative sketching exercises. Many of these do not insist on sketches of systems having to place a lot of emphasis on flow, change or process, or on how the system moves from a problem to a solution.

That said, the main contribution of rich picturing to the extensive world of collaborative sketching is that it attempts to show the relationships between stakeholders during a process. Relationship diagrams in systems thinking are often called 'influence diagrams'. The use of relationships, icons and flow distinguishes rich pictures. They therefore have at least two types of arrows, one showing relationships and the other showing flow, such as a flowchart or process map. The use of thought bubbles helps to maintain an appreciation of the distinction between human and technical systems.

## CONCLUSION

Collaborative sketching is used to help those designing solutions to present the solution concepts and related action plans. However, many picture forms do not insist on a lot of emphasis on the flow, the process of transformation inherent in problem-solving. Nor do they strongly show the relationship between stakeholders during a process of change. Solutions change things. Checkland's original rich pictures, for example of an insurance company, did show activities. There would seem to be a strong need to suggest that pictures showing how a solution is to be enacted should emphasize process or flow: how the past is to be changed to the future. Multiple-cause diagrams are a further option (Daellenbach 2003).

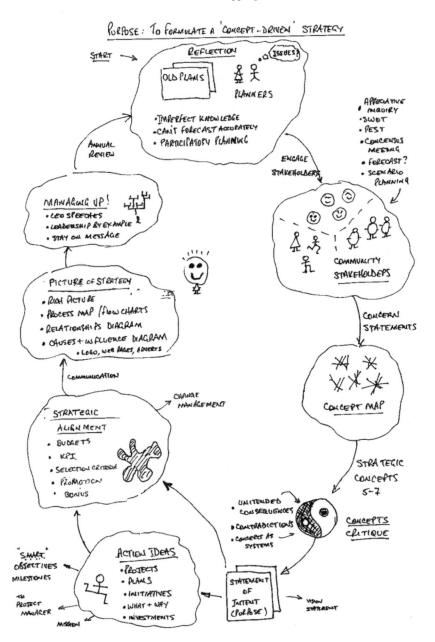

*Figure 11.9    Rich picture of strategy formulation using the concept-driven approach*

The Open University website (http://systems.open.ac.uk/materials/t552/index.htm) provides an excellent illustration and discussion of picturing systems. The Open University's academics talk of problem-solving as being thought of as a system that can be represented in a diagram showing its elements as icons, relationships and activities, and so on. For a wider discussion on sketching problems see http://openlearn.open.ac.uk/file.php/1290/formats/print.htm.

## APPLICATION

Prepare a graphic to represent how you conceptualized your problem.

## NOTE

1. This chapter is based on East and Metcalfe (2002).

# 12. Conclusion

## OVERVIEW

It seems appropriate to conclude by reflecting on what has been said previously. First, the concept that will be used for this reflection is 'process'. Hopefully the book has provided an explanation of why this process of problem-solving has been advocated. It is a process of making the concepts in use clear. Second, this chapter will reflect on the book using the concept of 'explaining human behaviour'.

## PROCESS TABLE

## PRAGMATIC EXPLANATION OF HUMAN BEHAVIOUR

This book has explained my understanding of how pragmatic concepts solve problems. However, partly because humans are problem-solvers, this book has therefore also explained why humans act as they do. It has provided a theory of human behaviour. For over a century the linguistic stream of pragmatism has been developing an explanation of our behaviour actions based on experienced actions, especially social interactions, which includes language. These interactions provide us with remembered, mutable, patterns of activity; packages of experiences remembered with their consequences. Smiling, justice, planning and innovation are examples. What seems like a reasonable future action depends on which of these patterns of activity we use to reflect on the world as it comes to hand. These patterns of activity can be named (pragmatic concepts) and used in reflection for complex reasoning. As a conclusion to this book, this linguistic pragmatic explanation of human behaviour, how we think and how we reason, will be restated in an alternative summarized form.

*Table 12.1    Process table*

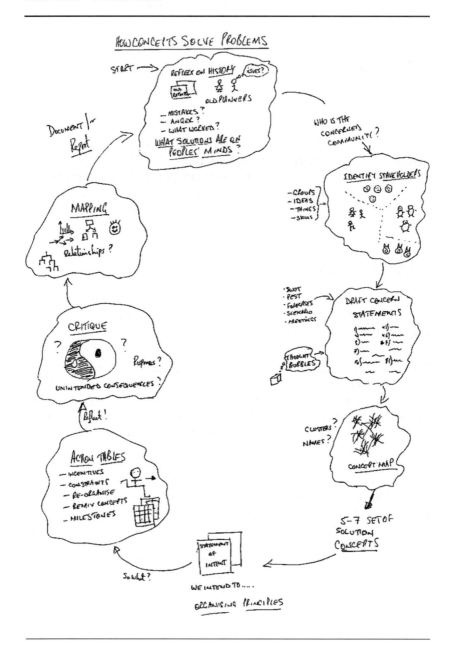

*Table 12.1*   (continued)

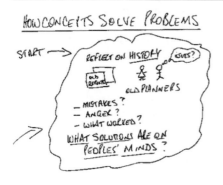

The starting point for using a process of making the concepts clear to solve problems, is to feel concern over something. The reflection literature argues that you will be very quickly able to formulate a conjecture of what needs to be done. This conjecture will contain the default concepts that are being used to interpret the problem. These default concepts come from your past experience. Solving the problem comes from thinking through the implications of applying the default concepts and looking for more useful ones.

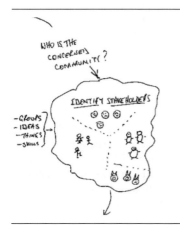

The source of alternative concepts is the stakeholders, others that will be interested in the problem. Identifying a wide range of stakeholders is crucial in generating novel concepts. It needs to include researchers and people working on analogous problems. Alternative ways of thinking 'who are the stakeholders' is required. Things might be anthropomorphized to generate more stakeholders. You are trying to draw on the stakeholders' past experiences.

You need to record the stakeholders' concerns related to your problem in the form of a conjecture or conditional statement. This will contain more information than a simple sentence. Number or code each statement and draft a table showing which statements are thought similar and why. The reasons different pairs of statements are linked can be many and varied (multidimensional).

*Table 12.1*   (continued)

| | |
|---|---|
| 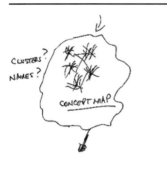 | Draft a concept map (statement or idea network) using software that makes the nodes repel (springiness), as this encourages clusters. Look for about five clusters. After looking at the statements in each cluster, give each cluster a representative name or label – a meta-narrative. These are potential concepts for how to react to the problem. |
| 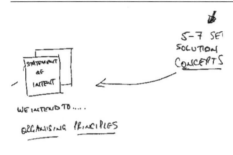 | Reflect on the relationship between the concepts. There should be a slight tension between them; they should make up a complementary set – a system of concepts. Record the concepts, with brief descriptions, in a Statement of Intent. Treat the concept as being the organizing principles for the response to the problem. |
| 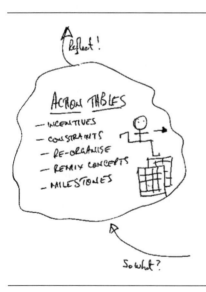 | Now draft a set of actions of what needs to be done classified under each concept, the action plan. These might include the removal of constraints or the implementation of incentives. This is your response to the problem. |

*Table 12.1*   (continued)

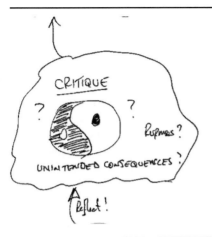

Before acting on your response, reflect on the possible paradoxical consequences. How will intelligent others react to stop you successfully achieving your response?

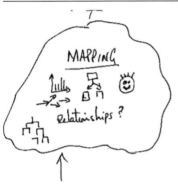

Draft a picture of your response. This is to provide an overview of your response and to think more about relationships between elements in your response. If done appropriately it might also quickly demonstrate to stakeholders what you intend to do.

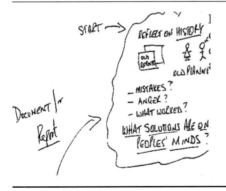

Having attempted to enact the response your set of concepts or organizing principles suggest, you may want to use the experience to have another attempt at identifying a problem and coming up with ways to react to it.

# PART I:   MIMICKING

## Problem Statement

In a TedTalks presentation, Kirby Ferguson argues that 'everything is a remix' and that this is a better way to think about creativity. Copying, transforming and combining, he proclaims, are how we create. He is mainly talking about music being presented as new, when it clearly is not. He quotes Blind Willie McTell as saying, 'I jump 'em from other writers, but I arrange 'em my own way'. But Ferguson also quotes Henry Ford as saying, 'I invented nothing new. I simply assembled the discoveries of other men, behind whom were centuries of work'. Ferguson also uses Steve Jobs making his keynote speech in 2007, introducing the multi-touch on the iPhone. Jobs says, 'We invented it, and *boy* are we going to patent it'. Ferguson compares this to a TedTalk from a year earlier, showing Jeff Han demonstrating the same multi-touch screen technology and saying, 'This isn't new. It's the small pieces that are different'. Ferguson is arguing that the iPhone is simply the remix of the multi-touch screen into phones. However, Ferguson's argument is itself a remix. There is a century-old, if not well-known, philosophy explaining human behaviour as copying (mimicking or imitating).

Plato's notion of hidden and abstract ideal forms represents the classic explanation of how we think, and therefore how we act. This argues that we should think by making a comparison with ideal forms. The theory of ideal forms encourages an endless quest to reveal the Grail. It is the mystical, invisible, behind the veil, ghosts in the machine, souls and the essence; a quest to reveal the ideal form in analysis, behaviour, organization, bodily form or in scenery. Plato thought geometry and algebra to be the greatest examples, their pure form abstractions being preferable to the confused reality of the physical material world. Truth and theory are two further examples of his idealism – iconic, universal and untouchable by the confusions of mankind. It is easy to see the appeal of idealism to the early Christian theologians. Seeking goals or visions and the use of numbers, statistics and mathematics in planning are modern managerial manifestations of idealism, as are aspiring to the actions of gurus, heroes or saints.

In the modern era, Descartes refined Plato's idealism. His mind–body dualism introduces the mind as the ideal form of the brain; the soul of the brain. We think with our God-given minds. Immanuel Kant divided this mystical mind into compartments and assigned it default functions. These process the before-experience functions of ethics, space, time and causality. Kant's British contemporary Jeremy Bentham looked more to explaining how we think by comparing alternative behaviours, those that result in pleasure and those that would avoid pain. More generically, we compare using our interests and fears. This raises, even with him, the question of why we take risks, whose interests and fears they really are, how we acquire them and how we choose an appropriate reaction. We can react the same or differently to repeated interests or fears in different contexts.

More recently, Skinner argued against the very presence of purposeful thoughts, rather that our actions are merely mechanistic responses, an explanation that takes no account of the past experience or any internal functions of an organism. He thought that we react rather than think. Charles Taylor elaborates on Chomsky's critique of Skinner, arguing that we need a more purposeful action-based explanation of our thoughts and actions. However, Chomsky and many others' functional localizations explanation of thought processing still assume thinking comes first from within an individual, a reasoning, or feeling, isolated entity. This inside-out explanation of how we think therefore suffers the same limitation as Descartes's abstract mind, Kant's notion of mental representations, Bentham's pleasure-seeking, or Freud's unfindable unconsciousness. It leads to assuming that human thinking is akin to a computer. Language and social interaction are relegated to the role of being how independently generated thoughts are communicated, how worded and to whom.

The computer metaphor of human thinking was encouraged by Herbert Simon in his influential work *Model of Man* (1975) and his chess-playing software. This encouraged the stream of artificial intelligence (AI) that tried to build a computerized version of an independent, calculative mind. The philosopher Hubert Dreyfus argued from the beginning that this whole project was ill-conceived. Rather, a more Heideggerian, social interaction, or outside-in interpretation of how we think was necessary. Dreyfus has been vindicated by the failure of the Descartes model of artificial intelligence and by modern brain scans. Neuroscience has, perhaps not surprisingly, failed to find anyone's mind, or consciousness, permanent localizations or any abstraction of our brains. However, our brain clearly allows us to interact intelligently with the world as it presents to us. Our masses of neuron connections somehow enable us to remember, recall and manipulate sense experiences. These memories can be chunked and recombined into unexperienced combinations as in dreams and imaged solution to problems. Brain scans have not found a mind function that processes images, nor one that builds computer-like calculative models of the world, to provide thoughts of how to act. Many neuroscientists, typically materialist or physicalists, reject the idealism agenda, seeking an earthly, physics or evolutionary interpretation of how we think and act. They want to do what Wittgenstein calls bringing the ideal into reality. Also, they seek to understand how we actually think, rather than how we should think to be either moral or scientific.

Before neuroscience, material philosophers such as Hume and Nietzsche sought ways of explaining our thinking and actions that could be explained without referring to mystical or spiritual mental abstractions. A formidable array of philosophers have aligned with this non-idealistic approach. They tend to draw on Aristotle's dialectic argument and Hegel's social and temporal approach to knowledge to provide their alternative explanation of how we know and act. Under this, what we think and do moves from comparison against ideals to what Richard Rorty (1982, 1989) calls a negotiated coherence with our physical and social world. Comparison still, but now between alternative past experiences.

Milgram's electrocution and Stanford's prison experiments found that our reasoning of how to act seems to be a consequence of social interactions and context. Participants acted out their randomly allocated social role to the extent that they were willing to hurt others. Rather than being isolated calculative individuals, inspired by ideals, passions or individual reasoning, some sort of social interaction effect was determining what the participant thought was appropriate action. This suggests the need for an explanation of our actions which includes that we are role-playing. These roles are learnt from observing others, and can be varied depending on the situation. This is a social interaction explanation of our actions.

It will be argued, more directly below, that our thoughts and behaviour can be explained as mimicking. What we mimic is experienced patterns of activity. To mimic is to compare. This capacity to compare forms the basis of thinking. We can choose what to mimic or what to compare. Our thoughts and subsequent actions are the result of which recombinations of these patterns of activity we choose to compare: we jump 'em from others, but arrange 'em in our own way. This social interaction (outside-in) explanation of human behaviour explains our actions using only the earthly concepts of comparison, sense experiences, pattern recognition and a memory capable of remixing past experiences.

## Mimicking

That we mimic (imitate, copy or reuse) the actions of others does not seem too hard to argue. Much of what we do personally and as management practice is clearly one of copying the perceived actions of others: perhaps parents, peers, professionals, heroes, fashion leaders and cultural icons. What we wear, what we say and what we do can easily be traced to a combination of others. Business schools mimic each other. Thomas Kuhn's scientific paradigms, or schools of thought, for example, can be seen as groups that mimic similar theories. The problem is explaining how much of our behaviour is mimicking and what exactly we are mimicking. This then needs to provide a means of thinking and role of language in that thinking. Perhaps the most influential writer arguing for the mimicking explanation of human behaviour is Heidegger in his *Being and Time* (2008). Despite his politics, he seems to have influenced most of the late-twentieth-century Continental philosophers including the later pragmatists such as Richard Rorty and Stephen Toulmin (Toulmin 1972). Heidegger explains our thoughts and actions as knowing how, not what. This sets up knowing as being about actions, not the characteristics of objects.

Written before Heidegger, the early pragmatists such as William James, the first Professor of Psychology at Harvard University, were also interested in the issue of how our reasoning (logic, thinking) informed our selection of alternative actions. They concluded that actions came before thoughts; we experience actions then think, not think then act. This aligns to the notion that we first mimic and then think. These pragmatists were aware of the work of the nineteenth-century European critical social theorists, but rather than looking at revolutionary politics, Peirce, James and Dewey looked to emancipation of human action from a study of how we reason, and thus of knowledge. The pragmatic maxim was that we conceive of things in terms of their effects; things are what they do, their actions, that is, the consequences of their existing. The effects, actions or consequences are temporal, they involve time, and so are patterns of activity. For example, a mother's smile takes time to enact so is a pattern of activity. A management decision is a pattern of activity, as is professional ethics. Even a face or building can be seen to be a pattern of activity if seen to be what it does. A face provides recognition and a building protects.

Like reproduction, mimicking is our replication, often imperfectly, of others – our abstraction of their actions. It provides our pre-thought actions as experiences. After sensing an experience our innate pattern-recognition abilities are thought to kick in and abduct, or abstract, a pattern of activity that we attempt to replicate. So after seeing examples of smiling, running, jumping and so on, we copy them but also abstract a remembered pattern for recognizing each of these activities. This may involve use of our mirror neurons. Smiling is an obvious example of what we mimic as a child, but language may be a more significant example. Language is at first the imperfect mimicking of the sound patterns of others. It is an imperfect mimic and mutation of what we hear others doing. When we try talking as a child, we get encouraging feedback, if only as getting others to understand our wants. But we develop our own distinctive voice because of our imperfect copying and by choosing what and who to mimic.

Mimicking, as acting, therefore places action as prior and central to language and thinking, as suggested by Heidegger. It provides memories through our senses as experience, which includes their consequences in different contexts. Apparently, these memories can be separated into discrete parts and recombined. This may be done without self-control, as in dreams. Else it can be done purposely, as in thought experiments. Scientific physical experimentation is a controlled remixing of mimicked past actions that can result in novel combinations and findings. The evolutionary mechanism of mimicking seems obvious; those babies who mimicked their parents more closely had more offspring. They were using the experience of their parents. Camazine et al. (2001) see mimicking in their empirical work with social insects, using it to explain how they make strategic responses to environmental threats with no leadership structure. Successful outcomes occur if the insects mimic the actions of the successful. Humans becoming self-conscious at around seven years of age can be seen as becoming critically competent at being aware of choosing who to mimic when, of mimicking reasoning, and of being able to extract novel mimics from events or stories. Free will, following from self-consciousness, can be seen to be the ability to choose what to mimic when.

Rene Girard's mimetic desire considerably extends the discussion on mimicking, using it to explain numerous human actions including aggression and envy. Aggression is initiated against those who mimic others rather than ourselves, and material envy is explained as envy of those who have means of acting in ways that we do not. Mimicking can be used to interpret social theory. Bruno Latour's actor network theory and Gabriel Tarde's social theory mention imitation. Our social network provides an abstraction of who we mimic. Our lives and our societies are made up of networks of influences. These include historical, media and mythical characters. Our actions reflect this network of influences, providing those we mimic. Asch's famous social pressure experiments can be read to explain the relationship between empirical evidence and mimicking. Unsuspecting subjects are often found to repeat what others say rather than the evidence of their own eyes. Social mimicking can blind us to our own observations of the physical world. Axelrod's work on the evolution of cooperation can be read as mimicking. Cooperation is close to mimicking. Those that mimic the successful are expected to outperform those who do not.

What we mimic, our actions, these are patterns of activity. Humans and other animals need, and seem to have, a capability to recognize movement and see pattern in it, for example which direction something is moving. Babies are attracted to movement. We have a particular mental sensitivity to movement. Our brains seem to have a strong pattern recognition capacity. They can see patterns in everything, even where there are none. Being able to see everything as patterns of activity provides the source of what can be remembered, remixed and compared. Colours are seen as patterns, their wavelength or their impact. Mathematics can be seen to be a pattern recognition exercise (Resnick 1999). Herbert Simon thought intuition was explained as implicitly recognizing novel and useful patterns. This is very similar to Klein's (1999) findings that experienced nurses and firemen had a skill in recognizing important patterns even if they could not articulate them. Camazine et al.'s (2001) insect studies, Heidegger and activity theory (Engestrom 1987) seem to agree that we can not only identify patterns in the actions of others but also action patterns in physical structures and tools. Camazine et al call this stigmergy, pointing to experiments where ants respond apparently instinctively to structures common in an ant nest, such as half complete arches. Heidegger mentions hammers and doors, how we can extrapolate the actions required by the presence of something which can be extended by our experiences of patterns of similar things. James aligns with Heidegger, objects are pattern of activities, things are what they do, their consequences of being. We see everything as a pattern of activities, able to be remembered, remixed, mimicked, and compared.

**Social Consequences**

The choice of what to mimic may be random but past consequences play a role. Selection of our action by past consequences is something both Charles Darwin (1871) and Skinner (1981) report from their observations. They argue that if we mimic something and like the consequences, then we are likely to repeat it. Biological species can learn by the consequences of their actions: feedback loops. Darwin observed this in the young, when learning about both actions and language. Skinner's box for training pigeons with food rewards can be seen as being their using consequences to learn. This connects consequences with responses and reactions. Consequences, including what leads to pain or rewards, can be seen to be an extended end part to any experienced pattern of activity. When this happens, this seems to follow.

The use of consequences, rather than causes, to explain anything is also to take the pragmatic turn. James argued that we do and should interpret everything in terms of consequences. As in evolution, function leads form. He uses this to define pragmatism. Using consequences extends the pattern of activity recognizable in everything. For example, a plan can be defined and evaluated by what it does: the consequences of its existing. This is in contrast to evaluating it by its characteristics, by comparing it to an ideal form. Prediction inherent in the plan is interpreted as anticipating the future from reflection on past experiences. The use of consequences, the actions subsequent to an event, was a deliberate move by the pragmatists to overcome the blocking effect of thinking about science as a study of inherent properties, or in terms of cause and effect. They used Hume's point that causes are not directly observable, only effects: outcomes or consequences. This made causes unscientific. The preferred alternative was to argue that science is about the study of effects, outcomes or consequences. Nietzsche seems to have started the modern concern over causes as being the basic study of science when he noticed that causes suggest prediction but could only be recalled as an *ex post*-experienced pattern of activity, a historic sequence of events. This suggests that causes be thought of historically, as consequences. Much of science drew on Kant's arguments that cause-and-effect is hardwired into our illusive minds, along with the concept of time and space. These were therefore obvious concepts to use as the basis of scientific investigation. Nietzsche saw this as a circular argument. James, who called Hume the father of pragmatism, took up this disagreement with Kant. He wanted rather to use past experiences, and their consequences, as the basis of all thinking.

The consequences of our mimics that we remember seem mainly to be the social rather than the physical consequences. Rorty draws on Dewey's book *Experience and Nature* (1958 [1929]) to argue for the importance of social interactions in determining our actions. He points out that Dewey seems to have regretted not calling the book *Experience and Society*. It does include mention of the role of art. Dewey used the book to make the argument that our thoughts and actions are the result of interactions with others. The 'others' he usually refers to are people, so the interactions are social rather than with the physical world. Spinoza agrees that thinking starts with us remembering (Rosenfeld 1988) some pattern of activity. This could be the actions of others. Our memory recognizes a pattern along with its associated sensations (precepts) as its consequences – how satisfying it was. Actions plus sensation consequences provide experiences, most of which are inter-social, that is, learnt from those we connect with. Heidegger and Rorty argue that for mimicking humans, the social consequence or response is more telling than the physical. For example, if we harm someone physically or economically, then our social conditioning tells us whether we are a hero or not. Children have to learn embarrassment. Our responses to events that occur to us have to be learnt from those around us. Parents teach children how to respond to pain.

**Thinking and Knowing**

Getting from mimicking to thinking seems a simple enough step. Mimicking is the capacity to copy or imitate patterns of activity, by first comparing your actions to those of others. After comparing what someone else is doing to your own actions, mimicking, it is possible to use this comparison capacity to compare any experienced activity with any other. For example smiling can be compared with running, or one measurement with another, or smiling with a measurement. An infinite pairing becomes possible. Extending the examples, the activity of organizing can be compared to almost anything: democracy, power, evolution, technology or boundaries. Whichever is used will make alternative responses seem rational. So from mimicking we have comparison and therefore thinking, and reaction. Comparing is an extension of pattern recognition, comparing this pattern to that. Dewey explains this comparison as 'reflection'. We reflect one mimic or pattern of activity on another. Richard Rorty talks directly of comparison and mirrors. Douglas Hoftstader talks about 'analogy' as core to cognition. Analogy is comparison. Thinking seems to be a process of comparison. One pattern of activity is compared to another. This aligns with the scientific method generally. Measurement is a comparison against agreed standards. Pragmatism suggests these comparisons not be with ideals but with experienced patterns of activity. Reasoning and dialectic argument can be explained as being mimics. It is another learnt pattern of behaviour, which will be used depending on the consequences of doing so. The concepts in a proposition are compared and contrasted.

Thinking, under this pragmatic explanation, involves using one experienced pattern to compare (reflect on, interpret, give meaning to) another. Dewey, in *How We Think* (1982 [1910]), uses the example of needing to select the appropriate form of transport to get across town to a meeting (see Chapter 1, this volume). He has several experiences of getting across town before, and several experiences of the consequences of using a bus, taking a taxi and driving his car. He has heard other people's experiences. From these experiences he has chosen to use the three patterns of activity speed, convenience and cost to compare with the activity of arriving at meetings. Choosing now how to get across town involves reflecting on each of these alternatives. This could be done implicitly, without his explicitly choosing which to use. Or the choice of which pattern to use might be purposeful. He could set up a table and write down his thoughts after reflecting off each in turn. In his classic article 'How to make your ideas clear', Charles Peirce (1878), and later John Dewey, argue that clear or rigorous thinking (interpretation, reflection) involves explicitly selecting and applying which patterns to use. Unclear thinking means applying a pattern without being explicitly aware of doing so, automatic thinking, almost a reflex. This will be an implicit mimic from unreflected prior influences. With clear thinking, the mimicked pattern will be explicitly chosen. Unclear thinking about what is an organization might assume the legal definition of an organization. Clear thinking would appreciate that this default concept is being assumed. It would then explicitly use other concepts such as networks, machines, prisons and power struggles.

To argue that comparing experiences is thinking, and that those experiences include consequences, has significant implications for the definition of knowing. It suggests that we know with memories of experiences, with their associated consequences. We know how actions can be taken. Saying 'I know your address' is saying, 'I know how to use the experience of people having homes, to interpret how to find you'. Knowing is what one experience tells you about another. This is seeing patterns in the comparison. Actions, patterns of activity, or rather past experiences, therefore define knowledge (knowing how). To be consistent, knowing needs to be evaluated by the actions (experiences) it suggests. This provides underpinning to Karl Marx and John Dewey wanting knowledge to be useful, to provide advice on how to improve the world (Rytina and Loomis 1970). The act of searching for new knowledge, inquiry, becomes one of searching for past experiences that have not yet been used to reflect on the world.

**Recap**

Rorty and Toulmin use Heidegger to elaborate their pragmatism. They argue that pluralist pragmatism is more optimistic, and communal, than his stream of Continental philosophy. But all agree that thoughts and actions are a social act learnt and evaluated from interactions with others. Knowing is memories of knowing how. They minimize the idea that thinking is about acquiring objective facts and goes behind any distinction between explicit and tacit knowledge. What we think and how we act depends on the concerns, interests or beliefs of those around us. These come from their social interactions. We learn how to act from socialization with beings that have an ability to inquire into their own thoughts and lives (*dasein*; mainly humans). Mimicking satisfies this socialization process. In *Being and Time* Heidegger (2008) distinguishes unappreciated entities (present to hand) from entities we have recognized as having a use (ready to hand). Things move from being around but not appreciated (present to hand) to being useful (ready to hand) by coming to our attention; they are brought into our attention. This occurs due to a change in our concerns (a disturbance). This awareness of new patterns of activity is brought to our notice, and shared through the process of socialization. These new patterns then provide a reinterpretation of events occurring around us. What comes to our attention is the result of the concerns and subsequent actions of others, including their language noises. These move what we often call objects from our unappreciated surroundings into being something conceived. Heidegger extensively uses the example of hammers as a process technology. Watching and listening to other beings makes us interpret how hammers can be used: their possible actions.

Rejecting the subject–object Cartesian divide, including mind and body separation and thus us having an unconscious, Heidegger and the modern pragmatists therefore explain our thoughts and actions as being the result of observing and then mimicking selected actions of other beings. This provides our means of knowing how to act in the universe and our social world. There are not any self-defined objects out there, rather mimicked classifications. Our thoughts emerge out of experiencing the actions of other beings. Individual differences in our thoughts are explained by the combination of whom we copy. Knowledge is knowing how, actions (patterns), not what: we are how we act, what we act, which we get from a social interaction process that itself is changing. For example, gravity is knowing how to explain falling objects to whom, which can be expected to change over time. Heidegger reflexively includes time in his thoughts about social interactions. Everything is in a rate of activity, seeing so-called 'objects' as static is only because they are changing at a slower rate than the actions taken on those objects. An object is what it does. All of which suggests an explanation of our thoughts and actions being the result of a dynamic interactive socialization processes. This 'outside-in' social interaction explanation of our thinking is in contrast to the notion of an independent calculating brain, reasoning out its own actions.

**Application**

This section has explored what has been called the pragmatists' argument that our thoughts can be explained as compared remixes of mimics. We recognize and compare patterns of activity. Comparison is thinking. What we compare makes subsequent reactions appear reasonable. For example, reflecting on strategy formulation using sociology rather than economics leads to different yet still reasonable responses of how the formulation process needs to be undertaken. Accepting that our behaviour is based on mimicking, comparison and knowing how, has significant implications for management practice. Management itself, how it is done, or not, and how much impact it has on others can be explained by mimicking. The pragmatic explanation of organization theory is that they mimic the actions of other perceived successful organizations. Universities are presently mimicking commercial organizations. Salaries, job titles, clothing, product mix, organizational structures, marketing strategies, leadership styles and workplace practices can be explained by who is being mimicked. Decisions can be explained by who is being mimicked rather than by the use of either reasoning or emotions (sensations). Put another way, decisions and other management actions can be understood by asking where those involved got their ideas, from whom. Innovation is in mimicking and remixing from a novel source. The extensive experimental evidence behind the use of goal (target, objectives) setting can also be explained as mimicking. The goal states what is to be mimicked: sales quantity or return on capital. Whether the goal is strived for is predicted to depend on what respected others are doing. If there were financial rewards for achieving the goals, then deciding to mimic respected others would include whether there was a desire to mimic the rich generally. The mimicking explanation of human behaviour predicts that someone's behaviour is determined by who they mimic either implicitly or explicitly. Explicitly identifying who we are mimicking and why, what pattern of activity, is expected to be informative.

Kahneman and Klein (2009) wrote a comparison of their individual empirical findings on intuitive decision-making. They both agree with Herbert Simon that intuition involves the implicit recognition of patterns. The examples of Kahneman's work used in this paper involve how well subjects make selections at interviews and of stock market purchases, compared to the use of simple mathematical heuristics. People do not do very well. Using pattern recognition, the findings confirm that our identifying pattern in one situation does not provide a reliable basis for predicting pattern in another. Prediction can only be reflection on past experience. Meanwhile, Klein studied experienced firemen and nurses making intuitive and fast decisions at work. He found their expertise required that they noticed and responded appropriately to subtle patterns in fires or in medical conditions. They did this well. Pattern recognition would expect this as they are only being asked to recognize patterns in the situation before them. It predicts that humans can only be expected to make skilful decisions when asked to recognize patterns they have experienced. Expertise is an ability to recognize very particular or subtle patterns. Kahneman and Klein mention the estimate that a chess master will have access to over 20 000 end-game patterns. Pattern recognition offers a researchable distinction between why Kahneman and Klein get such different results. It also explains Klein's work on sense-making, where sense-making is a process of explicitly looking for new patterns in whatever is presenting itself. It also explains Kahneman's work on framing if a frame is the pattern of activity used to reflect on a problem.

## Language

Humans have language. This evolved long after animals' ability to think and act. It has a significant impact on our ability to perform and respond to complex thinking (Vygotsky 1986). For the pragmatic explanation of human behaviour to have weight, it needs to explain the role of language in our thinking in relation to mimicking. This can be done. Briefly, the pragmatists' argument is that mimicked patterns of activity can be named. Smiling has been mentioned. This is a named pattern of activity. Patterns that have been named can be compared; smiling with running, for example. When named, patterns can be shared with others. This provides us with new ways of thinking about old patterns of activity. Patterns of activity are called conceptions by James, and when named, concepts. Toulmin elaborates. Given the possible confusion with idealistic concepts, these named patterns of activity might best be called pragmatic concepts. The role of language and pragmatic concepts in thinking will be elaborated upon in Part II of this chapter.

**Conclusion**

This section has explored what has been called the pragmatic explanation of human behaviour. It used the concepts of mimicking, actions, comparion, consequences and memory remixing to reflect on how we think and therefore how we act. It argued that thinking can be explained from a starting position of our having a genetic ability to mimic. This requires us to be able to recognize patterns of activity, to compare, to remember and to remix those patterns. These capabilities can be justified using evolution theory, and do not contradict any empirical findings of modern neuroscience. Emotions are the sensations remembered with the patterns of activity. Reasoning is an example of mimicked behaviour, as is decision-making. Analysis can make explicit who is being mimicked. The social consequences of using a mimic influences which mimics we reuse. Mathematics, colours, things, emotions, and much of human information processing research can be explained through the notion of comparing patterns of activity; mimicking requires comparison. Whatever is used to compare patterns of activity determines what we think is a reasonable reaction. Knowledge is based in actions (experiences), it is knowing how. The main limitation to this pragmatic, social interaction, outside-in explanation of human behaviour is the role of language. Clearly language is actively involved in complex thinking. How can we discuss equity if we do not understand the word 'equity'? This will be discussed in Part II, but if words are named patterns of activity then the connection between mimicking and language is starting to be made.

# PART II:   INCLUDING LANGUAGE

### Pragmatic Concepts

This summary of the pragmatic explanation of human behaviour has so far explained human behaviour without consideration of language. This will now be included in a manner consistent with the earlier explanation. This part will therefore present an argument that pragmatic linguistic concepts explain the role of language in how humans think and therefore act.

Consider the classic management problem of trying to get a team of people to do something they would rather not do. How do pragmatic linguistic concepts solve this management problem? More generally, how can words help with this problem? The manager might draw up a list of possible actions. This might include: offer financial rewards, appeal to their membership in a special problem-solving team, threaten them with retribution under their employment contract, lead by example, and/or rationally explain what needs to be done and why they should want to do it. That is, the manager could use the concepts of money, inclusion, threat, leadership and/or explanation to solve the problem. If money is to be used then concepts such as piecework, hourly rates or incentive bonuses can be used to decide how they are to be paid. The concepts make sense of structure, labels, and a classification system for the problem; they provide organizing principles. Eventually an action will need to taken, but the concepts have determined which action would be rational. This example will raise the question of what is therefore meant by a 'concept'.

In Part I it was argued that humans have the ability to identify and compare patterns of activity. This enables young children and management practitioners to mimic the behaviours of those they think are successful. Young children may identify and mimic patterns such as smiling, running and how to alter the behaviour of others. Management practitioners may identify and mimic patterns such as problem-solving, leadership and innovation. As well as comparing our own patterns of actions to those of others, these patterns can be compared with each other. This is thinking. So a baby may compare (reflect) on how to change the behaviour of others using smiling and running. Each will make different future actions seem reasonable. A practitioner may compare (think about) the act of problem-solving using the patterns identified as the act of leadership. These patterns of activity may or may not be named. Douglas Adams provides books full of examples of activities which have not been named in his amusing book series *The Meaning Of Liff* (Adams and Lloyd 1983). However, if named (turned into language) these patterns of activity can be pointed out to others, thus increasing the number of patterns that we can use in our comparisons. When named, the pragmatists call these named patterns of activity, concepts. To distinguish them from ideal concepts, they will be called pragmatic concepts.

Each pragmatic concept, as words or sequences of words, represents a pattern of activity. Smiling is what smiling does; the consequences of its existing. This does not exclude numbers, colours, abstractions and objects. These can all be interpreted as patterns of activity. Numbers and colours distinguish things. Numbers represent a quantity pattern; the number 6 divides whatever into six parts while the number 3 divides it into three parts. Numbering things enables them to be added to other things. The concept of $\pi$ is the act of dividing the circumference of a circle by its diameter. Colours are patterns of wavelengths. Blue distinguishes blue berries from red ones. Objects can be defined by what they do, understood by the consequence of their existing. Even an abstract question such as 'why' can be interpreted as asking for the cause and effect, and thus becomes an activity. A face smiles, democracy encourages voting. Shakespeare shows us how easily a noun can be changed into a verb, and vice versa. For pragmatism, words (and phrases) represent an activity; therefore knowledge is based on actions, including knowing itself.

**Mechanics**

William James first explains conception by distinguishing it from perception. Perception is external stimuli entering through our senses. Conception is experience that allows us to interpret what we perceive. Spinoza and Gilbert agree that we need these conceptions to make sense of perceptions, if only to determine whether they represent a threat or opportunity. The experiences that provide conceptions are patterns of activity remembered in our memory. The more patterns available to us, the greater is our ability to creatively interpret our perceptions. These patterns of activity can be remembered and used to interpret the world with or without our even being aware of their existence. If named, they are called concepts. We must be born with certain genetic capabilities such as the ability of pattern recognition and mimicking to provide and apply these patterns. Other capabilities may be empathy, hunger, pain, cooperation, and fight or flight. These, and protective parents, need to give us enough time to experience survival patterns if we are to avoid becoming food. However, there would be great evolutionary advantage if we could generate new patterns from combinations of patterns we had experienced. Mimicking requires comparison of what we do with the actions of others. An ability to compare means we can also compare patterns of activity to each other. We can compare running and walking and generate a remix such as jogging. Comparison allows us to generate new patterns – ideas. So we can remix new patterns but we could generate even more if we could learn from others. Language allows us to learn huge numbers of new patterns and remixes from others. We can learn from their experiences. We fail to notice patterns that others notice. Language exposes us to significantly more patterns than we would have time to recognize in one lifetime. Examples include relativity, the earth's roundness, its rotation around the sun, and species evolution. To use Heidegger's phrasing, naming concepts is how societies collectively bring the present to hand into ready to hand; bring them into our awareness. Mimicking, the comparison of patterns of activity, including those learnt through language, therefore provides us with a very expansive system for interpreting the world, one which provides a huge evolutionary advantage.

When a new word is explained to us our memories will attempt to draw on our own experiences to identify a pattern that compares to the explanation. For example the planning methods named Black Swan and Blue Oceans are meaningless until some attempt is made to explain them. For a pragmatist this explanation needs to be of what they do, the consequences of their existing. Black Swans is the name for a process of planning by looking for significant improbable events. Blue Oceans is the name for a process of looking for previously unrecognized markets. If the activity explained matches to our past experiences then the meaning of the new words becomes clear. If the consequences of our using these words are favourable, then we will start to use them in our language. A concept is useful because it provides a name for a pattern distinguished. It is hard sometimes to appreciate that some concepts had to be abducted by someone, named and explained to us. Examples include progress, individuality and numbers. Mathematical concepts such as the number one and zero, and integration, took a long time to be developed, as did many physical concepts such as objects, force and heat. Management-related concepts such as innovation, commodification, becoming, empathy, agility and justice had to be conceived, named and explained by someone we have listened to, someone who compared, reflected upon and abstracted a name for patterns from their experience. The distinction that is innovation, rather than creativity, perhaps came from experiencing the generation of new products, processes or services that were not successfully implemented. It includes the exploitation of new ideas. Pragmatic concepts are similar to conceptual ideas, as praised in poetry by Piaget (Gruber and Voneche 1995) and by Nietzsche (1979 [1873]), ideas such as empathy and justice. But not similar to Hume's ideas, which are mental images, as in remembering the idea of a lake (Hume 1975 [1777]). In pragmatism, ideas are patterns of activity, concepts. To have a new idea is to see a new pattern of activity and name it.

The pragmatic explanation of how language affects thought needs to deal with the tyranny of meaning. Words and sentences are said to carry meaning. The pragmatic explanation of meaning is to associate it with the word 'interpretation'. To give meaning to something is to interpret it in a particular way. Pragmatic concepts interpret the world as it presents itself to us. I can give meaning to management as leadership, using the concepts of problem-solving, as power, or as the meat in the shareholder–workers sandwich. Each gives different meaning to management. The meaning in a statement can be different to the literal interpretation of the words used. The exclamation, 'What do you think you are doing!' means, 'Stop doing that!' The speaker is using the pattern of activity of outrage to interpret whatever is going on. This may or may not work. The recipient will use their own concepts to interpret the situation.

**Empirical Psychology**

The relationship between words (linguistic concepts) and thinking has not escaped the interest of experimental psychologists. Tversky and Kahneman (1981), Kahneman and Klein (2009) and many others have conducted numerous student laboratory experiments that show how a slight rewording of a problem situation can act to alter subjects' response. Typically, imagined emergency plans for saving people from an island are presented to the subjects who have to decide between plan A and B. In one version, the plans are described by how many will be saved. In the other, by the number that will die. The numbers are identical, only the description changes. Subjects chose differently depending on the wording. This can be read as their response changing depending on whether they use the concept 'save' or the concept 'die' to reflect on the alternative plans. Tversky and Kahneman use the term 'frame' rather than concept, defining it as the 'conception of outcomes', and argue that frames are formed by how a problem is articulated and the personal characteristics (experiences) of the decision-maker. All of which sounds akin to the pragmatic explanation of thought and behaviour. The term 'frame' is often sourced to Bateson (1972) who briefly defines it as 'organising premises'. The term 'organizing principles' also seems appropriate. Goffman's sociology studies (1974) define frames as 'definitions of a situation that are built up in accordance with the principles of organisation which govern events'. Tannen (1993) in his discourse analysis defines them as 'structures of expectations'. Minsky (1975), from artificial intelligence research, defines them in terms of mindset and mental-models. Interestingly, to some framing is unwanted bias, and reframing is not thought possible; wanting to do is manipulative and a source of conflict. Yet there seems to be general agreement that it is experimentally observable that use of alternative words influences our interpretation of a situation, if only temporarily.

The pragmatic explanation might also claim some empirical support by drawing on the work of Vygotsky. He was a child language development experimental psychologist who died in 1935, but his work provides an extensive analysis of his and other empirical findings at the time. He concludes that words do not just communicate or signify thoughts, although there is a strong recursive relationship between them. However, he becomes stuck on which comes first, a thought or a word. This raises evolution questions, which he answers by arguing that thought came long before words, yet words are necessary for complex abstract thought. The sounds emitted by animals are more gestures than words. Apes can mimic human actions because they have similar bodies, and can mimic patterns of behaviour associated to noises or shapes. But they do not appear to be able to compare the patterns associated with different words and therefore perform complex abstract thought. Parrots can mimic the words of humans but they do not seem to see any associated pattern of activity. Vygotsky felt that science made a mistake when undertaking its usual task of picking things apart to understand them. Picking words and thoughts apart is not helpful. Rather, words need to be understood as carrying meaning. He uses the example of the statement that 'The clock has stopped because it fell over'. The meaning carried or interpretation given to this statement is to know that falling can result in damage. In the pragmatic explanation, falling is compared to (or used to interpret) the clock being stopped. The patterns of activity or consequences associated with falling include damage. Meaning is therefore given by the comparison of one pattern with another.

As Vygotsky (1986) points out, it is possible to randomly mix letters to create new words, but they have no meaning. To the pragmatic explanation this is because they have no associated pattern of activity that can be used in a comparison. But new words can be created, provided they are associated with a pattern of activity, that explains what they mean. Giving meaning and creating meaning is comparison, it is thinking. Vygotsky also argues that thoughts fulfil a function, they problem-solve. This is close to the pragmatic activity-based understanding of thinking. Words bring these functions (activities) into existence; sentences connect one function to another. The relationship of thought to words is one of process. This again is making the link between thought and actions.

To Vygosky it is of great significance that the meaning of words can change over time. We can develop a deeper or alternative understanding of a word as we get older. Social group usage changes the meaning of words over time. The same word can develop different meanings. He is confused that this undermines the notion that words represent some reality or ideal form. His subsequent studies of child development over time reveal other findings he finds hard to reconcile. Young children can use words such as 'because' and 'although', despite their not representing anything real. They seem to be grammatical abstractions. Development means that children have an increasing range of words, but also they that improve their capability to use these words in sentences and thus in comparison with each other. Being told a clock has stopped because it fell, is understood to be different to being asked what fell and being told it was a clock. The sequence is important for what is thought. Another finding is that children know that words cannot be interchanged: ink is not confused with cow, for example. This is because ink and cows do different things. Vygotsky tries to make sense of these and other findings while holding on to his idealism. He wants words to relate to ideal forms (lakes, women), assuming these forms really exist. The result is that he creates a distinction between inner speech and external speech; talking to yourself compared to talking aloud. Inner speech is comparison which turns words into thoughts. External speech turns thoughts into words. This distinction was reinforced by the historical finding that originally adults read written documents aloud. Reading quietly to oneself was invented later.

Vygotsky's distinction between internal and external speech seems a little forced today. Pragmatism rather than idealism may offer an alternative explanation to Vygotsky's findings. To run through his examples: the word 'ink' represents the activity of assisting writing, the word 'cow' represents the activity of providing milk; the word 'because' represents the activity of linking cause and effect, and the word 'although' represents the activity of pointing out exceptions to patterns. As mentioned earlier, the same is true of numbers and colour words. When words are associated to an experienced pattern of activity they are harder to confuse. Thought is a comparison of processes, between patterns of activity. This does not make sense if words represent ideal forms. As process or activity the order does matter. A different thought occurs when using falling to think about clocks compared to using clocks to think about falling. The first may encourage thoughts about damage, while the second may encourage thoughts about how long a fall takes.

**Not Mental Images**

As mentioned, pragmatic concepts are similar to conceptual metaphors and much of what has been written about the usefulness of metaphoric analysis also applies to concepts. The same is true of irony but the emphasis is on dissimilarity. Metaphors perhaps provide a useful means of explaining how comparing concepts acts in thinking. Comparing the concept of a computer with the concept of an elephant makes me think about memory and size. This is similar to saying 'a computer is like an elephant'. The resources theory of innovation argues that those with the more resources, including motivations and capabilities, will register more patents. I can think about innovation using the concept of resources. Doing so makes me think about the phrase 'Necessity is the mother of invention', and of the huge skills involved in designing and building something like a smartphone. It does not really work to use a metaphoric approach that 'innovation is like resources'. This makes talk of comparing concepts seem to have very much more scope. Note however that metaphors can compare two things that at first glance are not activities. Say, 'a book is like a picture': to pragmatism this would have to be understood to be saying that what a book does is like what a picture does.

Pragmatic concepts distinguish themselves from metaphors and mental images by not being able to be visualized. This aligns with the neuroscience finding of no picture processing function in our brains. It is possible to think of an example of something being agile but not of the concept of agility itself. The experienced pattern of activity known as being agile can be remembered as a visual memory of something seen. We can recall and remix these visual memories, purposefully in visual thinking and perhaps randomly in dreams. The same is true of other sense memories such as hearing, smell and touch.

Concepts, as named patterns of activity, are most likely remembered somehow in our brain as a particular path through our neural network. The modern Swype typing software provides a possible analogy. In Swype the keyboard keys are not pressed; rather your finger slides over them in a continuous path drawing out the word. The software recognizes the pattern or path taken past the keys as a path through a network. The word 'plan' forms a different path or shape through the keyword of keys compared to the word 'run' as your fingers run over the flat keyboard surface.

Networks remember patterns as paths through their nodes. The activities of a gymnast and an ape might create very similar patterns in our brains;

*Figure 12.1   Using Swype to draw out the word 'quick'*

drawing out a path named as 'agility' through our neural networks. But we cannot recall these neural network pattern paths as a mental image or memory. We can only recall visual memories of gymnasts and apes. When named, this path would need to include a path through sound memories so that we also know the sound of the name.

Problem sketching, drawing a picture to help think about a problem, is perhaps different to remixing visual memories to imagine a solution. Sketches show relationships; the sketch of a person shows the relationship of their body parts. The sketch of a flowchart shows the relationship between the activities. A map shows the relationship between the roads, buildings, hills and so on. Technical drawings are clear examples, including 'explosions' of parts as shown in maintenance manuals pictures. A sketch uses the comparison part of thinking. The parts are still 'what they do'. This can provide a means of finding new concepts from collections of parts found to be close to each other. New concepts are found by identifying new patterns. Pragmatic inquiry is a process of looking for patterns. This is a way of seeing any research and analysis work. Correlation statistics are a pattern found in columns of numbers. Qualitative research is a process of looking for patterns in what people have said. Christopher Alexander (1964), in his book *Notes on the Synthesis of Form*, presents a graphical means of doing this which is akin to cluster analysis. He suggests linking similar statements to produce a network, with statements as the node and similarity as the links: idea networking. The analyst or designer then looks for clusters (as patterns) in the resultant network diagram. Alexander is therefore using sketching to find new concepts from relationships.

## Other Theories of Knowing

By defining concepts in terms of experienced patterns of activity rather than ideal forms saves having to explain where the ideal forms come from. It also forces concentration on what things do rather than what they are. This has some useful outcomes. One of which is that it provides a useful understanding of concepts such as God. The pragmatic understanding of God is that someone abducted a pattern of activity across their experiences that they named God. On hearing about this concept, others found it useful for thinking about death; it alleviated their concerns. The concept of God therefore provides them with a new option of how to act in the future; that is, once identified it affects their consequent conduct. Naming and sharing the concept of God is therefore useful in pragmatism, although God cannot be observed, be explained by reasoning or measured.

Nietzsche's (1979 [1873]) makes the connection between knowledge and language. One of his famous quotes is: 'what then is truth, a mobile army of metaphors'. His metaphors are the same as the pragmatists' concepts, without the need for mental images. Donald Schon (1963) explains this by pointing out that to say an organization is like a machine can easily be restated as saying an organization can be compared to the concept of a machine. Truth is to use the concept of what actions physically happened in the comparison. To say it is true that an organization is bankrupt, is to use the concept (metaphor) of an actual physical action such as filing for bankruptcy to reflect on what the organization has done. It is true if they are comparable. Nietzsche's other famous quote, that 'there are no facts, only interpretations', aligns with pragmatism if the concepts provide the interpretations. They are what is used to interpret events. His quote, 'the doer alone learneth', reflects the pragmatic notion of actions (patterns) forming the basis of knowledge. We learn by trying to mimic the actions we see done. Nietzsche is making the connection between actions, language and thought. Pragmatism addes patterns of activity and comparison to this to flesh out the explanation.

The obvious person to mention when making the connection between language and thought is Wittgenstein. Rorty (1982, 1989) argues that philosophy can be split into before and after the Wittgenstein. Wittgenstein argues that there is no foundation to knowledge such as mathematics, logic or empirics, but rather there is just language. We need to explain scientific knowledge in terms of language games. James is one of the few philosophers cited by Wittgenstein in *Philosophical Investigations* (2001 [1953]). His argument of there being nothing but language as the basis of knowing aligns with James's explanation of concepts. Reasoning and empiricism can be seen to be learnt patterns of activity that has useful consequences. Mathematics, empirics, relativity, string theories and quantum mechanics can all be seen to be just words, patterns of activity, used to provide alternative interpretations of the physical world. As Rorty points out, relativism is avoided by justification, by dialectic argument using convincing evidence.

Dialectic argument ties pragmatic concepts to the theory of knowledge. Argument involves the use of dynamic tensions to create justified knowledge. It is a named pattern of activity and thus a pragmatic concept that can be experienced and mimicked. However, it is also a social interaction, language-based, method to assist people to think. Claims are compared. Comparing concepts is argument. To argue that X is A not B because of Y reasons, is to compare the use of concepts A and B against concept X. For example, the argument may be that leadership is about example not control. In this, the concepts of leadership, example and control are being compared in a particular order. Aristotle saw dialectic argument as between protagonists; Hegel saw it as between societies over time; and James argues that propositions contain concepts in opposition. Derrida's concern with polarization of concepts can be read as objecting to being restricted to only two contrasting concepts. Miller's magic number 7±2 from his cognitive capability research seems to suggest the maximum number we are likely to use implicitly. Habermas's book *Knowledge and Human Interests* (1972) has a chapter commending Peirce's writings. Habermas's book is an extension of the pragmatic notion of community (intersocial) generated knowledge. Popper's *Conjectures and Refutations* (1972) can be seen as further support for the use of argument as justification for what is claimed to be known and therefore as the basis of knowing and deciding. Argument, putting concepts in opposition, is the process of creative thinking used by science. The present-day debate between relativity, quantum mechanics and the many string theories is a modern example. Toulmin, a seminal writer on the structure of arguments, in his other book *Human Understanding* (Toulmin 1972) elaborated on pragmatic concepts and the role of argument to use these to generate and test our thoughts.

**Consequences**

The obvious question to ask about the pragmatic explanation of human behaviour is what difference it makes to management practice or related research. The pragmatic explanation predicts that if you manage the core concepts someone is using to interpret events, then you come closer to managing their behaviour. Determining what set of concepts you want used can act to coordinate and direct an organization. A statement of core or strategic concepts (or intent), states what the organization intend to become by stating what handful of concepts it will use when making future decisions. The seminal example reported is of Komatsu, a global, Japanese, construction equipment corporation that outgrew the large US industrial machinery provider, Caterpillar. It is claimed that Komatsu improved considerably when it explicitly articulated the use of the concepts of growth, global, and wanting to surpass Caterpillar, to coordinate its large corporate divisions. More generally, the becoming of any organization has been demonstrated by its change in expressed core concepts over time. The commodification of public goods such as education and pleasure can be understood by the shift in core concepts away from responsibility to community to more business-related concepts such as competition and product growth. Gustensen et al. (1996) studied 400 development organizations, finding those that explicitly identified the concept they wanted to drive change outperformed those who used other means of planning. All of which suggests that pragmatic concepts can be a practical management tool.

Strategic visions might be better understood to be concepts. The vision to be the best would be understood to be using the concept of 'bestness' to evaluate the future actions of an organization. Visions without supportive performance measures or decision criteria can be ineffectual rhetoric. Having only one concept misses out on the opportunity to use the creative dialectic of a handful of concepts. Strategic concepts give pattern to an organization. Mission statements can be interpreted as action plans: what actions are to be undertaken if the strategic concepts are to be pursued. Goal, targets and objectives work by focusing people onto the concepts they contain. A target to improve quality says quality is the concept to use when making future decisions. The advantage of explicitly identifying all the concepts in use in vision, mission and objectives is to ensure they are aligned.

The pragmatic explanation also suggests that many of the social pressure, behavioural economics, decision-making and information processing experiments could be repeated, focusing on the concepts in use. The Asch line experiment could, for example, first ask students to settle on the set of concepts that should be used to decide which of a set of lines is the longest. After the experiment the concepts actually used could be explored. The same is true of the Milgram electrocution experiments and the Stanford prison experiments. It is predicted that knowing or setting the concepts will determine what actions are taken. Of interest will be how easily new concepts can replace default ones long established in someone's behaviour, and how they can be changed.

The notion of 'searching for patterns' can be used to guide research, planning and forecasting. This might be quantitative or qualitative. Of course, this is already done, so what is being suggested is a change in emphasis, one aligned to a theory of behaviour. Moreover, concept could replace theory; consequences can replace prediction. What are the consequences of thinking about management using the concept of contingencies, rather than asking what contingency theory predicts? Deductive research studies theories to examine whether they hold up in different situations and what they reveal about the world. The definition of what a theory is has been very confusing, with some arguing against their use on social research. The usefulness of a concept can be studied directly or the research can induct what concepts are in use. For example, the BP Gulf of Mexico oil spill can be explicitly studied using the concepts of leadership, control or risk management; or the concepts in use by those involved could be induced from looking at patterns in their conversations. In place of predicting what will happen in the next oil spill, the consequences of managers and regulators using particular concepts can be examined. All of this happens somewhat already. The pragmatic explanation approach merely provides more emphasis on the concepts or words involved. This is to make the linguistic turn. Understanding management by what is said provides a credible pluralism to just the use of numbers.

The main attraction of using pragmatic concepts to design research and management practice is that it provides a complete explanation of human behaviour including an explanation of the role of language. It aligns with the modern empirical evidence and combines action with conceptions, while avoiding the excesses of idealism. Pragmatism argues that humans use these linguistic concepts, words, to conceive, to have a conception. We perform complex thinking by comparing concepts (patterns of activity) to each other. Thinking, including scientific, practical and complex problem-solving, is an act of comparing or reflecting one concept off another. The cosmos can be thought about by using the concepts of attraction, relativity or strings. These concepts are sourced from past experiences, mainly social interaction. Comparing pragmatic concepts provides an explanation of how we think. If these patterns are named, then it also provides an explanation of how language helps us think.

# Appendix: networking statements

## STATEMENTS

Start with over 100 statements, preferably conditional statements. Underline the key words in these statements. To draft the network you need to link similar statements. For example, you might feel statements 12, 27 and 37 below are about the need for innovation but statement 21 is not. This means 12, 27 and 37 are to be considered as linked. In practice this job is best done by the planner, or a very small group of knowledgeable managers, tracking through each statement comparing it with all those below it.

*No 12: We need to develop innovative new products to compete in the global marketplace.*
*No 21. If we do not make a concentrated effort to improve our safety record then our future is insecure.*
*No 27: If we do not find ways to encourage suppliers to provide new products and services we will be unable to compete in the future.*
*No 37: Useful creativity is the key to our future.*

You should aim for all of your statements to be linked to one or two statements and for some to be linked to four or five other statements. There needs to be a strong, clear, auditable connection between statements for any two statements to be recorded as linked. A common mistake is to have too many links.

## MATRIX

This linking can be recorded in a table:

Statement 1 is linked (paired) to 12, 27, 31 as they are about innovation
Statement 2 is linked 15, 21, 23, 45, 57 as they are all about suppliers
Statement 3 is linked 11, 32, as they are all about the weather
Statement 4 is linked 14, 29, 43, 59 as they are all about skills

Statement 5 is linked 5, 22, 27, 45, 51 as they are all about diversity
Statement 6 is linked 12, 27, 28, 49, 77 as they are all about the future
Etc etc to the final statement number

Part of the reason you are putting the links into the matrix is that it is required in this format for UCINET6.

Therefore, you need to download this software onto your computer and then enter the links in the spreadsheet matrix it provides (see below). This will then generate the right file format for drawing the concept map from your linkages matrix. You can import from EXCEL.

**UCINET6**

Below assumes you are using UCINET6. An alternative is NODEXL with works directly inside EXCEL, is free, and has a Mac version unlike UCINET6. Mac users need something like Parallels before downloading UCINET6.

After installing UCINET6 software you should get a page like this:

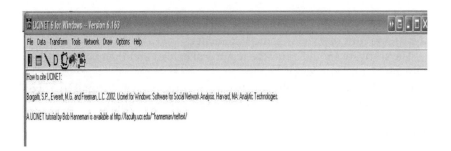

Click on the spreadsheet icon and you get this:

Your column and row headings are your statement numbers (1–60)

Set the mode on the right to symmetric and click 'FILL' from the top menu, then select 'missings with symmetric counterparts'. This means you will only have to enter the links between statements once.

Now you can enter the relationship links you think exists between the statements as discussed above. A '1' in the body of the matrix represents a linkage and a zero represents no linkage.

For example you may have the statements 3 and 7 linked so this would be entered in column 3 row 7 as a 1 to indicate a link. Zeros indicate no link:

Enter all your relationship links, perhaps two or three for most statements and four or five for some statements.

The software should enter the reciprocal entries and then you can FILL missing blanks with zeros.

Click SAVE, which will save two files with unusual formats (i.e. you cannot replace the above with an Excel spreadsheet, sadly).

**NETDRAW**

Now close the spreadsheet (matrix) page (click top right red cross) and you will be left with the original UCINET6 page:

Now click on the coloured network icon (Launch NETDRAW) and get:

Click on the folder icon and browse [. . .] your spreadsheet (.##h) filename, click OK.

And hopefully get something like the network diagram below but with only 60+ nodes. If not, then click the 'Lightening' (spring embedded recalculation) icon button from the top menu. This makes the nodes repulse each other. Then turn off the arrow heads also from a top menu icon.

Network diagram:

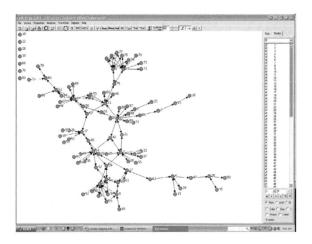

If you cannot see four to six 'clusters' of statements (as in the above and below diagrams) then you need to go back and either add more relationships or remove some. Otherwise the software can make suggestions accessed via 'Analysis Subgroups Girvan-Newman'. Set the number of clusters required to a minimum of four and maximum of six.

Draw a line freehand around the different clusters in your network diagram (concept map). Try to find about five clusters in your map. The figure that follows has six:

List separately the statements that make up each cluster (i.e. sort your statement list into the five or clusters). Look for common phrases through each cluster of statements: what are they about, what makes them a distinct cluster?

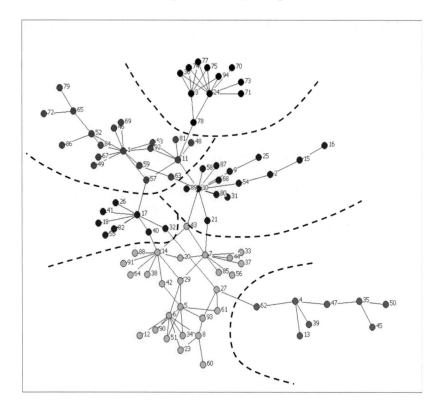

Think up a summary name for each your clusters of statements, a name that reflects what they have in common. This name or label we might call a meta-narrative, concept or frame. This is an important task in need of some very careful creative thinking. Choose the names carefully, be imaginative.

   List the five or so clusters of statements separately and explain in a sentence or two why you choose that name for those statements.

# References

Ackoff, R. (1971), 'Towards a system of system concepts', *Management Science*, 17(11), 661–71.

Ackoff, R. (1994a), 'From mechanisitic to social systemic thinking', available at http://ackoffcenter.blogs.com/ (accessed 6 June 2005).

Ackoff, R. (1994b), *The Democratic Corporation: A Radical Prescription for Recreating Corporate America and Rediscovering Success*, New York: Oxford University Press.

Ackoff, R. (2000), 'Making a difference, systems thinking – systems change', available from http://www.judgelink.org/Presentations/GirlsLink/ (accessed 1 August 2007).

Ackoff, R. (2007), *Best of Ackoff*, New York: Wiley.

Ackoff, R. and F.E. Emery (1972), *On Purposeful Systems*, Chicago, IL: Aldine-Atherton.

Adams, D. and J. Lloyd (1983), *The Meaning of Liff*, London: Pan Books.

Aiman-Smith, L. (2002), 'Implementing new manufacturing technology: the related effect of technology characteristics and user learning activities', *Academy of Management Journal*, 45(2), 421–30.

Aiman-Smith, L. and S.G. Green (2002), 'Implementing new manufacturing technology: the related effect of technology characteristics and user learning activities', *Academy of Management Journal*, 45, 421–30.

Alexander, C. (1964), *Notes on the Synthesis of Form*, Boston, MA: Harvard University Press.

Al-Kodmany, K. (1999), 'Using visualization techniques for enhancing public participation in planning and design', *Landscape and Urban Planning*, 45(1), 37–45.

Allport, G. (1954), *The Nature of Prejudice*, Reading, MA: Addison-Wesley.

Arend, U., K.P. Muthig and J. Wandmacher (1987), 'Evidence for global feature superiority in menu selection by icons', *Behaviour and Information Technology*, 6(1), 411–26.

Argyris, C. (1977), 'Double loop learning in organizations', *Harvard Business Review*, 55(5), 115–25.

Argyris, C. (1994), 'Good communication that blocks learning', *Harvard Business Review*, Jul–Aug, 77–85.

Argyris, C. and D.A. Schon (1978), *Theory in Practice*, San Francisco, CA: Jossey-Bass.

Argyris, C. and D.A. Schon (1996), *Organizational Learning II*, Boston, MA: Addison Wesley.

Aristotle (n.d.), *Nicomachean Ethics*, Internet Classic Archive, http://classics.mit.edu/Aristotle/nicomachaen.html.

Armstrong, J. (ed.) (2000), *Principles of Forecasting*, Norwell, MA: Kluwer.

Arnold, M. (2003), 'On the phenomenology of technology', *Information and Organization*, 13, 231–56.

Asch, S.E. (1955), 'Opinions and social pressure', *Scientific American*, 193, 31–5.

Ash, J.S. and E. Coiera (2004), 'Unintended consequences of information technology. *Journal of American Medical Informatics Association*, 11, 104–12.

Axelrod, R. (1976), *The Structure of Decisions*, Princeton, NJ: Princeton University Press.

Baggini, J. (2005), 'Pragmatism', *History of Ideas*, London: BBC Radio 4, available from http://www.bbc.co.uk/radio4/history/inourtime/inourtime_20051117.shtml (accessed 18 March 2007).

Bailin, S. (2003), 'Is argument for conservatives? Or where do sparkling new ideas come from?', *Informal Logic*, 23(1), 3–17.

Ball, H.G. (1982), 'Who is Snoopy?', *Cartoon and Comic in the Classroom: A Reference for Teachers and Librarians*, in J.L. Thomas (ed.), Littleton, CO: Libraries Unlimited, pp. 14–22.

Barley, S.R. (1986), 'Technology as an occasion for structuring', *Administrative Science Quarterly*, 31(1), 78–108.

Barnes, B. and D. Bloor (1982), 'Relativism, rationalism and the sociology of knowledge', in M. Hollis and S. Lukes (eds), *Rationality and Rationalism*, Oxford: Basil Blackwell, pp. 21–47.

Bartlett, C.A. and S. Ghoshal (1994), 'Changing the role of top management: beyond strategy to purpose', *Harvard Business Review*, November, 79–88.

Baskerville, R. and A.T. Wood-Harper (1998), 'Diversity in information systems action research methods', *European Journal of Information Systems*, 7, 90–107.

Bateson, G. (1972), *Steps to an Ecology of Mind*, Chicago, IL: University of Chicago Press

Bearman, P. and K. Stovel (2000), 'Becoming a Nazi: a model for narrative networks', *Poetics*, 27, 69–90.

Beer, M. and R. Eisenstat (2000), 'The silent killers of strategy', *Sloan Management Review*, 41(4), 29–40.

Benson, K.J. (1977), 'Organizations: a dialectical view', *Administrative Science Quarterly*, 22, 1−21.

Bergvall-Kåreborn, B., A. Mirijamdotter and A. Basden (2004), 'Basic principles of SSM modeling: an examination of CATWOE from a soft perspective', *Systemic Practice and Action Research*, 17(2), 55−73.

Blackmore, S. (1998), 'Imitation and the definition of a meme', *Journal of Memetics − Evolutionary Models of Information Transmission*, 2(2), 1−13.

Bloomer, C.M. (1976), *Principles of Visual Perception*, New York: Van Nostrand Reinhold.

Boland, R.J. and R.V. Tenkasi (1995), 'Perspective making and perspective taking in communities of knowing', *Organization Science*, 6(4), 350−72.

Borgatti, S.P., M. Everett and L.C. Freeman (2002), *Ucinet for Windows: Software For Social Network Analysis*, Harvard, MA: Analytic Technologies.

Braa, K. and R. Vidgen (1999), 'Interpretation, intervention, and reduction in the organizational laboratory', *Journal of Accounting, Management and Information Technologies*, 9(1), 25−47.

Brabetm, J. and M. Klemm (1994), 'Sharing the vision', *Long Range Planning*, 27(1), 84–94.

Brower, L. (1988), *Mimicry and the Evolutionary Process*, Chicago, IL: University of Chicago Press.

Brown, J.S. and P. Duguid (2000), 'Mysteries of the region: knowledge dynamics in Silicon Valley', in M. Lee (ed.), *Silicon Valley*, Stanford, CA: Stanford Books, pp. 16−46.

Bryson, J.M. and F. Ackermann (2004), *Visible Thinking: Unlocking Causal Mapping for Practical Business Results*, Chichester: Wiley.

Buchanan, M. (2002), *Nexus: Small Worlds*, New York: W.W. Norton.

Burt, R.S. (2002), 'Structural holes versus network closure as social capital', in N. Lin (ed.), *Social Capital*, Cambridge: Cambridge University Press, pp. 57−81.

Butcher, D. and S. Atkinson (2001), 'Stealth, secrecy and subversion', *Journal of Organizational Change Management*, 14(6), 554−69.

Byrne, M.D. (1993), 'Using icons to find documents: simplicity is critical', *ACM INTERCHI'93 Conference on Human Factors in Computing Systems*, 1(1), 446−53.

Camazine, S., J.-L. Deneubourg, R. Nigel, J.S. Franks, G. Theraulaz and E. Bonabeau (2001), *Self-Organization in Biological Systems*, Princeton, NJ: Princeton University Press.

Carroll, L. (1939), *The Complete Works of Lewis Carroll*, London: Nonesuch Press.

Chalmers, A.F. (1982), *What is this Thing Called Science?*, Brisbane: University of Queensland Press.

Chambers, R. (1994), 'Participatory rural appraisal', *World Development*, 22(9), 1253–68.

Chanin, M.N. and H.J. Shapiro (1985), 'Dialectical inquiry in strategic planning: extending the boundaries', *Academy of Management Review*, 10(4), 663–75.

Chaston, I. and E. Sadler-Smith (2011), 'Entrepreneurial cognition, entrepreneurial orientation and firm capability in the creative industries', *British Journal of Management*, 23(3), 415–32.

Checkland, P.B. (1981), *Systems Thinking, Systems Practice*, Chichester: John Wiley & Sons.

Checkland, P. (2000), 'Soft systems methodology: a thirty year retrospective', *Systems Research and Behavioural Science*, 17(1), S11–S58.

Chia, R. (1994), 'The concept of decision', *Journal of Managememt Studies*, 31(6), 781–806.

Chomsky, N. (1957), *Syntactic Structures*, The Hague, The Netherlands and Paris, France: Mouton.

Chomsky, N. (1959), 'A review of B.F. Skinner's *Verbal Behavior*', *Language*, 35(1), 26–58.

Churchman, C.W. (1971), *The Design of Inquiring Systems*, New York: John Wiley.

Churchman, C.W. (1979), *Systems Thinking and Its Enemies*, New York: Basic Books.

Churchman, C.W. and A.H. Schainblatt (1965), 'The researcher and the manager', 11(4), 69–87.

Clark, S.M. and S. Scrivener (1994), 'Sketching in collaborative design', in L. MacDonald and J. Vince (eds), *Interacting With Virtual Environments*, New York: John Wiley, pp. 95–118.

Clarke, I., W. Kwon and R. Wodak (2011), 'A context-sensitive approach to analysing talk in strategy meetings', *British Journal of Management*, 23(4), 455–73.

Cohen, H.F. (1994), *The Scientific Revolution: A Historiographical Inquiry*, Chicago, IL: University of Chicago Press.

Cowan, N. (2001) 'The magical number 4 in short-term memory: a reconsideration of mental storage capacity', *Behavioral and Brain Sciences*, 24, 87–185.

Coyle, G. (2000), 'Qualitative and quantitative models in systems dynamics', *System Dynamics Review*, 16(3), 225–44.

Crosswhite, J. (1996), *The Rhetoric of Reason*, Madison, WI: University of Wisconsin Press.

Cummings, S. and J. Davies (1994), 'Mission vision and fusion', *Long Range Planning*, 27(6), 147–50.

Cziko, G. (2000), *The Things We Do*, Boston, MA: MIT Press.

Daellenbach, H.G. (2003), *Systems Thinking and Management Science*, Christchurch, New Zealand: REA Publications.

Damasio, A.R. (1994), *Descartes' Error: Emotion, Reason, and the Human Brain*, London: Putnam Publishing.

Daniels, K., G. Johnson and L. de Chernatony (1994), 'Differences in managerial cognitions of competition', *British Journal of Management*, 5(1), S21–S29.

Darwin, C. (1859), *Origin of Species*, London: John Murray.

Darwin, C. (1871), *The Descent of Man, and Selection in Relation to Sex*, London: John Murray.

Dawkins, R. (1989), *The Selfish Gene*, Oxford: Oxford University Press.

Delarue, A., V.G. Hootegem, S. Procter and M. Burridge (2007), 'Teamworking and organizational performance', *International Journal of Management Reviews*, 10(2), 127–48.

De Martino, B., B.D. Kumaran, B. Seymour and R. Dolan (2006), 'Frames, biases, and rational decision-making in the human brain', *Science*, 313(5787), 684–87.

Dennett, D.C. (1989), *The Intentional Stance*, Cambridge, MA: MIT Press.

Dennett, D.C. (1995), 'Review of Antonio R. Damasio, *Descartes' Error: Emotion, Reason, and the Human Brain*', *Times Literary Supplement*, 25 August, pp. 3–4.

Dennett, D.C. (1996), *Kinds of Minds*, New York: Basic Books.

Densten, I.L. (2005), 'The relationship between visioning behaviours of leaders and follower burnout', *British Journal of Management*, 16(2), 105–18.

Desombre, T., C. Kelliher, F. Macfarlane and M. Ozbilgin (2006), *British Journal of Management*, 17(2) 139–51.

Dewey, J. (1958 [1929]), *Experience and Nature*, New York: Dover Publications.

Dewey, J. (1982 [1910]), *How We Think*, Lexington, MA: D.C. Heath.

Do, Y.L.E. (2000), 'The right tool at the right time: investigation of free-hand drawing as an interface to knowledge based design tool', PhD thesis, Department of Architecture, Washington, DC: University of Washington.

Dodd, L., J. Moffat and L. Smith (2006), 'Discontinuity in decision making when objectives conflict', *Journal of the Operational Research Society*, 57, 643–54.

Dreyfus, H. (2007a), 'The return of the myth of the mental', *Inquiry*, 50(4), 352–65.

Dreyfus, H. (2007b), 'Why Heideggerian AI failed and how fixing it would require making it more Heideggerian', *Philosophical Psychology*, 20(2), 247–68.

Drucker, P. (1973), *Management*, New York: Harper Row.

East, C. and M. Metcalfe (2002), 'Rich picturing: a case study', IFIP 8.6 Conference, Sydney, August.

Eemeren, F.H.W., J.B. Anthony, A.W. Charles and A.S.H. Francisca (2003), *Anyone Who Has a View: Studies in Argumentation*, Dordrecht: Kluwer Academic Publishers.

Eemeren, F.H. and R. Grootendorst (2003), 'Pragma-dialectical procedure for a critical discussion', *Argumentation*, 17, 365–86.

Ellsworth, R. (2002), *Leading With Purpose*, Stanford, CA: Stanford University Press.

El-Namaki, M. (1992), 'Creating a corporate vision', *Long Range Planning*, 29(3), 25–9.

Elster, J. (1983), *Explaining Technical Change*, Cambridge: Cambridge University Press.

Emery, F.E. and E.I. Trist (1965), 'The causal texture of organizational environments', *Human Relations*, 18, 21–32.

Engels, F. (1964), *Dialectics of Nature*, Moscow: Progress Publishers.

Engestrom, Y. (1987), *Learning by Expanding: An Activity-Theoretical Approach to Developmental Research*, Helsinki: Orienta-Konsultit Oy.

Eulie, J. (1969), 'Creating interest and developing understanding in the social studies through cartoon', *Peabody Journal of Education*, 46, 288–90.

Farson, R. and R. Keyes (2002), *Whoever Makes the Most Mistakes Wins*, New York: Free Press.

Ferguson, E.S. (1992), *Engineering and the Mind's Eye*, Cambridge, MA: MIT Press.

Feyerabend, P.K. (1975), *Against Method*, London: Humanities Press.

Fischer, D.H. (2012), *Fairness and Freedom*, Oxford: Oxford University Press.

Fischer, F. and F. Forrester (1993), *The Argumentative Turn*, Durham, NC: Duke University Press.

Flyvbjerg, B. (2000), 'Ideal theory, real rationality: Habermas versus Foucault and Nietzsche', *The Challenges for Democracy in the 21st Century*, Political Studies Association's 50th Annual Conference, London School of Economics and Political Science.

Forbus, K.D. and J. Usher (2002), 'Sketching for knowledge capture: a progress report', *The 7th International Conference on Intelligent User Interfaces*. 13–16 January, San Francisco, CA, pp. 71–7.

Forgas, J.P. and J.M. George (2001), 'Affective influences on judgments and behaviour in organizations: an information processing perspective', *Organizational Behaviour and Human Decision Processes*, 86(1), 3–34.

Forrester, J.W. (1994), 'Systems dynamics, systems thinking and soft OR', *Systems Dynamics Review*, 10(2), 245–56.

Foster, J. (2000), 'Competitive selection, self-organization and Joseph A. Schumpeter', *Journal of Evolutionary Economics*, 10, 311–28.

Francis, D., J. Bessant and M. Hobday (2003). 'Managing radical organizational transformation', *Managment Decisions*, 41, 18–31.

Francis, G. and J. Holloway (2007), 'What have we learned? Themes from the literature on best-practice benchmarking', *International Journal of Management Review*, 9, 171–89.

Fuchs, C. (2003), 'Structuration theory and self-organization', *Systemic Practice and Action Research*, 16(2), 133–67.

Gilbert, D.T. (1991), 'How mental systems believe', *American Psychologist*, 46(2), 107–19.

Girard, R. (1977), *Violence and the Sacred*, Baltimore, MD: Johns Hopkins University Press.

Goel, V. (1995), *Sketches of Thought*, Cambridge MA: MIT Press, available at http://mitpress.mit.edu/catalog/item/default.asp?tid=7587&ttype=2 (accessed 2 October 2002).

Gombrich, E.H. (1966), *Leonardo's Method for Working Out Compositions. Norms and Forms*, London: Phaidon Press.

Gordon, W. (1961), *Synectics*, New York: Harper Row.

Gratton, L. (1996), 'Implementing a strategic vision', *Long Range Planning*, 29(3), 290–303.

Green, K. and S. Armstrong (2011), 'Role thinking: standing in other people's shoes to forecast decisions in conflicts', *International Journal of Forecasting*, 27(1), 69–80.

Grohowski, R., C. McGoff, D. Vogel, B. Martz and J. Nunamaker (1990), 'Implementing electronic meeting systems at IBM: lessons learned and success factors', *MIS Quarterly*, December, 369–83.

Gruber, H.E. and J.J. Voneche (eds) (1995), *Source: The Essential Piaget*, Lanham, MD: Jason Aronson.

Guindon, R. (1990), 'Designing the design process', *Human Computer Interaction*, 5, 305–44.

Gustavsen, B., B. Hofmaier, M. Ekman Philips and A. Wikman (1996), *A Concept-Driven Development and the Organization of the Process of Change*, Amsterdam: John Benjamins.

Haack, S. (1993), *Evidence and Inquiry*, Oxford: Blackwell.

Haack, S. (2003), *Defending Science*, New York: Prometheus Books.

Haack, S. (2006), *Pragmatism: Old and New*, New York: Prometheus Books.

Habermas, J. (1972), *Knowledge and Human Interests*, Boston, MA: Beacon Press.

Habermas, J. (1984), *The Theory of Communicative Action: Reason and the Rationalisation of Society Vol.1*, Boston, MA: Beacon Press.

Habermas, J. (1990), *Discourse Ethics in Moral Consciousness and Communicative Action*, Cambridge, MA: MIT Press.

Hamel, G. and C.K. Prahalad (2005), 'Strategic intent', *Harvard Business Review*, 83(7–8), 148–61.

Haney, C., W.C. Banks and P.G. Zimbardo (1973), 'Interpersonal dynamics in a simulated prison', *International Journal of Criminal Penalty*, 1, 69–97.

Hare, A.P. (1976), *Handbook of Small Group Research*, New York: Free Press.

Hatch, M.J. (1997), 'Irony and the social construction of contradiction', *Organization Science*, 8(3), 275–88.

Hayden, F.G. (1982), 'Social fabric matrix', *Journal of Economic Issues*, 16(3), 637–62.

Haynes, J. (2000), *Perspectival Thinking*, Palmerston North, NZ: ThisOne & Company.

Hegel, G.W.F. (1956), *Philosophy of History*, New York: Dover Publications.

Heidegger, M. (1968 [1817]), *What Is Called Thinking*, http://www.scribd.com/doc/40105022/Heidegger-Martin-What-is-Called-Thinking.

Heidegger, M. (2008), *Being and Time*, New York: Harper Perennial Classics.

Hillier, M. (2009), 'Using systems thinking to sense-make Australian Customs', PhD thesis, University of South Australia.

Hofstadter, D. (1979), *Godel, Escher, Bach: An Eternal Golden Braid*, London: Penguin.

Hookins, T. (2005), 'Developing a questioning model', PhD thesis, University of South Australia.

Hookins, T. and M. Metcalfe (2005), 'A systemic development of the interrogative pronouns and adverbs', *Systemic Practice and Action Research*, 18(6), 581–605.

Horn, M. (1980), *The World Encyclopaedia of Cartoons*, New York: Chelsea House.

Huff, A.S. and M. Jenkins (2002), *Mapping Strategic Knowledge*, London: Sage.

Hume, D. (1975 [1777]), *An Enquiry Concerning Human Understanding*, 3rd edn, Oxford: Clarendon Press.

Humphrey, N. (2006), *Seeing Red: A Study In Consciousness*, Boston, MA: Harvard University Press.

Hurvich, L.M. (1981), *Color Vision*, Sunderland, MA: Sinauer.

Hutzschenreuter, T. and I. Kleindienst (2006), 'Strategy-process research', *Journal of Management Studies*, 32(5), 673–720.

Iyer, P. (2004), *Sun after Dark – Flight into the Foreign*, New York: Allen & Unwin.

Jacques, M. (2003), 'Ackoff interview from March Jacques', *Strategy and Leadership*, 31(3), 19–26.

James, W. (1890), *Principles of Psychology, Vol 1*, New York: Henry Holt.

James, W. (1910 [1907]), *Pragmatism*, Cleveland: World Publishing (Meridian).

James W. (1996 [1909]), *The Pluralistic Universe*, Cleveland, NE: University of Nebraska Press.

James, W. (1996 [1911]), *Some Problems of Philosophy*, Cleveland, NE: University of Nebraska Press.

Jarzabkowski, P. and A.P. Spee (2009), 'Strategy-as-practice', *International Journal of Management Reviews*, 11(1), 69–95.

Jenkins, M. and G. Johnson (1997), 'Linking managerial cognition and organizational performance: a preliminary investigation using causal maps', *British Journal of Management*, 8(1), 77–90.

Joham, C. (2006), 'Self organization for understanding policy formulation', PhD thesis, University of South Australia, Adelaide.

Juarrero, A. (2002), *Dynamics in Action: Intentional Behavior as a Complex System*, Boston, MA: MIT Press.

Kahneman, D. and G. Klein (2009), 'Conditions for intuitive expertise', *American Psychologist*, 64(6), 515–26.

Kant, I. (1974 [1781]), *The Critique of Pure Reason*, London: Dent.

Kanter, R.M. (1983), *The Change Masters*, London: Unwin.

Kaplan, S. (2011), 'Cognition and strategy', *Journal of Management Studies*, 48(3), 665–95.

Katzenbach, J. and D. Smith (1993), 'The discipline of teams', *Harvard Business Review*, March–April, 111–19.

Keen, P. (2000), Staff seminar, Georgia State University, USA.

Keeney, R.L. (1994), 'Creativity in decision-making with value-focused thinking', *Sloan Management Review*, Summer, 33–41.

Killworth, P.D. and H.R. Bernard (1979), 'A pseudomodel of the small world problem', *Social Forces*, 58(2), 477–505.

Kipling, R. (1902), 'The Elephant's Child', *Just So Stories*, http://www.gutenberg.org/files/2781/2781-h/2781-h.htm.

Klein, G.A. (1989), 'Recognition primed decisions', in W.B. Rouse (ed.), *Advances In Man–Machine Systems Research*, Greenwich, CT: JAI Press, pp. 47–92.

Klein, G. (1999), *Sources of Power: How People Make Decisions*, Boston, MA: MIT Press.

Klein, G. (2009), *Streetlights and Shadows*, Boston, MA: MIT Press.

Kluge, J., W. Stein and T. Licht (2001), *Knowledge Unplugged: The Mckinsey & Company Global Survey on Knowledge Management*, Basingstoke: Palgrave.

Knowles, R.N. (2002), 'Self-organizing leadership', *Emergence*, 4(4), 86–97.

Kolli, R., R. Stuyver and J.M. Hennessey (1993), 'Deriving the functional requirements for a concept sketching device: a case study', *Proceedings of Conference on Human Computer Interaction*, Vienna.

Kuhn, T.S. (1970 [1962]), *The Structure of Scientific Revolutions*, 2nd edn, Chicago, IL: University of Chicago Press.

Lakoff, G. (1993), 'The contemporary theory of metaphor', in A. Ortony (ed.), *Metaphor and Thought*, Cambridge: Cambridge University Press, pp. 202–51.

Landry, M. (1995), 'A note on the concept of problem', *Organizational Studies*, 16(2), 315–27.

Larkin, J. and H. Simon (1987), 'Why a diagram is sometimes worth ten thousand words', *Cognitive Science*, 11(1), 65–99.

Larwood, L., C. Falbe, M. Kriger and P. Miesing (1995), 'Structure and meaning of organizational vision', *Academy of Management Journal*, 38(3), 740–89.

Latour, B. (1986), 'Visualization and cognition', *Knowledge and Society*, 6, 1–40.

Latour, B. (2005), *Reassembling the Social: An Introduction to Actor-Network-Theory*, Oxford: Oxford University Press.

Latour, B. and S. Woolgar (1986), *Laboratory Life: The Construction of Scientific Facts*, Princeton, NJ: Princeton University Press.

Lewis, M.W. (2000), 'Exploring paradox: towards a more comprehensive guide', *Academy of Management Review*, 25(4), 760–76.

Liebl, F. (2002), 'The anatomy of complex societal problems', *Journal of Operational Research Society*, 53, 161–84.

Linstone, H.A. (1999), *Decision Making for Technology Executives: Using Multiple Perspectives*, Boston, MA: Artech House.

Lissack, M. and J. Roos (2001), 'Be cohent not visionary', *Long Range Planning*, 34, 53–70.

List, D. (2001), 'The consensus group technique in social research', *Field Methods*, 13 (2), 277–90.

List, D. and M. Metcalfe (2004), 'Sourcing forecast knowledge through argumentative inquiry', *Technological Forecasting and Social Change*, 71, 525–35.

Locke, E.A. and G.P. Latham (1990), *A Theory of Goal Setting and Task Performance*, Englewood Cliffs, NJ: Prentice Hall.

Locke, J. (1690), *An Essay Concerning Human Understanding*, available at http://www.ilt.columbia.edu/publications/locke_understanding.html (accessed 20 March 2007).

Lugt, R. (2000), 'Developing a graphic tool for creative problem-solving', *Design Studies*, 21, 505–22.

Luscher, L.S. and M.W. Lewis (2008), 'Organizational change and managerial sensemaking: working through paradox', *Academy of Management Journal*, 51(2), 221–40.

Lynch, M. and M. Metcalfe (2006), 'Reflection, pragmatism, concepts and intuition', *Journal of Information Technology Theory and Application*, 7(4), 1–10.

Lysenko, T. (1948), *The Science of Biology Today*, New York: International Publishers.

MacCoun, R. (1998), 'Biases in the interpretation of research results', *Annual Review of Psychology*, 49, 248–57.

Malaska, P. and K. Holstius (1999), 'Visionary management', *Journal of Future Studies*, 1(4), 45–52.

Mao, T. (1967), *On Contradiction*, Vol. 1, Peking: Foreign Languages Press.

Mareschal, D., P.C. Quinn and S.E.G. Lea (2010), *The Making of Human Concepts*, Oxford: Oxford University Press.

Margolis, E.L. and J. Stephen (2010), 'Concepts', *Stanford Encyclopedia of Philosophy*, Stanford, CA: Stanford University, available at http://plato.stanford.edu/entries/concepts/.

Markus, M.L. (1994), 'Finding a happy medium: explaining the negative effects of electronic communication on social life at work', *ACM Transactions on Information Systems*, 12(2), 119–49.

Markus, M.L. and A. Bjorn-Andersen (1987), 'Power over users: its exercise by professionals', *Communications of the ACM*, 30(6), 498–504.

Martin, C., M. Metcalfe and H. Harris (2009), 'Developing an implementation capacity: justifications from prior research', *Journal of Operational Research Society*, 60(6), 859–68.

Marx, K. (1992), *Capital: Volume 1: A Critique of Political Economy*, transl. B. Fowkes, London: Penguin.

Mary, K. and Trochim M.K. William (2007), *Concept Mapping for Planning and Evaluation*, New York: Sage Publications.

Mason, R.O. (1996), 'Commentary of varieties of dialectic change processes', *Journal of Management Inquiry*, 5(3), 293–300.

Mason, R.O. (1969), 'A dialectical approach to strategic planning', *Management Science*, 15(8), B-403–14.

Mason, R.O. and I.I. Mitroff (1981), *Challenging Strategic Planning Assumptions (SAST)*, New York: Wiley.

Massey, A.P. and W.A. Wallace (1996), 'Understanding and facilitating group problem structuring formulation: mental representations, interaction, and representation aids', *Decision Support Systems, Special Issue on Model Formulation*, 17, 253–74.

Matsuo, Y., Y. Ohsawa and M. Ishizuka (2001), 'A document as a small world', available at www.miv.t.u-tokyo.ac.jp/~matsuo/homepageeng. html (accessed 2003).

McDougall, S.J.P., O.D. Bruijn and M.B. Curry (2000), 'Exploring the effects of icon characteristics on user performance: the role of icon concreteness, complexity and distinctiveness', *Journal of Experimental Psychology*, 6(4), 291.

McDougall, S.J.P., M.B. Curry and O.D. Bruijn (2001), 'The effects of visual information on users' mental models: an evaluation of path-finder analysis as a measure of icon usability', *International Journal of Cognitive Ergonomics*, 5(1), 59–84.

McKim, R.H. (1980), *Thinking Visually*, Belmont, CA: Wadsworth.

Menand, L. (2002), *The Metaphysical Club: A Story of Ideas in America*, New York: Farrar Straus & Giroux.

Metcalfe, M. (2006), 'Churchman's guarantors of knowledge claims', *Systems Research and Behavioral Science*, 23, 51–9.

Metcalfe, M. (2007a), 'Pragmatic inquiry', *Journal of Operational Research Society*, 59, 1091–9.

Metcalfe M. (2007b), *Why Good Argument is Critical to Useful Research*, Cardiff: Mellon Press.

Metcalfe, M. (2007c), 'Problem conceptualisation using idea networks', *Systemic Practice and Action Research* 20(2), 141–50.

Metcalfe, M.A. (forthcoming), 'System of decision criteria', *Systems Research and Behavioral Science*.

Metcalfe, M. and E. Hobson (2001), 'Concern solving for ISD', *Socio-technical and Human Cognition Elements of Information Systems*, Harrisburg, PA: Idea Group Publishing.

Metcalfe, M. and P. Powell (1995), 'Information: a perceiver-concerns per-spective', *European Journal of Information Systems*, 4, 121–9.

Meyers, R.A. and D.R. Seibold (1989), 'Perspectives on group argument', *Communications Yearbook*, 14, 268–302.

Midgley, G. (2003), 'Science as systemic intervention', *Systemic Practice and Action Research*, 16(2), 77–97.

Milgram, S. (ed.) (1992), *The Individual in a Social World: Essays and Experiments*, New York: McGraw-Hill.

Miller, G.A. (1956), 'The magical number seven, plus or minus two: some limits on our capacity for processing information', *Psychological Review*, 63, 81–97.

Mintzberg, H. (1987), 'The 5 P's for strategy', *California Management Review*, Fall, 11–24.

Mintzberg, H. (1994), 'The rise and fall of strategic planning', *Harvard Business Review*, 72(1), 107–14.

Mintzberg, H. and F. Westley (2001), 'It's not what you think', *Sloan Management Review*, Spring, 89–93.

Miron-Spektor, E., M. Erez and E. Naveh (2011b), 'The effects of conformist and attention-to-detail members on team innovation', *Academy of Management Journal*, 54(4), 740–60.

Miron-Spektor, E., F. Gino and L. Argote (2011a), 'Paradoxical frames and creative sparks', *Organizational Behavior and Human Decision Processes*, 116, 229–40.

Mitroff, I.I. and J.R. Emshoff (1979), 'On strategic assumption-making: a dialectical approach to policy and planning', *Academy of Management Review*, 4(1), 1–12.

Mitroff, I.I. and R.H. Kilmann (1975), 'Stories managers tell: a new tool for organizational problem-solving', *Management Review*, July, 18–25.

Mohr, L.B. (1982), *Explaining Organizational Behaviour (Process vs Variance Theory)*, San Francisco, CA: Jossey-Bass.

Morden, T. (1997), 'Leadership as vision', *Management Decision*, 3(9), 668–78.

Morgan, G. (1986), *Images of Organizations*, Thousand Oaks, CA: Sage Publications.

Muecke, D.C. (1982), *Irony and the Ironic*, New York: Methuen

Mullins, P. (2002), 'Peirce's abduction and Polanyi's tacit knowing', *Journal of Speculative Philosophy*, 16(3), 198–224.

Murch, G. (1984), 'The effective use of color: cognitive principles', *TEKniques*, 8(2), 25–31.

Murphy, N. and W.S. Brown (2007), *Did My Neurons Make Me Do It? Philosophical and Neurobiological Perspectives on Moral Responsibility and Free Will*, Oxford: Oxford University Press.

Nelson, T.P. (1975), *Cartooning*, Chicago, IL: Contemporary Book.

Newell, A. and H.A. Simon (1972), *Human Problem-Solving*, New York: Prentice Hall.

Niederman, F. and G. DeSanctis (1995), 'The impact of the structured argument approach on group problem formulation', *Decision Sciences*, 26(4), 451.

Nielsen, R.P. (1996), 'Varieties of dialectic change processes', *Journal of Management Enquiry*, 5(3), 276–93.

Nietzsche, F. (1979 [1873]), 'On truth and lies in a nonmoral sense', in Daniel Breazeale (ed.), *Philosophy and Truth: Selections from Nietzsche's Notebooks of the early 1870's*, New York: Humanities Press International, pp. 79–93.

Novak, J.D. and A.J. Cañas (2009), 'The theory underlying concept maps', Technical Report, Florida Institute for Human and Machine Cognition, available at http://cmap.ihmc.us/Publications/ResearchPapers/TheoryUnderlyingConceptMaps.pdf.

O'Brien, F. and M. Mathews (2007a), 'Developing a visioning methodology', *Journal of the Operational Research Society* 58, 557–75.

O'Brien, F.A. and M. Meadows (2007a), 'How to develop visions', *Systemic Practice and Action Research*, 14(4), 495–515.

O'Brien, F.A. and M. Meadows (2007b), 'Corporate visioning: a survey of UK practice', *Journal of the Operational Research Society*, 51, 36–44.

Ordonez, L.D.M., E.A. Schweitzer, D. Galinsky and H. Bazerman (2009), 'Goals gone wild: the systematic side effects of overprescribing goal setting', *Academy of Management Perspectives*, February, 6–16.

Ormerod, R. (2006), 'The history of pragmatism', *Journal of Operational Research Society*, 57, 892–909.

Oswick, C.T., T. Keenoy and D. Grant (2002), 'Metaphor and analogical reasoning in organization theory', *Academy of Management Review*, 27(2), 294–303.

Palmer, I. and T. Dunford (2008), 'Organizational change and the importance of embedded assumptions', *British Journal of Management*, 10, 20–32.

Peirce, S.C. (1878), 'How to make our ideas clear', *Popular Science Monthly*, 12 January, pp. 286–302, available at http://www.peirce.org/writings/p119.html (accessed 1 November 2005).

Perelman, C. and L. Olbrechts-Tyteca (1969), *The New Rhetoric: A Treatise on Argumentation*, Notre Dame, IN: University of Notre Dame.

Perry-Smith, J.E. and C.E. Shalley (2003), 'The social side of creativity: a static and dynamic social network perspective', *Academy of Management Review*, 28(1), 89–106.

Polanyi, M. (1966), *The Tacit Dimension*, London: Routledge.

Polya, G. (1945), *How To Solve It*, Princeton, NJ: Princeton University Press.

Poole, M.S. and A. Van de Ven (1989), 'Using paradox to build management and organizational theories', *Academy of Management Review*, 14(4), 562–78.

Popper, K. (1972), *Conjectures and Refutations*, London: Routledge & Kegan Paul.

Popper, K.R. (1971 [1945]), *The Open Society and Its Enemies*, Princeton, NJ: Princeton University Press.

Pratt, P. (1996), 'Visionary management', *Home Healthcare Management Practices*, 8(4), 78–9.

Price, T.L. (2000), 'Explaining ethical failures of leadership', *Leadership and Organization Development Journal*, 21, 177–84.

Purcell, A.T. and J.S. Gero (1998), 'Drawing and the design process', *Design Studies*, 19(4), 389–40.

Purcell, F.J.B. (2000), 'Value engineering: a tool for our times', Boynton Beach, FL: Purcell Associates.

Putnam, H. (2001), *Enlightenment and Pragmatism*, Assen: Koninklijke Van Gorcum.

Quine, W.V. (1961), *The Ways of Paradox*, New York: Random House.

Quinton, A. (1966), 'The foundations of knowledge', in B. Williams and A. Montefiore (eds), *British Analytical Philosophy*, London: Routledge & Kegan Paul, pp. 55–86.

Raynor, M. (1998), 'That vision thing. Do we need it?', *Long Range Planning*, 31(3), 368–76.

Raynor, M. (2007), *The Strategy Paradox*, New York: Currency.

Reichertz, J. (2009), 'Abduction: the logic of discovery of grounded theory', *Forum Qualitative Sozialforschung / Forum: Qualitative Social Research*, 11, Art. 13.

Rescher, N. (1979), *Cognitive Systematization: A Systems-Theoretic Approach to a Coherentist Theory of Knowledge*, Oxford: Basil Blackwell.

Rescher, N. (2005), 'Pragmatism at the crossroads', *Transactions of the Charles S Peirce Society*, 41(2), 355–65.

Resnik, M.D. (1999), *Mathematics as a Science of Patterns*, Oxford: Oxford Scholarship.

Richards, L.A. (1936), *The Philosophy of Rhetoric*, New York: Oxford University Press.

Richardson, K.A. and M.R. Lissack (2001), 'On the status of boundaries both natural and organizational: a complex systems perspective', *Emergence*, 3(4), 32–49.

Rittel, H.W.J. and M.M. Webber (1973), 'Dilemmas in a general theory of planning', *Policy Sciences*, 4, 155–69.

Rodgers, P.A., G. Green and A. McGown (2000), 'Using concept sketches to track design progress', *Design Studies*, 21(5), 451–64.

Rorty, R. (1982), *Consequences Of Pragmatism*, Minneapolis, MN: University of Minnesota Press.

Rorty, R. (1989), *Contingency, Irony and Solidarity*, Cambridge: Cambridge University Press.

Rosenfield, I. (1988), *The Invention Of Memory*, New York: Basic Books.

Rost, K., K. Hölzle and H.-G. Gemunden (2007), 'Promoters or champions: pros and cons of role specialisation for economic process', *Schmalenbach Business Review*, 59, 340–63.

Rottger, E. and D. Klante (1976), *Creative Drawing*, London: Batsford.

Ruben, D.-H. (1993), *Explanation*, Oxford: Oxford University Press.

Rytina, J.H. and C.P. Loomis (1970), 'Marxist dialectic and pragmatism: power as knowledge', *American Sociological Review*, 35 (2), 308−18.

Saku, M. and J.A.A. Sillance (2007), 'Strategic intent as a rhetorical device', *Scandinavian Journal of Management*, 23, 406–23.

Schon, D.A. (1963), *Displacement of Concepts*, London: Tavistock Publications.

Schon, D.A. and G. Wiggins (1992), 'Kinds of seeing and their function in designing', *Design Studies*, 13(2), 135−56.

Schumpeter, J. (1942), *Capitalism, Socialism and Democracy*, New York: Harper & Brothers.

Schwarz, G.M. and G.P. Huber (2008), 'Challenging organizational change research', *British Journal of Management*, 19, 1–6.

Scott, J. (1996), 'Software review: a toolkit for social network analysis', *Acta Sociologica*, 39, 211−16.

Scudder, S.H. (1874), 'In the laboratory with Agassiz', *Every Saturday*, 16, 369–70.

Seo, M-G. and D.W.E. Creed (2002), 'Institutional contradictions, praxis and institutional change: a dialectical perspective', *Academy of Management Review*, 27(2), 222−47.

Sexton, C. (1994), 'Self-managed work team: TQM technology at the employee level', *Journal of Organizational Change Management*, 7(2), 45−52.

Shields, P.M. (1998), 'Pragmatism as philosophy of science', *Research in Public Administration*, 4, 195−225.

Shields, P. (2005), 'Classical pragmatism does not need an upgrade', *Administration and Society*, 37(4), 504−18.

Sillince, J.A.A. (1995), 'Extending the cognitive approach to strategic change in organizations: some theory', *British Journal of Management*, 6(1), 59–76.

Simon, H.A. (1975), *Model Of Man*, New York: Wiley.

Simon, H. (1996), 'The sciences of the artificial Boston', Boston, MA: MIT Press.

Skinner, B.F. (1981), 'Selection by consequences', *Science*, 213, 501−4.

Sminia, H. (2009), 'Process research in strategy formulation theory', *International Journal of Management Reviews*, 11(1), 97–125.

Smith, A. (2006), *Wealth Of Nations*, London: Book Jungle.

Smith, W.K. and M.K. Lewis (2011), 'Towards a theory of paradox', *Academy of Management Review*, 36(2), 381−403.

Sowell, T. (1985), *Marxism*, New York: William Morrow & Co.

Stanwick, P.A. (1996), 'Mental imagery: an alternative to top management team replacement for declining organizations', *Journal of Organizational Change Management*, 9(2), 47−65.

Sterman, J. (2000), *Business Dynamics*, New York: McGraw Hill.

Stove, D. (1998), *Anything Goes*, Sydney: Maclay Press.

Stylianou, D.A. (2002), 'On the interaction of visualization and analysis: the negotiation of a visual representation in expert problem-solving', *Journal of Mathematical Behavior*, 21(3), 303−17.

Suddaby, R. (2006), 'What grounded theory is not', *Academy of Management Journal*, 49(4), 633−42.

Surowiecki, J. (2005), *The Wisdom Of Crowds*, New York: Anchor.

Suwa, M. and B. Tversky (1996), *What Architects See in Their Sketches: A Protocol Analysis. Artificial Intelligence in Design*, Stanford, CA: Stanford University.

Swan, J. (1997), 'Using cognitive mapping in management research: decisions about technical innovation', *British Journal of Management*, 8(2), 183–98.

Tannen, D. (1993), *Framing in Discourse*, Oxford: Oxford University Press.

Thornberry, M. (1997), 'A view about vision', *European Management Journal*, 15(1), 28–34.

Tichy, N.M. and S. Sherman (1994), *Control Your Own Destiny Or Someone Else Will*, New York: Harper Business.

Tidd, J., J. Bessant and K. Pavitt (2001), *Managing Innovation: Integrating Technological Market and Organisational Change*, Chichester: Wiley.

Todorova, G. and B. Durisin (2007), 'Absorptive capacity: valuing a reconceptualization', *Academy of Management Review*, 32(3), 774–86.

Toulmin, S. (1964), *The Uses of Argument*, Cambridge: Cambridge University Press.

Toulmin, S. (1972), *Human Understanding: The Collective Use and Evolution of Concepts*, Princeton, NJ: Princeton University Press.

Tovey, M., S. Porter and R.M. Newman (2003), 'Sketching, concept development and automotive design', *Design Studies*, 24(2), 135−53.

Tracey, T.J.G. and C.E. Glidden-Tracey (1999), 'Integration theory, research design, measurement and analysis', *Counselling Psychologist*, 27(3), 299−324.

Tullis, T. (1981), 'An evaluation of alphanumeric, graphic, and color information displays', *Human Factors*, 23(5), 541−50.

Tversky, A. and D. Kahneman (1981), 'The framing of decisions and the psychology of choice', *Science*, 211(4428), 453–58.

Tyre, M. and E. von Hippel (1997), 'The situated nature of adaptive learning in organisations', *Organisational Science*, 8, 71–4.

Ulrich, W. (1983), *Critical Heuristics of Social Planning: A New Approach to Practical Philosophy*, Chichester: John Wiley & Sons.

Ulrich, W. (2002), 'A bibliography of C. W. Churchman's writings from

1938 to 2001', Werner Ulrich's Home Page, available at http://wulrich. com/ (accessed 1 July 2013).

Unsworth, K. (2001), 'Unpacking creativity', *Academy of Management Review*, 26(2), 289–87.

Van de Ven, A. and M.S. Poole (1995), 'Explaining development and change in organizations', *Academy of Management Review*, 20(3), 510–40.

van Gelder, T. (2003), 'Enhancing deliberation through computer-supported argument mapping', in P. Kirschner, S. Buckingham Shum and C. Carr (eds), *Visualizing Argumentation: Software Tools for Collaborative and Educational Sense-Making*, London: Springer-Verlag, pp. 97–115.

Verstijnen, I.M. (1997), 'Sketches of creative discovery – a psychological inquiry into the role of imagery and sketching in creative discovery', PhD thesis, Universiteit Delft.

Vygotsky, L. (1986), *Thought and Language*, Cambridge, MA: MIT Press.

Walsh, J.P. (1995), 'Managerial and organizational cognition: notes for a trip down memory lane', *Organization Science*, 6(3), 280–321.

Walther, H. (1963), *Proverbia sententiaeque Latinitatis Medii Aevi: Lateinische Sprichwörter und Sentenzen des Mittelalters in alphabetischer Anordnung*, 6 vols, Göttingen: Vandenhoeck & Ruprecht.

Walton, D. (1998), *The New Dialectic*, Toronto: Toronto University Press.

Walton, D. (2004), 'A new dialectical theory of explanation', *Philosphical Explorations*, 7(1), 71–89.

Watts, D.J. (1999), 'Networds, dynamics and the Small World phenomenon', *American Journal of Sociology*, 105(2), 493–527.

Weber, M. (1997), *The Theory of Social and Economic Organization*, New York: Free Press.

Weick, K.E. (1995), *Sensemaking in Organizations*, Thousand Oaks, CA: Sage.

Weick, K.E. (2006), 'The role of imagination in the organizing of knowledge', *European Journal of Information Systems*, 15, 44652.

Wenger, E.C. and W.M. Snyder (2000), 'Communities of practice', *Harvard Business Review*, January, 139–45.

Werhane, P.H. (2002), 'Moral imagination and systems thinking', *Journal of Business Ethics*, 38(1–2), 33–42.

Westley, F. and H. Mintzberg (1989), 'Visionary leadership and strategic management', *Strategic Management Journal*, 10, 17–32.

Wheeler, S. (2006), 'An analysis of combined arm teaming for the Australian defence force', *Journal of the Operatational Research Society*, 57, 1279–88.

Wilhelm, H. and S. Bort (2012), 'How managers talk about their consumption of popular management concepts: Identity, rules and situations', *British Journal of Management*, DOI: 10.1111/j.1467–8551.2012.00813.x.

Wilson, P. (1983), *Second Hand Knowledge*, Westpost, CT: Greenwood Press.

Wittgenstein, L. (2001 [1953]), *Philosophical Investigations*, London: Blackwell Publishing.

Zeitz, G. (1980), 'Interorganizational dialectics', *Administrative Science Quarterly*, 25(March), 72–88.

## FURTHER READING

Alvesson, M. and K. Skoldberg (2000), *Reflexive Methodology*, Thousand Oaks, CA: Sage.

Berger, P.L. and T. Luckmann (1967), *The Social Construction of Reality*, New York: Anchor.

Bertalanffy, L.V. (1975), *Perspectives on General Systems Theory*, New York: Brazilier.

Boland, R. and F. Collopy (eds) (2004), *Managing As Designing*, Stanford, CA: Stanford University Press.

Boulding, K.E. (1956a), *The Image: Knowledge in Life and Society*, Ann Arbor, MI: University of Michigan Press.

Boulding, K. (1956b), 'General system theory – the skeleton of science', *General Systems Yearbook of the Society for the Advancement of General Systems Theory*, 1(1), 11–17.

Bronte-Stewart, M. (1999), 'Regarding rich pictures as tools for communication in information systems development', *Computing and Information Systems*, 6, 83–102.

Bruner, J.S. and L. Postman (1949), 'On the perception of incongruity: a paradigm', *Journal of Personality*, 18, 206–23.

Coker, R. and J. Coker (2004), 'This room has 20 chairs: prediction and complexity in considering design expertise and design education', International Engineering and Product Design Education Conference, 2–3 August, Delft.

Cross, R., A. Parker and S.P. Borgatti (2002), 'Making invisible work visible: using social network analysis to support strategic collaboration', *California Management Review*, 44(2), 25–46.

Darwall, S.E. (2002), *Consequentialism*, Oxford: Blackwell.

Dewey, J. (1938), *Logic: The Theory of Inquiry*, New York: Holt Rinehart & Winston.

Dewulf, A., B. Gray, Linda Putnam, Roy Lewicki, Noelle Aarts, Rene Bouwen and Cees van Woerkum (2009), 'Disentangling approaches to framing in conflict and negotiation research', *Human Relations*, 62(2), 155–93.

East, C. (2007), 'Information system flexibility using the concept of space', PhD Thesis, University of South Australia.

Eden, C. (1992), 'On the nature of cognitive maps', *Journal of Management Studies*, 29(3), 261–5.

Fiol, C.M. and A.S. Huff (1992), 'Maps for mangers: where are we? Where do we go from here?' *Journal of Management Studies*, 29, 267–85.

Girvan, M. and M.E.J. Newman (2002), 'Community structure in social and biological networks', *Proceedings of National Academy of Science USA*, 99, 7821–6.

Goffman, E. (1974), *Frame Analysis: An Essay on the Organization of Experience*, London: Harper & Row.

Gubrium, J.F. and J.A. Holstein (eds) (2000), *Handbook of Interview Research: Context and Method*, Thousand Oaks, CA: Sage.

Hanneman, R.A. and M. Riddle (2005). 'Introduction to social network methods', University of California Riverside, http://faculty.ucr. edu/~hanneman/.

Hatch, M.J. and S.B. Ehrlich (1993), 'Spontaneous humour and an indicator of paradox and ambiguity in organizations', *Organization Studies*, 14(4), 505–26.

Hodgkinson, G.P. and A.J. Maule (2002), 'Further reflections on the elimination of framing bias in strategic decision making', *Strategic Management Journal*, 23, 1069–76.

Hofstede, G. (1984), *Culture's Consequences*, Beverly Hills, CA: Sage Publications.

Houghton, L., and M. Metcalfe (2009), 'Synthesis as conception shifting', *Journal of the Operational Research Society*, 61, 953–63.

Huff, A.S. and M. Jenkins (2002), *Mapping Strategic Knowledge*, London: Sage.

Jensen, J.V. (1978), 'A heuristic for the analysis of the nature and extent of a problem', *Journal of Creative Behaviour*, 12(3), 169–81.

Kaplan, S. (2008), 'Framing contests: strategy making under uncertainty', *Organization Science*, 19(5), 729–52.

Katada, T. (1994), 'Strategic intent to corporate purpose: the remaking of Komatsu', *Harvard Business Review*, 72(6), 83–5.

Kelly, W.E. (2002), 'An investigation of worry and sense of humor', *Journal of Psychology*, 136(6), 657–66.

Keren, G. (2011), *Perspectives on Framing*, New York: Psychology Press

Langley, A., H. Mintzberg, P. Pitcher, E. Posada and J. St-Macary (1995), 'Opening up decision making: the view from the black stool', *Organization Science*, 6(3), 260–79.

Linstone, H. (2003), 'Technology, terrorism, and the multiple perspective approach', *Technological Forecasting and Social Change*, 70, 283–96.

Luhmann, N. (1995), *Social Systems*. Stanford, CA: Stanford University Press.

Mason, D. (1994), 'Planning an English course for students of health care', http://exchanges.state.gov/forum/vols/vol32/no2/#special_ret_41.

Maule, J. and G. Villejoubert (2007), 'What lies beneath: reframing framing effects', *Thinking and Reasoning*, 13(1), 25–44.

McGhee, P.E. (1979) *Humor: Its Origins and Development*, New York: Freeman.

Millikan, R.G. (2000), *On Clear And Confused Ideas: An Essay About Substance Concepts*, Cambridge: Cambridge University Press.

Minsky, M. (1975), 'A framework for representing knowledge', in P. Winston (ed.), *The Psychology of Computer Vision*, New York: McGraw-Hill, pp. 211–77.

Mitchell, R.K., B.R. Agle and Donna J. Wood (1997), 'Toward a theory of stakeholder identification and salience', *Academy of Management Review* 22(4), 853–86.

Mizruchi, M.S. (1994). 'Social network analysis: recent achievements and current controversies', *Acta Sociologica*, 37, 329–43.

Monk, A. and S. Howard (1998), 'The rich picture: a tool for reasoning about work context', *Interactions*, March/April, 21–30.

Morgan, G. (1996), 'Is there anything more to be said about metaphor?' in D. Grant and C. Oswick (eds), *Metaphor and Organization*, London: Sage, pp. 227–40.

Rosenhead, J. (1996), 'What's the problem? An introduction to problem structuring methods', *Interfaces*, 26(6), 117–31.

Rosenhead, J. and J. Mingers (eds) (2001), *Rational Analysis for a Problematic World: Problem Structuring Methods for Complexity, Uncertainty and Conflict*, Chichester: Wiley.

Schon, D. (1983), *The Reflective Practitioner*, New York: Basic Books.

Schumacher, E.F. (1977), *A Guide for the Perplexed*, London: Jonathan Cape.

Stephen, M.E.L. (2010), 'Concepts', *Stanford Encyclopedia of Philosophy*, available at http://plato.stanford.edu/entries/concepts/ (accessed April 2011).

Tayor, C. (1967), *The Explanation of Behaviour*, London: Routledge.

Trochim, W.M.K. (1989), 'Introduction to concept mapping for planning and evaluation', *Evaluation and Program Planning*, 12(1), 1–16.

Watson, T.J. (1997), 'Theorizing managerial work: a pragmatic pluralist approach to interdisciplinary research', *British Journal of Management*, 8(1), 3–8.

Weick, K., K. Sutcliffe and D. Obstfeld (2005), 'Organizing and the process of sensemaking', *Organization Science*, 16(4), 409–21.
Wright, G. and P. Goodwin (2002), 'Eliminating a framing bias', *Strategic Management Journal*, 23, 1059–67.

# Index